NEW TO NORTH AMERICA

WRITING BY U.S. IMMIGRANTS, THEIR CHILDREN AND GRANDCHILDREN

Second Edition

Abby Bogomolny, Editor
Chapter Introductions by John Isbister

Burning Bush Publications
New York • Santa Rosa

ISBN-10: 0-9650665-6-8
ISBN-13: 978-0-965-06-656-3

Library of Congress Cataloging-in-Publication Data

New to North America: writing by U.S. immigrants, their children and grandchildren / Abby Bogomolny, editor. -- 2nd ed.
    p.   cm.
Includes index.
ISBN-13: 978-09650665-6-3 (pbk. : alk. paper)
1. Immigrants' writings, American. 2. American literature--Minority authors. 3. Ethnic groups--Literary collections.
4. Children of immigrants--Literary collections. 5. Children of immigrants--United States. 6. Immigrants--Literary collections.
7. Immigrants--United States. I. Bogomolny, Abby, 1953- II. Title.

PS508.I45N49 2007
810.8' 09220691--dc22

                                                    2006021865

For more information, write to the publisher:
Burning Bush Publications
P.O. Box 4658
Santa Rosa, California 95402
http://www.bbbooks.com

Cover Painting by Florin Ion Firimita.
Cover design by Annie Browning.

Dedicated to my parents,
Frances and Samuel Bogomolny

ACKNOWLEDGEMENTS

Grateful acknowledgement is made to the following authors, publishers, and agencies for permission to reprint the works in this collection.

Opal Palmer Adisa, "Will the Real Island Please Stand Up," "Attack At Dawn," and "We Have It" from *Tamarind and Mango Women*, Sister Vision Press. Copyright © 1992 by Opal Palmer Adisa. Reprinted by permission of the author.

Abby Bogomolny, "From City to Suburb America" from *Nauseous in Paradise;* "Dad" and "We are the miracle" from *People Who Do Not Exist*. Copyright © 1986 and 1997 by Abby Bogomolny. Reprinted by permission of HerBooks and Woman in the Moon Publications.

Eva Metzger Brown, "No Memories at all" adapted from original printing in *Reunion of a Very Special Family: Yesterday-Today-Tomorrow*. Reprinted by permission of the author.

Cecilia Manguerra Brainard, "Butterscotch Marble Ice Cream" from *AA Literary Realm, dIS*Orient Journalzine*; also from *Acapulco at Sunset and Other Stories*. Copyright © 1995 by Cecilia Manguerra Brainard. Reprinted by permission of the author.

José Antonio Burciaga, "The Great Taco War," and "He Who Serves Two Masters Disappoints One . . . or Both" from *Drink Cultura*. Copyright © 1992 by José Antonio Burciaga. Reprinted by permission of the author.

Hayan Charara, "When It Happens It Seems Altogether Impossible." Published in *The Chiron Review* under the title "Camel Jockey." Reprinted by permission of the author.

Tony Diaz, "All Educated With No Place To Go" was first published in the *Los Angeles Times*. Reprinted by permission of the author.

Charles Fishman, "Bungalow People" is reprinted from *Mortal Companions*. Copyright © 1977 by Charles Fishman. By permission of Charles Fishman.

Joey Garcia, "Choosing Camps" from *The Caribbean Writer, Volume 10*. Reprinted by permission of the author.

Dan Georgakas, "Funny Sounding Names" from *The GreekAmerican*. Reprinted by permission of the author.

CONTENTS

Chapter 4
First Generation
Language, Identity, Achievement *163*

Chapter 5
Second Generation
Assimilation and Amnesia *235*

Chapter 6
Looking to the Future** *309*

Index of Authors *373*

Editor's Preface

When we think of immigrant literature, we usually expect to hear the voices of the most recent newcomers to these shores; however, to some extent most of American literature is immigrant literature. I have always been captivated by stories that seek to understand the forces that have prompted migration. Reading immigrant literature prompts us to think about cultural identity, assimilation, language, history, and the struggle to be accepted and reach what has been called the "American Dream." While national headlines oversimplify the complex pros and cons of immigration policy, a debate as old as the United States itself, too often the voices of immigrants are excluded, and we close ourselves to valuable stories of the human experience. The strategies families use to retain their values, identities and cultures through migration, dispersal, diaspora, or conquest form the soul of our most dramatic historical fiction. Their perspectives confront us with universal needs for dignity, equality and achievement. Some rejoice; others express that bittersweet mix of despair and hope. Voices like these, while not given center stage in American literature, are nonetheless profoundly American in their yearnings to succeed and transform our society. This anthology presents a diverse group of writers spanning three generations.

All of the fiction, poetry and essays refer to events that occurred after 1840, and all of the authors have an intimate knowledge of the cultures they represent. I have chosen "first generation American" to mean the first generation born on United States soil. Accordingly, "second generation American" refers to the second generation born here. Each chapter represents the chronological process of adjustment to the United States. "The Other Side" views conditions back in the old country. "Passages" describes the tumultuous physical and psychological experiences of geographic movement. "Immigrant Dreams, Survival, Reflection" explores the American reality that the immigrant must negotiate in order to be successful. "First Generation-Language, Identity, Achievement" chronicles the issues, both internal and external, that children of immigrants face. "Second Generation-Assimilation and Amnesia" looks at the conflicts between generations as a result of assimilation, a persistent tug toward issues of the past that can plague or benefit us. And finally, "Looking to the Future" poses new visions and informs us of the many changes put into effect after September 11, 2001.

I would like to acknowledge one problematic implication of our title *New to North America: Writing by U.S. Immigrants, Their Children and Grandchildren*, which was chosen for its alliterative quality. While most immigrants who come to the U.S. are indeed "new to North America" (unless they are from Canada), I do not wish to imply that the U.S. alone occupies North America. Still the current title is a better choice than *New to America*, which would inaccurately claim "America" to be the sole the province of the United States, thereby erasing Central and South America's presence in this hemisphere.

Another challenge in compiling this collection concerns each author's use of accent marks. Because expressions of identity and culture or degree of assimilation are central to this anthology, I made no attempt to standardize each selection. Any inconsistencies noted by readers, for example in Spanish language names, are indicative of the author's preference.

In this volume, we find the experiences, pleas, misgivings, candor, advice and humor of those who have contributed to the building of the United States, representing a variety of perspectives, concerns, challenges and solutions. A process begins with the crossing of a border: Contained in the immigrant experience are essential multiple perspectives, multigenerational conflicts, and firsthand historical testimonies that need to be told. The United States could not have been built without the work of immigrants from Africa, Europe, Asia, Latin America, the Middle East, and the indigenous people of North America. This literature is a map to understanding the past and a prescription for our future.

I am thankful to John Isbister who wrote the first five contextual chapter introductions and contributed information that became the sixth chapter introduction. His book, *The Immigration Debate*, is a valuable aid toward unraveling conflicting rhetoric over immigration. Others who have inspired and nurtured this project are Déborah Berman Santana, whose book *Kicking Off the Bootstraps: Environment, Development, and Community Power in Puerto Rico* presents an important case history of grassroots activism for environmental and social justice; Marian Knox, whose board game *Coming Home* increases family communication in the context of discussing African American migration out of the South; my students, whose efforts to research and write their families' migration stories keep history alive; and of course, all of the authors in this volume whose writing, enthusiasm and generosity make it possible to present this anthology to you.

Abby Bogomolny
Santa Rosa, California, 2006

NEW TO NORTH AMERICA

WRITING BY U.S. IMMIGRANTS, THEIR CHILDREN AND GRANDCHILDREN

Chapter 1
The Other Side

Over a million people immigrate to the United States every year. Why have people come to North America? In a way, the answer is simple. With the exception of those who migrated involuntarily, most people have come for a better life. But that is only the beginning of the story. What really makes people pull up stakes and start a new life in a strange country? Is it the promise of a better job, a higher income, professional advancement, more security, a freer society, reunification with one's family? Is it fear of what will happen to them if they stay at home—perhaps destitution, persecution, torture or death? Do they make a definitive decision to immigrate, or do they come just for a visit and then get more connected to the U.S. than they had expected?

The answer is all of these and much more. Each immigrant has a different story. Immigrants remember their home countries in remarkably different ways, and they understand their reasons for changing countries in equally different ways. The selections in this section—and the whole book—only begin to hint at the varieties of the immigrant experience.

One of the lessons we have learned from studying the history of immigration is that people usually do not leave home just because they are poor. Most people in the world have been poor, most of the time, and the great majority have not migrated. Their life choices are clear and well defined in a society that is familiar to them. Migration becomes an alternative only when their lives are dislocated. When commercial agriculture and market forces transform a previously self-sufficient peasant community, for example, the old ways are destroyed and people have to search for new options. One of those options might be emigration, perhaps to the nearest town, perhaps to the United States. When foreign investment intrudes into a poor country, average incomes may actually rise, but people's lives are thrown into disarray. Invasions and civil wars generate refugees. Chih Hao Huang writes about uncovering the truth of how his family was shattered by the arrival of the Nationalist Chinese in Taiwan. Alberto Angel writes of discovering a village that was destroyed—and its people massacred—in the struggle with the Shining Path movement in Peru. These are the sorts of experiences that can lead a person to start over again in a new place.

Some immigrants to the U.S. understood that they were making a definitive break with the old country, but some expected no break at all. Most Jewish immigrants were in the first category. They were fleeing persecution in Russia and Central Europe, persecution which culminated in the European Holocaust. Most Jews understood that while their hearts might be left behind, they could never return to Europe. Many of today's newer Mexican immigrants are in the second category. They move back and forth across the border, sometimes several times a year. In other words, many new Mexican immigrants retain a presence on both sides of the border; they work in both places, have family, even own property in both the U.S. and Mexico. For part of their lives they are immigrants, but they have made no break with Mexico. Some of them gradually and imperceptibly change their places of work and residences from Mexico to the United States, but they do so without ever having made a major life decision to leave their home country.

Many immigrants fall in an in-between category. It was common in the late nineteenth century, for example, for Italians to work in the United States but to return to Italy: some annually, some only upon retirement. Their children grew up in the United States, however, and when the young people went back to Italy it was only for a visit.

We can see these variations in the selections. Florin

Ion Firimita has made the break: "I am more and more a part of my new country," he writes. Minh Ta, on the other hand, has not separated himself from Vietnam. He recalls his teacher telling him, "On the day when you come back to this land from the United States, if you can make this field to have good harvest, so that children do not have the nightmare and cry at midnight by the hunger, then I will never forget your name." To which his heart replies, "A time to study, a time to serve and a time to be welcomed home." We cannot know where Minh will be in twenty years, but for now in his soul he is but a temporary sojourner in the United States.

The Old People and the Old Story
Chih Hao Huang

Is it right for parents to keep information from their children in order to protect them? In this short story Chih Hao Huang discovers the truth about his family.

There is an old Chinese proverb that says, "Life starts to be stressful when people learn how to read." When we realize the name of everything, good or bad, we learn that there is anxiety, grief, pain and suffering in this world and in our life. From then on, we can not forget. We will remember everything; every moment of our past.

I was born into a lower middle-class family in Taiwan which had once been wealthy. My father used to tell me that once my family was very, very rich in the 1920s, when Taiwan was still under the rule of Japan. My family around that time did business with the Japanese. We sold sugar, bananas, and many things to Japan and we made a lot of money. We had a big family; my great grandfather had five sons and three daughters, and they also had their own children. There were about thirty people in the family, and they all lived in a big house in Keelong. When my father was ten years old, my great grandfather was already dead and my grandfather, who was the eldest son of the family, took care of the business. During that time my father realized that there was something wrong in the family, even though he was only a little boy.

"Family," he told me, "is the core of our existence, our life. When the members of the family stop willing to gather together, when every one of them starts considering himself first, and the family next, when a family is broken, there is nothing but hatred."

It did happen. My aunt told me. When my grandfather died of cancer at the age of thirty-six, his brothers and sisters took over the business and broke up the family. Everybody had a portion of the property except my grandmother. "It was a shock," she said, "your grandmother sat in the chair. I stood beside her. My uncles kept saying something I didn't understand. Suddenly your grandmother grabbed my hand and held it so tight that I started to cry. But there were no tears in her eyes; she didn't even say a word. The next morning a wagon came, and we left the house without a penny in our pockets and moved to the other side of Keelong; I never saw the house again. And she told me that the house was the biggest house in Keelong; it contained twenty rooms on each side. A few years ago when I had a chance to visit the place in Keelong where the house was located, I didn't see a big house, but a lot of four story apartments, and the other side of the city which used to be a ghetto had been turned into the commercial section."

My father never told me the story in such detail. His story always ended at the time my grandfather died; it seemed to him that after that there was nothing to talk about. "Be proud of your grandfather and your family," he always said. "The man could deal with the Japanese well and gained their respect at such a young age, and your family made tremendous progress in that crucial and turbulent time." My grandmother, while she was alive, never said a word about the past. But I could feel that she had thought about the past a great deal. When she would sit in a chair, looking at a portrait of my grandfather which hung on the wall, I would see that there were tears in her eyes.

What happened in the past? I asked my father, my aunt, my uncles; none of them had given me a clear picture of the story. All I know was that there is some deep hatred in the hearts of my father, my aunt and my uncles. And there was reason for them to have that kind of feeling, I thought, because these brothers and sisters of my grandfather had kicked my grandmother and her children out of the family and took their money and land away. And then my grandmother worked in the banana fields. My eldest uncle quit school and worked in the port of Keelong as a coolie. My aunt never had the chance to finish her education, for she had to take care of my father and my younger uncle. My father, after twenty years of working hard and struggling, finished a college degree when he was nearly forty years old. Only my little uncle could finish his education and have a nice job while he was still young.

I was never aware how deep the hatred could be until the day my grandmother passed away. I saw them kneel down on the ground and cry. It was a real shock to me; I never saw my father cry. He cried and blamed himself that his mother suffered so much, that because her husband died so young she had to care for four children on her own, that because of her uncles, she, a well-educated young woman, couldn't find a decent job and had to work for slave wages. My sister and I hid in the other room and did not dare do anything. I didn't feel sorry for my grandmother, which was strange, yet all I could feel was the guilt and the anger my father had. My sister suddenly said, "All this is their fault." I knew whom my sister meant. "They," the people we never saw, but had heard about, the relatives who put my grandfather into the dust and stole everything my poor grandmother had. We hated them; it was their fault that my grandmother lay there dead and my father was crying like a baby. Yes, they deserved to die and they will all go to hell.

Years after my grandmother died, one day, when I came home from school, my mother brought me a cup of ice cream and told me not to enter the sitting room, for we had some guests and father was talking to them. I sat on the chair of the dining room beside my sister, who was making a funny face to me because she already had finished one cup and was going on to the second; I made the same face back to her, and we kicked each other under the table as we were still little kids. Without any warning, father came in, and there were some other people behind him, a very old man carried by two young women. We stood up. My father introduced them to me and my sister. "This is your great uncle and his granddaughters," he said. I looked at my father and wondered to myself, "What did you mean my great uncle?" and then I realized that this old man is one of "them"! Dear god, this was the guy who caused my grandmother's suffering and my father's crying, and now father brings him to our home and talks to him! I looked at my sister and she looked at me; we stood there not able to say a word. My mother, who was behind us, touched our backs and said,

"They are stupid children." The old man laughed and raised his hand to pat my shoulder. "He looks just like your father," he said to my father. And they all laughed. "Yes, he does, doesn't he?" my father said.

That night the old man and his granddaughters stayed for dinner with us. He kept talking about my grandfather and grandmother, about the Japanese, about the disagreeing and fighting between their brothers, and about their life in Taiwan during those years. Father listened and responded to his questions. They talked and laughed. At the dining table that night, we looked just like a family.

Father didn't tell me why he invited "them" to have dinner with us. Actually, such questions never occurred to his mind. But I had to know why; he had to give me a reason to explain why he did this. Two days after the dinner, I knocked on the door of his study and entered. As usual, he was having an after-dinner coffee and reading a book. I asked my question; he stared at me, "What kind of question is that? He is your great uncle; he came from Keelong to Taipei to visit us and take a look at your grandmother's grave. What's the problem with that?"

"But they . . . ," I couldn't finish my question.

"What is it in your mind?" he said.

"No, I just wonder why we never had contact with them 'til now . . . "

"We have kept contact with them, actually," he moved his eyesight to another place. "Well, it is a long story. After the second world war, the Japanese were gone and the Kuomintang came; some of your great uncles had been arrested during the February 28th event, for we had been so close to the Japanese. They said we betrayed our country. Your grandfather's youngest brother had been killed, and the great uncle who you had dinner with had been imprisoned and stayed in jail for quite a long time."

I stared at him, "They stole our money and land . . . "

"What money? What land? There was no money and no land for our family under the domination of the Koumintang. They took it all."

"But aunt said . . . "

"Your aunt never knew what happened; no child could understand what happened at that time. Even I myself only began to know exactly what had happened when I was thirty years old. Your grandmother and her brother-in-law decided to separate the family. Everyone lived on their own to protect their children."

"Why didn't they tell you about this? Why have you never told me?"

He looked at me; then he stood up, put his book back into the bookshelf, and looked at those volumes. Most of them were history books. "Sometimes," he said, "the best way to protect the people we love is to not let them know everything; let them forget their past." He turned his face back to me, "That is what your grandmother chose, and she chose right; you should be proud of her."

I couldn't say anymore; I learned that the people I should hate were the Kuomintang, our government. Father seemed to read my mind. "Don't feel angry at them; don't hate anybody; it won't work. Things are so complicated that the more facts you know, the less hatred you have. You will understand more as you get older. Everybody does right and wrong; everybody has problems and they also bring other people problems. The best way to live on is to forget everything or to forgive everything."

At that moment, I understood my father more. I understood his anger and his crying; I had thought it was because of hate, but it was not; it was because of the heartbreak of my grandmother's life. Because at that time in our country, an intelligent woman became nobody, but an old woman who used to work in the banana fields. And she was not the only one; the fact is a whole generation of Taiwanese were wasted and now nobody remembers them.

And that was the end of our conversation. Father never said any more to me and I never asked him more. However, years later, when I enrolled in college and chose Chinese Historiography as my major, father smiled and said, "So, after all, you do not choose to forget your past; but can you forgive?"

Can I?

Nameless Place
Alberto Angel

Between 1980 and 1992, hundreds of thousands of Peruvians fled their homes to escape a brutal war between Maoist Shining Path rebels and the government. Many rural communities were turned into ghost towns. Civilians at various times have described members of the Shining Path, the police and the army as agents of persecution. Persons at risk have included "persons suspected by the authorities of helping the Shining Path," as well as "persons suspected by the Shining Path as helping the authorities." In this selection Alberto Angel looks back at his two months as a Peruvian army soldier in a deserted mountain village.

There is a special place in my life. It is a beautiful place that I have tried to forget unsuccessfully. I do not want to say its name because it is of no importance, but it is located in the heart of a country—Peru. This place is located high in the mountains, perhaps 13,000 feet above sea level. It is on the border of two different worlds, the border of the jungle and the sierra. It is one of the most beautiful places that I have ever been to, yet it is also one of the saddest places that I do not ever want to see again.

I arrived there by helicopter in June of 1984. After my arrival, I learned that the nearest road that could connect us with civilization was five days away, five days of hiking through the mountains. I got there and somebody told me that this place was "the rear end of the world." There was no electricity, no television, no nothing; not even a store to buy a cookie. I started to think like the others, this place was so lonely that it was a punishment to be there. We had money but could not buy anything; we were dying for a piece of bread but there was none to be found. However, after awhile we got used to this place and our new style of life. We had to because we were soldiers, and we were there for a specific reason, to take care of that place for it was a strategic geographic point in the war against the terrorist group "Shining Path."

The first morning after my arrival, I got up early and went out to look at this new place where I was going to live. The house where we slept was on top of a hill; from there

the whole valley could be observed. I started to watch as
the sun rose over the tall mountains that surrounded the
valley. Everything was green. I looked to my right and there
were the mountains and by its side, the path that could con-
nect us with the nearest civilization. The path went uphill,
always going up, surrounding the mountains and following
the course of a river whose pure and crystalline waters irri-
gated the valley in front of me. The path disappeared in the
distance, always by the side of the mountains that seemed
like sleeping giants. In front of me were more mountains
but between them was a beautiful green valley and the river
whose waters were born high above. As I watched this calm
river, the sunlight illuminated the pools of water that this
river had made, and the water brightly reflected the sun's
rays. The scene was magical; the river like a big mirror cross-
ing the valley, and suddenly the valley was awake. I heard
the sound of water against the rocks coming down from the
mountains and the birds opened their throats as if some-
body had just told them to sing. And the combinations of
the water's sound and the bird's songs gave me an intense
sense of tranquility. I followed the river with my eyes and
saw something magnificent; the river went into the jungle.
At that moment I could clearly see the boundaries of the
sierra and the jungle, a line making its limits—to the left
were big trees and exuberant vegetation; to the right was
the sierra covered mainly by grass and small bushes scat-
tered here and there.

The day was clear, but as I continued to watch, a dense
fog ascended, like a gentle monster that slowly ate every-
thing in its path. Soon the green jungle was only a dense
and thick cloud of white fog that covered the whole valley
and rose up to the place where I was standing. At that mo-
ment I turned my eyes rapidly toward my right and saw the
fog covering a group of houses. The fog reached the top of
the hill and soon everything around me was white; the air
was humid but its smell was like a sweet perfume.

Three hours passed and the fog started to dissipate,
and a group of soldiers including myself went to explore the
abandoned village. We walked down the hill, crossed the

river and approached the village. We walked through the narrow streets and all around us was only destruction. The houses had been destroyed; the walls that were made of dirt and stone had been toppled and their straw roofs had been burned. We went inside the houses, and in one of them we saw rotten furniture, broken dishes and baby's clothes lying around. I picked up a small red sweater and it crumbled in my hands. The few partial standing walls were black in color; perhaps they were the only witnesses remaining since the destruction of this place. We kept on walking and we arrived at the center of the village. There the spectacle was even worse; human bones were lying around. Skulls, hip bones, hand bones and more were lying on the dirt; some of those bones still had some dried meat attached to them. The smell was terrible, like someone had thrown sulfur there. We kept on walking and more human bones were scattered on the ground, here and there, everywhere; some of them were partially covered by fallen walls. The day was still foggy and cloudy and suddenly it started to rain, and the bones were being washed by the rain when we left this sad place.

That night I could not sleep. It was a full moon and the valley was well illuminated. The river reflected the moonlight and the jungle seemed like a giant black shadow threatening to strike any time it wished. The desolate village seemed even sadder under the light of the moon. The air was cold and I wrapped myself with a blanket; at that instant I thought about those bones. Could they feel the cold that I was feeling? I could not answer, but I felt even colder, a chill in my bones. The next morning, we buried the bones, and life continued its course. Two months passed and we were replaced by another group of soldiers that were also brought by helicopters. I got on a helicopter to be transported, and when it rose I could see from above the valley where I had spent two full months of my life. The valley from above looked beautiful; there was the river telling me goodbye; there was the destroyed village that perhaps some day would have people again, and there were the mountains sheltering the whole valley saying goodbye for the last time.

Will the Real Island Please Stand Up
Opal Palmer Adisa

Born in Jamaica, Opal Palmer Adisa is a literary critic, writer and Professor at the California College of Arts. Her latest published works include *Caribbean Passion* (2004), *The Orishas Command the Dance* (2004), *Until Judgement Comes* (2004), *Leaf of Life* (2000) and *It Begins With Tears* (1997).

De grass
is no longer green
de palm trees are dead
de sea is full of weeds
and de white sandy beaches
are covered with rubbish

Eight year old girls
stand by the Carib Theatre
late night show begging ten cents;
in Ochos Rios straw-makers
argue with tourists
arms akimbo
hands a flailing
"yuh come from rich America
come tief me off"
Negril women show their navels
buy panties for dem daughters,
still I can't leave
connected through birth pains
this island of tamarind and mango

Attack at Dawn*
Opal Palmer Adisa

These are dangerous times.

There is no one within reach.

I am too far
away from home.

I am a slave.
This is the law of
the land.

The man who fathered me
is a tyrant
his rape of my mother
is celebrated.
This is the law
of the land.
I am holding
my breath;
my chest cracks and crumbles
under the strain

All my blood
is drained
They have killed my boy.
Maurice Bishop is dead.
Dead.
Dead.
Suddenly,
the meaning of my name
is a task.
The market is empty.
They have killed my boy.
Maurice Bishop is dead.
Dead!

Dead!

The yearning
for my name to pave roads,
water nutmeg
is brushed aside
like some idle fly.
My boy is dead.
I am a slave.
This is the law of
the land.

There must be another word,
synonym
for pawn,
imperialism,
capitalism,
communism,
democracy.

Maurice
a man
helping us believe
we could govern
our own lives.

These are dangerous times
I let out my breath:
sweat, splinter and bones
scrape my mouth.

My boy is dead.
Once more
We are roped
and battered.

*Attack at dawn refers to the invasion of Grenada by U.S. troops on
October 25, 1983.

The Occupied Zone
Geneviève Duboscq

Geneviève Duboscq's family came to the U.S. in 1966 from the Basque region of France. The clash of cultures, languages, and expectations has been a source of her writing for a long time.

We carry the stories of our parents' wars inside us, and so we are careful. We store up food. Provisions pile up in the cabinets: canned tuna, canned peaches. We hoard cardboard boxes and paper bags in the closets for future use. We are mindful of shoe leather and wear cloth slippers around the house. We know how to drive any kind of a car because Papa says in a war, in a disaster you have not the luxury of finding an automatic transmission. All right, we say, *bon*, teach us.

In our minds we live in a small village where every minute invaders may arrive and change our lives completely. Men with harsh voices, uniforms. We are prepared to surrender if they will allow us to go back to our parents on the trains full of terror and live together as a makeshift family. My brother they will have sent to a work camp where there is no work, in Poland or Czechoslovakia, no work but digging holes and filling them in again. Like the rest of us he will be hungry, but he will not have even the comfort of the familiar.

As my mother did when she was ten, we will accept a gift of oranges from the soldier who requires all the potatoes our garden produces. We will say the most quiet thank you so that he will think only that we are shy. We will eat the fruit somewhere far from his eyes, give him no pleasure for this small favor. Behind the barn we will tear into the orange skin with our teeth, lick the ridges of fruit and eat section by section every bit that is orange and white, even the seeds. Save the skin to dry and put in the herbal tea. Afterwards we will not wash our hands for awhile; we will brush our faces with them repeatedly to arouse our hungers with that lingering smell.

I Remember Haifa Being Lovely But
Lyn Lifshin

Lyn Lifshin's grandparents came from Russia, but her father was born in
Lithuania. She has edited four anthologies of women's writing and written
more than one hundred books of poetry. She is the subject of the award-
winning documentry film *Not Made of Glass,* which is also the title of the
collection from which this selection is taken.

there were snakes in the
tent   my mother was
strong but she never
slept, was afraid of
dreaming. In Auschwitz
there was a numbness,
lull of just staying
alive. Her two babies
gassed before her, Dr.
Mengele, you know who
he is? She kept her
young sister alive
only to have her die
in her arms the night
of liberation. My mother
is big boned, but she
weighed under 80 lbs.
it was hot, I thought
the snakes lovely. No
drugs in Israel, no
food. I got pneumonia
my mother knocked the
doctor to the floor
when they refused,
said I lost two in
the camp and if this
one dies I'll kill
myself in front of
you. I thought that
once you became a

mother, blue numbers
appeared, mysteriously,
tattooed on your arm.

He Read He Was
Ebrahim Wahab

Ebrahim Wahab immigrated to the U.S. from Afganistan. He explains, "The experience of the war from which I barely escaped alive has had a deep effect on my attitude, art, personality, and life in general. It resembles a deep scar on my face that I see every time I have to look in the mirror. Please know that my poems are not the voice of sorrow and self-pity: I consider myself a content person and life has given me so much that I am eternally thankful. They are a reflection of what it means to come out alive from a war-torn location."

Frustrated
Situated
Aggravated
Conjugated
Infiltrated
Terminated
Stimulated
Permeated
Subjugated
Insinuated
Agitated
Irradiated
Incarcerated
Alienated
Stipulated
Consummated
Irradicated
Asphyxiated

Knowing the Teacher
Minh Ta

Minh Ta wrote this essay as a student in an English class at DeAnza College. He was born in Vietnam.

Emile Capouya says: "A high school teacher, after all, is a person deputized by the rest of us to explain to the young what sort of world they are living in and to defend, if possible, the part their elders are playing in it." This idea perfectly explained my old high school teacher who I respected so much. Throughout his life as a teacher, he helped make many people useful to society. One of them created the rice, IR-34, which helped the farmers in my country to have good harvests in the fields that in the past were a place of war with blood, fire and tears from the AK-47 machine guns, the B-52 bombers, and the K-54 tanks. He was the teacher who always assisted me when I felt hopeless or wanted to quit school. He often told me that "You can not fail . . . unless you quit." He was the point, the mirror that I wanted to follow. However, the way he communicated with others made me unable to understand him. He had an excellent memory, but he often forgot the names of famous people right away, even those who had just visited him the day before. When they returned, he often asked them again, "Who are you?" He was a gentleman, but he often scaled down a welcome to someone when he or she wanted to visit him. Many people thought that he was an arrogant teacher, and at that time, I had to agree with them.

And then there came a certain night. I was getting ready to leave my country to come to the United States to study. That night, the sky was wonderful with a light moon and bright stars. I went to my teacher's house to say goodbye. My teacher, being tired after a long day of working, was sitting under the old bamboo. We sat in quiet for a long time, not saying a word. At last, while I was adding hot tea to his cup, he pointed at the sky and asked me which stars I liked the best and if I remembered their names. I pointed at the

Triones, the stars I loved very much.

He said, "I love them too. I love them because they are beautiful stars, but I know their names because they are useful stars for people to find out where is the North." And then he showed me the rice field far beyond his home and said, "On the day when you come back to this land from the United States, if you can make this field to have good harvest, so that children do not have the nightmare and cry at midnight by the hunger, then I will never forget your name; I will be very happy to ask you 'Minh, how are you?' Otherwise, if you cannot do anything good for this field and our children, then I will hardly remember your name because you will have nothing for me to touch."

Now, under the night sky of California, walking home from school, I miss my teacher very much. I want to hear, "Minh, how are you?" I am looking at the Triones and my heart sings, "A time to study, a time for service and a time to be welcomed home."

Chapter 2
Passages

Over the last five centuries, 60 million people have immigrated to the U.S. They have come in waves: sometimes a great flood of newcomers, sometimes a trickle. Historians identify four waves—the colonial period (1607 to 1789), the middle of the nineteenth century (the 1840s to the 1870s), the turn of the century (the 1880s to the 1920s) and the current wave (1965 to the present). About two thirds of the immigrants have come from Europe, yet there was never a time when the U.S. population was exclusively European.

By today's standards, the first wave was just a ripple. In the entire colonial period, fewer than a million people arrived to make new lives on the North American shore. Although they were few in number compared to the immigrants who came after them, their descendants constitute approximately half the country's current population. About 600,000 of the colonial immigrants were European settlers. Among them the English predominated, but significant numbers of Scots, Dutch, Germans, Swedes, Irish and French arrived as well. Almost 300,000 of the immigrants were West Africans, brought as involuntary participants in the slave trade. The Africans taken came mostly from the Yoruba, Dahomey, Ashanti, Ife, Congo and Oyo peoples. The slave trade was made illegal by Congress in 1807, but slavery itself continued until the Civil War. The immigrants of the colonial period did not encounter an empty continent, but rather one populated with indigenous nations and mestizo communities in territories controlled by Spain. Thus, from the beginning immigration created multiethnic relationships.

The Europeans responded to the earlier inhabitants by dispossessing them of their lands.

After the independence of the United States in 1776, immigration slowed, but it picked up again in the 1840s. In the middle of the nineteenth century, immigration formed a higher proportion of the U.S. population than at any time since. The majority of the second-wave immigrants were also European. Some still came from England, but they were now outnumbered by the Irish and the Germans. The great potato famine and the policies of Great Britain sent millions of destitute Irish to America, while the expansion of the industrial revolution to central Europe destroyed the agricultural feudalism there and sent rural Germans on their way to find new lives. Although the immigrants of the second wave came mostly from the European countryside, few of them ended up on American farms. They provided, instead, the labor for the new American industrial civilization. They built the canals and the railways. They worked in the new factories and served in the Civil War. Not all of these immigrants were European, however, especially on the West Coast.

The peak years of early Chinese immigration were 1848 to 1882, an era that began with the Gold Rush in California and continued with the building of the transcontinental railroad. Most of the Chinese immigrants of the second wave came from seven districts of southern China, in the province of Kwangtung, and from the vicinity of Canton. They sought work in this country; many had the intention of returning home with their savings. Chinese males comprised nearly one-quarter of the wage laborers of California in the 1870s. Chinese immigration was abruptly halted by the passage of the Chinese Exclusion Act of 1882, an explicitly xenophobic measure designed to ensure that West Coast opportunities be reserved for those of European descent.

Japanese immigrants came to the U.S. for similar reasons. Many had migrated to Hawaii, and from Hawaii they came to the West Coast. Originally from the southern parts of Hiroshima, Kumamonto, Wakayame, Fukuoka and Yamaguchi, most had been farm laborers or small farmers who were pushed out by economic change.

The annexation of the Southwest following the Mexican-American War in 1848—under the Treaty of Guadalupe Hidalgo and in 1853 with the Gadsden Purchase—incorporated several hundred thousand Spanish speakers into the United States. Most Mexican Americans, who held title to lands under earlier Spanish Land Grants, lived in relative isolation in the border states of Texas, New Mexico, Arizona, and California. Most Mexican Americans, who were mestizo—of Spanish and Indian descent—never made a decision to come to the United States; the United States came to them.

The third wave, from the 1880s to the 1920s, was the period of the largest immigrant flow. Approximately 25 million people arrived during those decades. This time they came from southern and eastern Europe: from Italy, from Greece, from the territories of the Austro-Hungarian Empire and from Poland and Russia. Every corner of Europe was being transformed by the scientific, commercial, and capitalist revolutions that mark the modern era. Persecution drove out thousands as well.

During this period, the open border with Mexico allowed U.S. agriculture and Mexican labor to develop in tandem. The Mexican Revolution also sent about one million persons fleeing north across the border between 1910 and 1920. The conquest of the Philippines by the United States during the Spanish-American War also brought thousands of Filipinos to the expanding U.S. agricultural sector in California and Hawaii.

Throughout most of the first, second and third waves, immigration into the U.S. was essentially unrestricted by the laws of the country. The passage was expensive, difficult and often life-threatening and the conditions the immigrants met upon arrival were often bleak—but if they wanted to come, the authorities did not stand in their way. This began to change as a result of the third wave. Anti-immigrant and nativist forces, always present, grew in number and influence and are with us today. The poet Thomas Bailey Aldrich wrote in 1882:

In street and alley what strange tongues are these,
Accents of menace in our ear;
Voice that once the Tower of Babel knew.

Gradually, Congress shut immigration down. The first measure was the Chinese Exclusion Act of 1882, an explicitly racist measure. Decades later, a series of quota acts in the 1920s reduced the annual flow of immigration from a million a year to just a few hundred thousand and skewed the source countries strongly toward Britain, Ireland and Germany. The door was closed tight to the relatives of most of the people who made up the great third wave.

The door stayed tight through the Depression, the second world war and the immediate post-war period. Then it was slowly opened again in the 1960s, making possible the current, fourth wave. The irony of the fourth wave is that Congress made no explicit decision to resume the tradition of welcoming immigrants. The Immigration Act of 1965 was thought at the time to be a measure to remove the racism inherent in the quota acts and to allow refugees from Communism to enter the country. The act was a response to both the civil rights movement and the cold war. No politician at the time expected the number of immigrants to explode and the source countries to shift radically, yet that is what happened.

Immigration rose steadily from the 1960s through the 1990s, reaching in some years the numbers achieved during the third wave. Today's fourth-wave immigrants come mostly from Latin America (especially Mexico and the Caribbean basin) and from Asia. Most of the Latin American immigrants are poor and working class. They work in the fields, and they take the lowest paying, lowest status jobs in the cities: hotel maid, dishwasher, street cleaner, as immigrants have always done in this country. Some of the Asians are poor as well but many are well educated and some have professional skills. They come from China, Taiwan, Korea, Vietnam, the Philippines, Indonesia, India and Pakistan.

   Some of today's immigrants are admitted because they help to meet a specific labor shortage in particular industry in the United States, while others qualify because they are refugees who fear persecution in their home countries. Some come without authorization. Most, however, enter legally because of a family relationship with an American resident.

   Today's immigrants are remaking the nation, changing its ethnic composition and bringing new languages, cultures and ideas to its communities. In countless ways, they are making the diversity of the United States reflect the diversity of the world.

In the Land of the Free
Sui Sin Far

Sui Sin Far, (1865–1914), was the first Asian American writer of fiction to be published in the U.S. The eldest of fourteen children, she was born Edith Maud Eaton in England to a Chinese mother and an English father. Her short story collection *Mrs. Spring Fragrance* was published in 1912. This short story dramatizes the anti-Chinese immigration policies of the period.

"SEE, LITTLE ONE—THE HILLS IN THE MORNING SUN, THERE IS THY home for years to come. It is very beautiful and thou wilt be very happy there."

The Little One looked up into his mother's face in perfect faith. He was engaged in the pleasant occupation of sucking a sweetmeat; but that did not prevent him from gurgling responsively.

"Yes, my olive bud; there is where thy father is making a fortune for thee. Thy father! Oh, wilt thou not be glad to behold his dear face. 'Twas for thee I left him."

The Little One ducked his chin sympathetically against his mother's knee. She lifted him on to her lap. He was two years old, a round, dimple-cheeked boy with bright brown eyes and a sturdy little frame.

"Ah! Ah! Ah! Ooh! Ooh! Ooh!" puffed he, mocking a tugboat steaming by.

San Francisco's waterfront was lined with ships and steamers, while other craft, large and small, including a couple of white transports from the Philippines, lay at anchor here and there off shore. It was some time before the *Eastern Queen* could get docked, and even after that was accomplished, a lone Chinaman who had been waiting on the wharf for an hour was detained that much longer by men with the initials U.S.C. on their caps, before he could board the steamer and welcome his wife and child.

"This is thy son," announced the happy Lae Choo.

Hom Hing lifted the child, felt of his little body and limbs, gazed into his face with proud and joyous eyes; then turned inquiringly to a customs officer at his elbow.

"That's a fine boy you have there," said the man. "Where was he born?"

"In China," answered Hom Hing, swinging the Little One on his right shoulder, preparatory to leading his wife off the steamer.

"Ever been to America before?"

"No, not he," answered the father with a happy laugh.

The customs officer beckoned to another.

"This little fellow," said he, "is visiting America for the first time."

The other customs officer stroked his chin reflectively.

"Good day," said Hom Hing.

"Wait!" commanded one of the officers. "You cannot go just yet."

"What more now?" asked Hom Hing.

"I'm afraid," said the customs officer, "that we cannot allow the boy to go ashore. There is nothing in the papers that you have shown us—your wife's papers and your own—having any bearing upon the child."

"There was no child when the papers were made out," returned Hom Hing. He spoke calmly; but there was apprehension in his eyes and in his tightening grip on his son.

"What is it? What is it?" quavered Lae Choo, who understood a little English.

The second customs officer regarded her pityingly.

"I don't like this part of the business," he muttered.

The first officer turned to Hom Hing and in an official tone of voice, said:

"Seeing that the boy has no certificate entitling him to admission to this country you will have to leave him with us."

"Leave my boy!" exclaimed Hom Hing.

"Yes; he will be well taken care of, and just as soon as we can hear from Washington he will be handed over to you."

"But," protested Hom Hing, "he is my son."

"We have no proof," answered the man with a shrug of his shoulders; "and even if so we cannot let him pass without orders from the Government."

"He is my son," reiterated Hom Hing, slowly and solemnly. "I am a Chinese merchant and have been in business in San Francisco for many years. When my wife told to me one morning that she dreamed of a green tree with spreading branches and one beautiful red flower growing thereon, I answered her that I wished my son to be born in our country, and for her to prepare to go to China. My wife complied with my wish. After my son was born my mother fell sick and my wife nursed and cared for her; then my father, too, fell sick, and my wife also nursed and cared for him. For twenty moons my wife cared for and nurse the old people, and when they die they bless her and my son, and I send for her to return to me. I had no fear of trouble. I was a Chinese merchant and my son was my son."

"Very good, Hom Hing," replied the first officer. "Nevertheless, we take your son."

"No, you not take him; he my son too."

It was Lae Choo. Snatching the child from his father's arms she held and covered him with her own.

The officers conferred together for a few moments; then one drew Hom Hing aside and spoke in his ear.

Resignedly Hom Hing bowed his head, then approached his wife. " 'Tis the law," said he, speaking in Chinese, "and 'twill be but for a little while—until tomorrow's sun arises."

"You too," reproached Lae Choo in a voice eloquent with pain. But accustomed to obedience she yielded the boy to her husband, who in turn delivered him to the first officer. The Little One protested lustily against the transfer; but his mother covered her face with her sleeve and his father silently led her away. Thus was the law of the land complied with.

2

Day was breaking. Lae Choo, who had been awake all night, dressed herself, then awoke her husband.

" 'Tis the morn," she cried. "Go, bring our son."

The man rubbed his eyes and arose upon his elbow so that he could see out of the window. A pale star was visible in the sky. The petals of a lily in a bowl on the windowsill were unfurled.

" 'Tis not yet time," said he, laying his head down again.

"Not yet time. Ah, all the time that I lived before yesterday is not so much as the time that has been since my Little One was taken from me."

The mother threw herself down beside the bed and covered her face.

Hom Hing turned on the light, and touching his wife's bowed head with a sympathetic hand inquired if she had slept.

"Slept!" she echoed, weepingly. "Ah, how could I close my eyes with my arms empty of the little body that has filled them every night for more than twenty moons! You do not know—man—what it is to miss the feel of the little fingers and the little toes and the soft round limbs of your little one. Even in the darkness his darling eyes used to shine up to mine, and often have I fallen into slumber with his pretty babble at my ear. And now, I see him not; I touch him not; I hear him not. My baby, my little fat one!"

"Now! Now! Now!" consoled Hom Hing, patting his wife's shoulder reassuringly; "there is no need to grieve so; he will soon gladden you again. There cannot be any law that would keep a child from its mother!"

Lae Choo dried her tears.

"You are right, my husband," she meekly murmured. She arose and stepped about the apartment, setting things to rights. The box of presents she had brought for her California friends had been opened the evening before; and silks, embroideries, carved ivories, ornamental lacquer-ware, brasses, camphorwood boxes, fans, and chinaware were scattered around in confused heaps. In the midst of unpacking the thought of her child in the hands of strangers had overpowered her, and she had left everything to crawl into bed and weep.

Having arranged her gifts in order she stepped out on to the deep balcony.

The star had faded from view and there were bright streaks in the western sky. Lae Choo looked down the street and around. Beneath the flat occupied by her and her husband were quarters for a number of bachelor Chinamen, and she could hear them from where she stood, taking their early morning breakfast. Below their dining-room was her husband's grocery store. Across the way was a large restaurant. Last night it had been resplendent with gay colored lanterns and the sound of music. The rejoicings over "the completion of the moon," by Quong Sum's firstborn, had been long and loud, and had caused her to tie a handkerchief over her ears. She, a bereaved mother, had it not in her heart to rejoice with other parents. This morning the place was more in accord with her mood. It was still and quiet. The revellers had dispersed or were asleep.

A roly-poly woman in black sateen, with long pendant earrings in her ears, looked up from the street below and waved her a smiling greeting. It was her old neighbor, Kuie Hoe, the wife of the gold embosser, Mark Sing. With her was a little boy in yellow jacket and lavender pantaloons. Lae Choo remembered him as a baby. She used to like to play with him in those days when she had no child of her own. What a long time ago that seemed! She caught her breath in a sigh, and laughed instead.

"Why are you so merry?" called her husband from within.

"Because my Little One is coming home," answered Lae Choo. "I am a happy mother—a happy mother."

She pattered into the room with a smile on her face.

The noon hour had arrived. The rice was steaming in the bowls and a fragrant dish of chicken and bamboo shoots was awaiting Hom Hing. Not for one moment had Lae Choo paused to rest during the morning hours; her activity had been ceaseless. Every now and again, however, she had raised her eyes to the gilded clock on the curiously carved mantelpiece. Once, she had exclaimed:

"Why so long, oh! why so long?" Then, apostrophizing herself: "Lae Choo, be happy. The Little One is coming! The Little One is coming!" Several times she burst into tears, and several times she laughed aloud.

Hom Hing entered the room; his arms hung down by his side.

"The Little One!" shrieked Lae Choo.

"They bid me call tomorrow."

With a moan the mother sank to the floor.

The noon hour passed. The dinner remained on the table.

3

The winter rains were over: the spring had come to California, flushing the hills with green and causing an ever-changing pageant of flowers to pass over them. But there was no spring in Lae Choo's heart, for the Little One remained away from her arms. He was being kept in a mission. White women were caring for him, and though for one full moon he had pined for his mother and refused to be comforted he was now apparently happy and contented. Five moons or five months had gone by since the day he had passed with Lae Choo through the Golden Gate; but the great Government at Washington still delayed sending the answer which would return him to his parents.

Hom Hing was disconsolately rolling up and down the balls in his abacus box when a keen-faced young man stepped into his store.

"What news?" asked the Chinese merchant.

"This!" The young man brought forth a typewritten letter. Hom Hing read the words:

"Re Chinese child, alleged to be the son of Hom Hing, Chinese merchant, doing business at 425 Clay Street, San Francisco.

"Same will have attention as soon as possible."

Hom Hing returned the letter, and without a word continued his manipulation of the counting machine.

"Have you anything to say?" asked the young man.

"Nothing. They have sent the same letter fifteen times before. Have you not yourself showed it to me?"

"True!" The young man eyed the Chinese merchant furtively. He had a proposition to make and was pondering whether or not the time was apportune.

"How is your wife?" he inquired solicitously—and diplomatically.

Hom Hing shook his head mournfully.

"She seems less every day," he replied. "Her food she takes only when I bid her and her tears fall continually. She finds no pleasure in dress or flowers and cares not to see her friends. Her eyes stare all night. I think before another moon she will pass into the land of spirits."

"No!" exclaimed the young man, genuinely startled.

"If the boy not come home I lose my wife sure," continued Hom Hing with bitter sadness.

"It's not right," cried the young man indignantly. Then he made his proposition.

The Chinese father's eyes brightened exceedingly.

"Will I like you to go to Washington and make them give you the paper to restore my son?" cried he. "How can you ask when you know my heart's desire?"

"Then," said the young fellow, "I will start next week. I am anxious to see this thing through if only for the sake of your wife's peace of mind."

"I will call her. To hear what you think to do will make her glad," said Hom Hing.

He called a message to Lae Choo upstairs through a tube in the wall.

In a few moments she appeared, listless, wan, and hollow-eyed; but when her husband told her the young lawyer's suggestion she became electrified; her form straightened, her eyes glistened; the color flushed to her cheeks.

"Oh," she cried, turning to James Clancy. "You are a hundred man good!"

The young man felt somewhat embarrassed; his eyes shifted a little under the intense gaze of the Chinese mother.

"Well, we must get your boy for you," he responded. "Of course"—turning to Hom Hing—"it will cost a little money. You can't get fellows to hurry the Government for you without gold in your pocket."

Hom Hing stared blankly for a moment. Then: "How much do you want, Mr. Clancy?" he asked quietly.

"Well, I will need at least five hundred to start with."

Hom Hing cleared his throat.

"I think I told to you the time I last paid you for writing letters for me and seeing the Custom boss here that nearly all I had was gone!"

"Oh, well then we won't talk about it, old fellow. It won't harm the boy to stay where he is, and your wife may get over it all right."

"What that you say?" quavered Lae Choo.

James Clancy looked out of the window.

"He says," explained Hom Hing in English, "That to get our boy we have to have much money."

"Money! Oh, yes."

Lae Choo nodded her head.

"I have not got the money to give him."

For a moment Lae Choo gazed wonderingly from one face to the other; then, comprehension dawning upon her, with swift anger, pointing to the lawyer, she cried: "You not one hundred man good; you just common white man."

"Yes ma'am," returned James Clancy, bowing and smiling ironically.

Hom Hing pushed his wife behind him and addressed the lawyer again: "I might try," said he, "to raise something; but five hundred—it is not possible."

"What about four?"

"I tell you I have next to nothing left and my friends are not rich."

"Very well!"

The lawyer moved leisurely toward the door, pausing on its threshold to light a cigarette.

"Stop, white man; white man, stop!"

Lae Choo, panting and terrified, had started forward and now stood beside him, clutching his sleeve excitedly.

"You say you can go to get paper to bring my Little One to me if Hom Hing give you five hundred dollars?"

The lawyer nodded carelessly; his eyes were intent upon the cigarette which would not take the fire from the match.

"Then you go get paper. If Hom Hing not can give you five hundred dollars—I give you perhaps what more that much."

She slipped a heavy gold bracelet from her wrist and held it out to the man. Mechanically he took it.

"I go get more!"

She scurried away, disappearing behind the door through which she had come.

"Oh look here, I can't accept this," said James Clancy, walking back to Hom Hing and laying down the bracelet before him.

"It's all right," said Hom Hing, seriously, "pure China gold. My wife's parent give it to her when we married."

"But I can't take it anyway," protested the young man.

"It is all same as money. And you want money to go to Washington," replied Hom Hing in a matter-of-fact manner.

"See, my jade earrings—my gold buttons—my hairpins—my comb of pearl and my rings—one, two, three, four, five rings; very good—very good—all same much money. I give them all to you. You take and bring me paper for my Little One."

Lae Choo piled up her jewels before the lawyer.

Hom Hing laid a restraining hand upon her shoulder. "Not all, my wife," he said in Chinese. He selected a ring—a gift to Lae Choo when she dreamed of the tree with the red flower. The rest of the jewels he pushed toward the white man.

"Take them and sell them," said he. "They will pay your fare to Washington and bring you back with the paper."

For one moment James Clancy hesitated. He was not a sentimental man; but something within him arose against accepting such payment for his services.

"They are good, good," pleadingly asserted Lae Choo, seeing his hesitation. Whereupon he seized the jewels, thrust them into his coat pocket, and walked rapidly away from the store.

4

Lae Choo followed after the missionary woman through the mission nursery school. Her heart was beating so high with happiness that she could scarcely breathe. The paper had come at last—the precious paper which gave Hom Hing and his wife the right to the possession of their own child. It was ten months now since he had been taken from them—

ten months since the sun had ceased to shine for Lae Choo.

The room was filled with children—most of them wee tots, but none so wee as her own. The mission woman talked as she walked. She told Lae Choo that little Kim, as he has been named by the school, was the pet of the place, and that his little tricks and ways amused and delighted every one. He had been rather difficult to manage at first and had cried much for his mother; but children so soon forget, and after a month he seemed quite at home and played around as bright and happy as a bird.

"Yes," responded Lee Choo. "Oh, yes, yes!"

But she did not hear what was said to her. She was walking in a maze of anticipatory joy.

"Wait here, please," said the mission woman, placing Lae Choo in a chair. "The very youngest ones are having their breakfast."

She withdrew for a moment—it seemed like an hour to the mother—then she reappeared leading by the hand a little boy dressed in blue cotton overalls and white-soled shoes. The little boy's face was round and dimpled and his eyes were very bright.

"Little One, ah, my Little One!" cried Lae Choo.

She fell on her knees and stretched her hungry arms toward her son.

But the Little One shrunk from her and tried to hide himself in the folds of the white woman's skirt.

"Go 'way, go 'way!" he bade his mother.

When It Happens It Seems Altogether Impossible
Hayan Charara

Hayan Charara was born in Detroit to Lebanese Muslim immigrants. His first book of poems is titled *The Alchemist's Diary*. He is also the editor of the annual literary anthology, *Graffiti Rag*.

Your stomach lay flat
against the floor, the empty
beer bottles stacked
to the ceiling and
cigarettes in cardboard boxes.
You are unable to get over
a man as desperate as this,
to hold a gun to your back
and tell you as you stare
at the dirt between
the cracks of the floor tile,
after he is finished
robbing you,
he is going to shoot.
You decide it is because
you said to him
"Take what you want."
or "God bless you."
Perhaps he doesn't believe
in the one true church,
or the priest from
his parish slept with his wife.
Whatever the case, it seems
impossible. You cannot
give reasons for him.

Did you believe you could
be killed across the street
from the gas station where
police ate their lunches?
Suppose nobody heard

the sound of the bullet—
the old Polish lady
whose cousin is always drunk;
the trembling idiot
standing in front of cars
on Wyoming Avenue
wanting to get hit;
your father asleep in a brick house
built hundreds of years ago
on a hill in Lebanon
where the Phoenicians
built ships for Solomon,
Jesus rested his feet, the Turks
drank thick coffee and jiddi,
Hajj Ali, rolled his own cigarettes
from the tobacco leaves he grew?
You could die and nobody
would hear. And then?

How do you, my father's shadow,
the grocer, make sense of it all?
Perhaps it was
the dark color of your skin,
the photographs of famous Arabs
on the wall behind the counter,
your name, Abdul Karim,
or maybe because
the car parked outside
was not made here.
Did you imagine
the impossible, a grave
with your name on it
here in Detroit, not next to
your mother's in Bint Jubail,
and that is the reason
that the thief who believed
himself a failure
pulled away the pistol
in his hand and said as he left,
"This is your lucky day, Camel Jockey!"

On the Mountain, The Cathedral and the Fast-Food Culture (A Tale of Two Worlds)

Florin Ion Firimita

Florin Ion Firimita is a Romanian American visual artist who escaped death during the anti-communist uprising in December, 1989, and immigrated to the United States the following year. After becoming a U.S. citizen, he settled in a tranquil Connecticut community where he paints and writes almost every day. This essay contrasts the peace he found in the Carpathian Mountains with his first impressions of the United States.

Eighty miles away from Bucharest, surrounded by mountains, in the Romanian province of Transylvania, there is a medieval burg called Brasov, a place where people lived for generations in the same old stone houses and went out for drinks on Friday nights in pubs opened three hundred years ago. In Brasov, I established a base for my expeditions in the Carpathian Mountains with Tino, an old friend who was a meteorologist at one of the highest altitude stations in Romania. Many times he invited me to spend my vacations up there, away from the city, 8,200 feet above sea level, in a WW II building with large metal doors and steel window shutters, that always shook in the high altitude winds.

In the mornings, we would collect fresh snow in big pots, boil it and finally cool it for our water supply; then, occasionally, the electric generator would break down, and being too tired to repair it, we would use candles at dinner while talking about Bruce Springsteen, climbing techniques or books. At night, through the old-fashioned small radio station, under the crystal-clear sky, we listened to the voice of the world and made plans for leaving Romania. The place, quite inaccessible for tourists, was perfect for my readings from Goethe or Tolstoy, and many times during the winter, especially when the snow isolated us from the world for weeks, we went out and skied under the moonlight. Sometimes a helicopter would break the silence of the valleys and land on the small platform next to the building only for a few minutes to drop some blankets and canned food. Frequently, in the morning, we found our supply of seltzer water converted into bottled ice, and often scared and disoriented wolves, looking like faithful pets, showed up in search of food or maybe attention. There were never more than four or five people at the station, and somehow, that gave me a sense of owning my private Himalayas, away from the city and its daily circus.

Each of us had a laconic nickname: "the General," an elderly army officer; "Clapton," the Guitar Player; me, "the Painter," and a few others. Without noticing, we developed strong friendships for the simple reason that we were all looking for an escape, and conquering the mountain and talking about books or politics was the immediate and only available form of revolt. I never painted up there, except for the big red cross on the roof of the alpine refuge that could be seen from the rescue helicopter, but I would draw with my inner eye, using my memory as a sketch pad. When the weather permitted, I went outside on the roof to watch the fog and the colors, the eagles and the shadows, and often listened to classical music. In the winter it was always Bach, and since then I cannot separate his music from the songs of the avalanches, the power of the winds or the contrast between the rocks and the snow. Under that enormous and silent Sistine Chapel, I was closer to the sky than ever before. I could think about the things that frightened me. I found out how to read between the lines. And I learned how to listen. On top of the mountain I discovered how much I liked those quiet times, while trying to understand and know what "the verticals," the mountains represented.

From time to time we slid on our skis to Brasov, where Tino's family lived. Almost every weekend we went and listened to the organ concerts held in the town's cathedral, built in 1384 in the shadow of the mountain and named "The Black Church" because of a devastating fire that partially destroyed it in the seventeenth century. I never found too many natives inside, only a few peasants, the only beggar, who was the "official" one of the church, and sometimes a few German or French tourists. The organist played almost every Saturday, announced by a handwritten poster pinned to the massive oak and iron door, and I always had the feeling that he was never expecting anyone. Actually, I never saw him. With the profoundness of prayer, he was playing only for himself. There was nothing compared with the feeling of being in that unrestored church, with its Persian rugs, simple stained glass windows and old guild flags. The music gave me the same feeling of freedom, inner peace and security found on the top of the mountain. Listening to Bach was like climbing a never-ending spiral staircase; the notes sounded strong and upstanding and the echo lasted a long time after the music was gone until the sudden click of the wooden keyboard cover would wake me up from my reflections. All my childhood and adolescence was like that: surrounded by music, paintings, books and mountain villages, listening to the shepherds telling legends around campfires. Was this an immature attempt of survival by avoiding reality, or a desperate search for a divinity who seemed to be absent or hiding in books and organ concerts? Most of us were part of a rather unsophisticated underground culture: the dark humor, the political cabaret, Fellini's movies, Top 40 of Radio Free Europe, Xeroxed copies of *The Gulag Archipelago*, *Hamlet*; the evening concerts of classical music always sold out even when a minor piece was performed— they were all part of us.

Three years have now passed, and I have found myself among a different sort of "verticals" in America. I was told before coming here that this was a loud country without poets and cathedrals; a culture of doing rather than thinking, where the Gothic arches have been replaced by the McDonald's arches (as a businessman, Socrates would have failed here miserably). Seen from the other side of the Atlantic, and from the point of view of someone fed daily black and white television propaganda, my knowledge about the reality of the United States was limited to the *Voice of America* and the colorful posters in front of the foreign embassies in Bucharest. To my mind, the United States was a place where people communicated through fax machines with a God who supplied a type of soul-savings bond. On

the dollar bill, "In God We Trust" was a confusing state-
ment to me because I was born in a culture that did not
believe in money. I found myself immigrating to a society
that was too clever and too busy to just lay back and con-
template. It was Madonna versus Goethe, the political ver-
sus the poetical, the interviews of Geraldo Rivera versus
the confessions of Saint Augustine, mass communication
against simple dialogue, the image against the word. What
was I bringing to this new world? The shadows of a revolu-
tion, the names of Ceausescu, Nadia Comaneci and Dracula,
and an undefined desire to succeed?

In New York, walking near Saint Patrick's, I noticed
that this cathedral didn't seem to have too many ambitions.
The insurance company's headquarters, a skyscraper of
glass, mirrors and steel dwarfed the cathedral. The boxy
skyscraper was closer to God than Saint Patrick's. Was this
cathedral just a figurehead, a way of disguising the wealth
of a too-powerful nation trying to catch up with history and
culture-oriented Europe by tolerating a cathedral on some
of the most valuable real estate in Manhattan? What in the
European burg represented the heart of the social life of the
community, seemed to survive here as an empty symbol. In
my old and tranquil Transylvanian town, there was some-
thing magical about the Black Church, but in the American
cathedral, the chaotic city was the enemy of any contempla-
tive attempt. The cathedral was not a place of dialogue; Bach
was missing and God was missing as well. There was a loss
of mystery watching the Gothic shadows of the cathedral
projected on the tall, ultramodern building, among scream-
ing ambulances, elegant women and tourists eating their
french fries on the stairs. New York City was closer to a
factory than a temple. I have learned that it makes a differ-
ence if behind the cathedral you find a mountain or a well-
designed skyscraper.

I often remember how, years back, when I was looking
for myself throughout the Romanian mountains, I had of-
ten found, way up in the most reclusive monasteries, the
real signs of the past: forgotten names engraved on decayed
tombstones, ancient hermitages in which the only beautification

was innocent, fresh chrysanthemum bouquets and in which the only meaningful, yet silent individuality was the Transcendental One. Coming from my pastoral Eastern European culture, the aggressive "verticality" of the Western world shocked and overpowered the first days of my new life here. Seeing the skyline of Manhattan and all it represented was the prelude to my process of "switching cultures." And while this new financial world scared me because this country knew so well what to do with its investments, I realized it had no idea what to do with its soul. I discovered that in coming to this country, I had lost many things, but I was about to gain many others. Happily, I began to move towards myself and I started to paint almost every day. A year ago I gave up switching my TV channels and went back to books; and although an entire wall in my apartment is packed with volumes written in my native language, I rarely read in Romanian.

Once in a while I get a letter from my friend, Tino, the meteorologist. He gave up his intentions of leaving Romania, got married and now has a son. I write him that I am becoming more and more a part of my new country. The McDonald's arches have slowly stopped reminding me of European cathedrals, and I can even get used to making money. Would he understand all this? He is happy still chasing the clouds 8,200 feet above sea level, and this is all that matters.

The Rearview Mirror
Marja Hagborg

Marja Hagborg was born in Finland to Karelian parents and lived in Sweden before moving to the U.S. in 1985. She became a U.S. citizen in 1996. She has an M.F.A. from the University of Gothenburg, Sweden, and has studied Creative Writing at Northwestern University and The University of Iowa. She lives in Chicago with her Swedish American husband and two cats.

1

I drove slowly and carefully, thinking that whatever happens, I was not going to kill myself in an accident on the roads of a miserable country. I didn't have too many sentimental bonds to the place where I was born.

After driving a few miles from the airport, I started to realize that there really was a possibility of being killed on the road; maniacs in their motor vehicles were all over the place, scaring me out of my wits and giving me all imaginable international hand signs. Even people in these forests knew how to give the finger. Maybe not a big surprise, since MTV, videos and the information superhighway reach every corner, every mudhole in this world.

I tried to ignore the drivers and enjoy the view. I had always loved Finland's emerald-green forests and small lakes with clear water, shimmering like clusters of diamonds. The crimson sun on the horizon blinded me with its intensity and sad beauty when a sudden anxiety struck me. A cacophony of inner voices filled my head, aching from hangover and fatigue after a long flight over the Atlantic. My father's angry voice kept asking me why didn't I listen to my mother and behave, wear skirts, perm my hair, get a real job, marry a Finnish man, have children, be normal (whatever that means). Why did I have to become a painter, a disappointment, a disgrace, a damned stupid renegade?

2

It was years since I had been in the town. I realized that what I had been expecting to find was not there anymore, or rather, it was there but not as I remembered it.

Most of the old houses had disappeared, so it felt like a generic town. The building had sad, gray facades and square corners, neon signs, and parking lots like most other towns. There was a Shell station; there were billboards urging and seducing you to smoke, to drink, to buy a faster car, promising you happiness, respect and ultimately, love.

There were Cafe Oscar, Pizzeria Pronto, and the Länsipäijännehämeen Market and a hoard of unemployed, slouching guys drinking beer in the bar next to the bus station, still men enough to comment on the shapes of females passing by. They were men in their thirties and forties; some might have been dreaming of winning the Lotto, the only realistic way to get rich. Some were just too tired to dream of anything. Life went on but it went by, more demanding than ever and always in a hurry. Pissing in the bushes behind the bus station might have been the only relief, ultimate protest or solace at the end of a hard day in an endless string of tough, meaningless weeks.

I bought a pack of cigarettes, and the young, rye blond, beautiful girl behind the counter gave me a broad smile which made me suspicious: Finns have never smiled without a reason and buying cigarettes didn't seem like a good excuse to show feeling to a stranger. But things change. I smiled back, self-consciously wondering whether I had ketchup on my face.

There was a mumbling in the group of the beer drinking men; a half dozen pairs of watery blue eyes were directed at me. I was walking away from the counter, mildly confused by the sudden friendliness, when one of the guys, with a thinning ponytail and a scab on his nose, walked over to me, taking cautious but wobbling steps.

"Excuse me miss," he said. "May I ask you something?" He took a deep breath and leaned against the nearest table. "My friends and I would like to know where you are from. You don't look like you are from here."

"California," I said, knowing that it sounded as if I were bragging, so I added, "but I was born here."

"Really!" I heard the chorus of guys.

I explained my background and my recent life using

some broad strokes.

The guy with the scab looked at me, tilting his heavy-looking head, and asked me what had brought me there. For a moment I didn't really know why I had come. It seemed to me that it was my pattern to visit my parents every third year.

"My father is not well," I said, knowing that it wasn't really the reason but was a good enough explanation.

"It's not often we have visitors like you," he said, "just all those stuck-up skanks from Helsinki, all kinds of summer guests and assholes who buy up the land." He sighed. "You know, there is not a lake left without log cabins, speed boats and screaming stereos."

I smiled, thinking that what else could you expect. I didn't say anything, but he must have sensed what I felt because he touched my arm with a shaking hand and said, "Remember now, don't you ever change."

3

"Damned American music," my father muttered as his cheeks grew red. It was the third day of my visit and the formal politeness of the first days had worn out and we were on the old track.

"Mindless and stupid . . . made for idiots . . . makes me sick. Turn that terrible noise off. Damned . . . "

My mother looked at me, blinking helplessly and smoothed creases in her white and blue apron.

"But it's her tape . . . " she whispered almost inaudibly and stood in the middle of the room, between him and me.

I was waiting for him to tell me once again that he didn't fight in the war for the country's independence to see his only kid become a parasite in California. We should have let the Russians win, he used to say, and by now we would all be playing balalaika in Siberia.*

"I don't need this damned noise in my house," he continued while I picked up my tape from the cassette player.

---

* That was what happened to many Estonians who lost the war and their independence.

"Never mind," I said to my mother. "I can use the head-phones. No problem at all."

I didn't look at my father but I knew that he was about to explode in his chair. The worst thing for him was to be ignored. I had learned early on how to make his life miserable without uttering a single word. I sensed his helpless anger, the rising steam in his purple head and I felt the sweetness of victory in the same way I had always felt while gliding elegantly away out of reach of his anger and bitterness.

He grabbed a newspaper and hid behind it. I didn't know whether to hate or feel sorry for this skinny old man, consumed by his own rage. To my surprise, I didn't feel much, the old cramp of frustration in my midriff was gone and my palms were dry. It was like being an outsider, as if I were watching a quite uninteresting movie.

4

In the sunshine the cemetery looked beautiful. My mother and I walked slowly between the graves, she in front of me, bending forward to look at the names on the grave-stones.

"Do you remember Gustav and Hilda?" she asked and stopped in front of two small wooden crosses. "Here they are. Both died the same year your grandpa died."

Yes, I remembered. I had hardly visited the cemetery since then because the place had always given me the creeps.

"Do you know that when I was a kid I thought the dead could come out of their graves and try to catch us?" I asked. My mother blinked as if she thought I was just kidding.

"I thought they would come during the night and pull screaming people into their deep and cold graves."

"I didn't know." My mother sounded surprised. "What are you talking about? What kind of nonsense is that?" She had stopped walking to catch her breath. I saw that she was getting old and easily tired.

"Mom, I have always been so scared of everything."

"You scared?" My mother's voice was thin and clear like a silver bell.

"I have never seen you scared of anything."

I realized then that she didn't. I had hidden my fears so brilliantly under aloofness or anger; she didn't have a clue. There wasn't a point in talking about it now. My life had really been full of fear and standing in the graveyard—even though it was a beautiful day—I was thinking about my grandfather's funeral.

It was in November. I was five years old and I didn't really know what it meant to die. The wind was blowing cold and damp from the lake over the gray landscape. The big fir trees around the cemetery chapel swayed slowly back and forth, moaning, shaking off heavy drops of water on the mourners. I squeezed my mother's hand, afraid of any unexplainable powers snatching me, pulling me into the deep black hole in the snowy ground with the rattling stones and gravel over my grandfather who was lying, wearing his best suit, in a black casket in the bottom of it.

Now the sun was so bright between the foliage of the gigantic birches and maples that I felt almost light-headed. So odd the memory seemed. Then I looked at my mother, walking in front of me, mumbling about people, alive and dead, totally absorbed by her own thoughts. I saw her narrow shoulders, her graying hair. I saw my mother, bird-like and fragile as I had always seen her. And yes, she had grown old, but she hadn't changed, I had.

5

I looked into the rearview mirror and saw my mother and father standing in the driveway, she waving, he standing with slouching shoulders, hanging his head. There they were—my mother with tears in her eyes, secretly proud of me; my father angry and stubbornly rejecting me and my chosen life. But his goodbye hug convinced me that he couldn't help himself being the way he was.

These were my parents and I loved them, even though I, not being better than my father, was unable to tell them. What had really kept me avoiding them? Was I afraid that they would snatch me—like the dead would snatch the living ones in the cemetery—just to take me and keep me as a prisoner in their unbearably empty lives, force me to become an exact copy of them and stay that way? Or was it just weariness?

I put my foot on the gas and gave a last look into the rearview mirror: there they were like two small dots on the horizon, disappearing.

The whole town was soon behind me. I was back on the road, on my way back to the airport, annoying drivers in their power cars by my impulsive driving style. They honked and gave me the finger and I did the same, smiling and singing along with Travis Tritt's "Ten Feet Tall and Bulletproof," which I would never, in my right mind, do on the California highways.

6

When the plane took off jerking and rattling for a moment, I felt that I would get sentimental and burst into tears. It never happened, though, because hearing the English-speaking flight attendant's perky voice explaining how to float with one's seat in case of a crash, I forgot my "goodbye-to-the-past" ritual. It was like changing the floppy disk in my head: I was back in civilization, normality, stability. I was back in my own life.

The morning sky was partly covered by dark purple clouds, curiously compact and heavy over the sea in the south. I stared at them, prayed for inspiration for my next painting and I promised myself that I would send it to my mother for Christmas.

"Coffee or tea, ma'am?" a pleasant voice with a British accent asked, interrupting my silent prayer and I got an irresistible desire to say in the most mocking way: "But of course!" because there is something so amusing in the way they speak, those loveable Britons. They sound so sophisticated and civilized. The flight attendant was a man, tall and thin and he was absolutely loveable. I was happy; I was on my way home.

A Room With A View
by Qun Wang

An immigrant from China, Qun Wang is Associate Professor of Humanities at California State University, Monterey Bay. This short story describes the trauma of a young man who vicariously experiences the bloody events in Tiananmen Square on the eve of his return back to China. Sensing that the student democracy movement in China would require containment by force, the Chinese government in 1989 ordered all Chinese students living overseas to return to China immediately. The Chinese government hoped to prevent a deluge of applications for political asylum abroad—which is exactly what happened after Tiananmen Square.

Fifteen days after he received his Ph.D. in English, Tod Lu was notified by the Chinese Consulate in San Francisco that he was scheduled to leave for China on June 5, 1989. However for the last 48 hours, he had been glued to the television screen. Except for occasional trips to the kitchen, he hadn't moved. Not being able to sleep for two days straight had finally taken its toll. Mental fatigue and physical exhaustion had lowered his contact with reality to the minimal level but broadened his imagination to its maximum capacity. His mind started to take its own course. It threw him into a world that looked so familiar and yet so strange:

For a brief moment, he couldn't remember where he was. The room was large and clean. Its fragrant smell had an intoxicating effect on him. The soft colors of the walls and furniture made him sleepy. He knew this was not home, though. The bed was too soft. There was no traffic noise or dust. The television set, the VCR, the couch, the carpet, and the calmness of the air all suggested that he was in a foreign environment.

He wanted to explore and experiment. He wanted to stay. He wanted to become a permanent part of the room so badly, he wouldn't mind turning himself into an inanimate object. His time, though was limited. He knew he had to hurry.

He looked around the room surreptitiously and awkwardly moved his feet.

He walked on his toes.

He could feel the presence of other people in the room. He knew they were there. They were probably waiting for the right moment to jump on him and take him as their prisoner.

His heart started to pound like a rabbit's, so hard that he was afraid that someone would arrest him for disturbing the peace.

He decided to take the initiative:

"Come out, you bastards! Come and get me. I'm not afraid anymore. Let's get it over with!"

He prodded his invisible audience.

"Hey, wouldn't it be a tremendous relief to all parties involved if we get this thing over with? Come and get me. I'm tired of this shit."

The audience opted to remain silent.

He became frustrated and infuriated. He didn't know what move they were going to take next.

"How can I fight an invisible enemy and win?" he wondered to himself.

Now he could empathize with those who were taken to an execution ground without being told they would be executed. Anxiety alone could kill a person long before the bullets hit.

Then, he saw the soldiers.

"I know you bastards would come out from hiding someday. Come and get me," he defiantly shouted to the soldiers.

They marched on as if they were deaf.

"Why are there so many soldiers?" he wondered. "Don't they usually have one police officer aim his pistol at one prisoner?"

He recalled a popular television program in China: public execution. He hated the part where they put an iron stick in the bullet hole on the back of the prisoner's head and twisted it. A close friend who worked for the Public Security Bureau in Shanghai once told him that the stick was to make sure the person was dead. Sometimes the bullet wasn't lethal enough to kill a person. Twisting the stick in the hole would effectively destroy the brain.

"And Americans thought using water to persecute a person to a slow death was Chinese torture. Hah," he snickered. "Lighten up. We're not in the stone age anymore. "

He redirected his vision to the soldiers. "Why are there so many of them?"

They were not carrying pistols. They were carrying rifles with bayonets. He looked around the room and shuddered. He was living, to use an American cliché, on borrowed time. He looked around the room again and was hit by the urge to laugh. He had forgotten why he was in the room.

"Damn it! It's those soldiers. They interrupted my train of thought. Wouldn't it be funny if I were arrested and executed for doing something I forgot to do? You can't kill a billion people," he shouted at the soldiers.

He remembered that he was necrophobic as a child. Even the mention of the word "morgue" would upset his stomach and could keep him awake most of the night. Their house was located in the middle of Lu Village. Sometimes in the middle of the night, he could hear people play music. To the imagination of a child who was afraid of the dark, there was no difference between the music of mourning and that of celebration. He had developed the notion that people only played music at funeral processions.

Death didn't appear as formidable to him now as it did before. After his mother was tortured to death during the "Cultural Revolution," he started to like funeral music. It had become the connection of his awareness of this world and his understanding of the world of death, the connection of his sense of reality and his imagination, and the connection of the ontological significance of his existence and people like his mother who had left their worldly worries and woes behind them for good.

He heard a roaring noise.

Through the room's large glass window, he saw tanks moving toward him.

"There are things that are still sacred in this world," he shouted. "Human lives are sacred! The square is sacred! This room is sacred! I am sacred! Go back to where you came from. The game's over."

The tanks ignored his order. They kept moving toward the room. The roaring noise became louder.

He became frustrated and infuriated. He didn't know what move they were going to take next.

"If I can only remember why I'm here," he murmured to himself. "If I can only remember . . . "

Someone was firing at someone else outside the window now. He heard gun shots.

He turned his head to the television screen. His heart sank. He saw a large group of young people about his age. They wore jeans and shirts. He could see blood oozing out of the gauze that covered their foreheads and arms. He was greatly moved by what he saw. He wanted to salute those who were willing to die for an abstract idea, for a metaphysical concept, those who condemned totalitarianism with their own blood and lives, those who, while limping along, carried their comrades-in-arms on their backs. No relationship could be purer than the one that was formed in blood. No friendship dearer than the one that was sealed in front of bullets, bayonets and tanks.

Suddenly, he felt differently about himself. He was free. As free as the person whose brain had just been stirred by an iron stick. All his life, he had worried about how other people would react and respond to what he said or what he did. Now he didn't care anymore. He felt purified by their baptism of fire. Lines from Laozi popped into his mind:

> Human life is soft;
> but its death should be staunch and strong.
> The life of trees and grass is weak and delicate;
> but their death is haggard.

He decided to help the wounded instead of trying to recall why he was in that room.

A voice yelled at him. "It's dangerous here. You better leave. Take care of yourself."

"I know. That's why I'm here. I want to help, " he replied.

"The soldiers are here. They are opening fire on their own people."

"Don't worry. They can't kill a billion people. They don't have a billion iron sticks," he shouted.

"What are you doing here," an officer wearing a starched uniform asked him. "Is this your room?" It was impossible to tell if the officer was American or Chinese.

"C'mon man. We have a war on our hands. We need to defend our freedom. We need to defend the idea of democracy. We need to establish a government that works for people, " he said.

"Excuse me, where are you from? Why are you here?"

"I'm in the room to help. I want to help."

A young man with blood on his forehead screamed at him, "C'mon, you get out of here. Go tell people our government is crazy. Let the whole world know. You leave and take care of yourself."

He didn't know there was so many Chinese who could speak English.

"Hey, you. What are you doing in this room? Can I see some ID? Otherwise, I'm going to call security."

"You can call whoever you want. I don't care. Did you hear what that man just told us? The soldiers are here. I don't care anymore. I'm not afraid anymore. I'm free."

After the officer looked at his ID, he urged him to leave the room as soon as possible.

"But the funny thing is," he laughed to himself, "I can't remember why I'm here."

A loud voice in Chinese shrieked out of a loudspeaker.

"All people must evacuate Tiananmen Square in 15 minutes. We will start clearing the square in fifteen minutes. If you don't leave, you must face the consequences."

He turned his head to the window and waited.

He then began to frantically search in his suitcases. After going through several of them, he finally found the plaque he was looking for. The Chinese character "Endure" stared him in the face. Two small lines at the bottom said, "Endure and you'll have peace; Be content and you'll always be happy." He had seen the words millions of times. But this time, something was different. He saw blood dripping from the wood. The characters weren't painted in ink with brushes. They were painted in blood with broken human limbs.

The large glass window of the room then became streaked with red.

He wished it were the sunset's glow. A closer look made him see the red that covered everything, red was everywhere—on the bodies, the walls, the carpet, the screen of the television set. He turned his head to the television. The screen was as red as the window. The air became so thick and dense, it was suffocating. He was drowning in blood. The revolution was over. Long live the revolution! But what about him?

"I don't want to live in ignorance. I want a room with a view!" He suddenly realized that he was all packed but had no place to go.

He put some rags in the crack between the door to the room and its frame. He didn't know what his neighbors would say if they saw blood ooze out into the hallway.

After he realized all his efforts to stop the blood from getting out of his room were futile, he screamed, "But I tried. I really tried . . . "

The room was getting dark . . .

Before he closed his eyes, he saw his plane ticket sitting on top of the bookshelf. Waiting for him. He would have to leave.

***

Several months after students' hopes for a new China were crushed by tanks, then-President George Bush issued a presidential directive. It allowed all students and visitors from Mainland China who had come to the United States before April 11, 1990 to stay in the country indefinitely. Tod Lu would have been in that group. Four years later, he would have been eligible to apply for permanent residency.

To Be Viet Kieu Is to Be Santa Claus
Andrew Lam

Andrew Lam is a syndicated writer and editor with the Pacific News Service, author of the book *Perfume Dreams: Reflections on the Vietnamese Diaspora* (2005), and a regular commentator on NPR's *All Things Considered*. Born in Saigon, he came to the U.S. at the end of the Vietnam War, when he was eleven years old.

Saigon—The scrawny street vendor studies my eyes, my lips. "Brother," he observes, "yours is not a Vietnamese face. It's a face that has not known suffering." Then, after a long sign, he concludes: "Had I escaped to America, brother, maybe I too would have such a face—a Viet Kieu's face."

Viet Kieu: Vietnamese nationals living abroad, especially those living in America, who return to Vietnam to serve as a kind of romantic mirror in front of which an entire population measures its lost potential. "If I had escaped to America . . . " becomes the secular equivalent to that well-turned Vietnamese phrase (from ancient Hindu-Buddhist tradition): "When I am reborn into the next life . . . "

In Vietnam, my face and my body take on mythological proportions. A cousin proudly introduces me to a friend, someone who has tried a dozen times to escape but, alas, in vain. "Ah, a Viet Kieu," declares the failed escapee as he reaches over to squeeze my thigh. I have no doubt that his is an impersonal gesture. Visions of double-tiered freeways and glassy high-rises are to be extracted out of the Viet Kieu's flesh. Squeeze a little harder and, who knows, you might just see Disneyland.

Since a Viet Kieu is presumed to be omniscient, at a dinner party people ask me to explain the intricacies of virtual reality, American foreign policy and, while I'm at it, genetic engineering. Another time my American passport is read like a comic book by various relatives. As the welcoming passport stamps of Greece, France, Mexico, Thailand and a dozen other countries flutter past my cousin's eyes like butterflies, she declares: "Brother, such happiness. It's as if you have wings."

Indeed, if in the last 3,000 years it was generally understood that a Vietnamese soul is tied to home and soil, in the last two decades a new idea has subverted the poetry of retrenchment: escape. In the last two decades *vuot bien*— escape from Vietnam—has probably crossed every Vietnamese mind. When the Vietnamese diaspora began at the end of the Vietnam War, nationalism—that firebrand weapon that defeated the Chinese, Mongolians, French and Americans—seemed to wither from old age.

The border cannot hold. Old Vietnamese leaders continue to emphasize the finer points of collective strength, invoking memories of a war against invaders. But the young of Vietnam have moved away from a parochial us-vs.-them mentality. If Uncle Ho Chi Minh once preached freedom and independence to his compatriots, today it is the Viet Kieu, those persecuted by Uncle Ho's followers and forced to escape, who exude freedom and independence.

As a Viet Kieu, I am not an individual here but an icon against hopelessness, a character who took the high road and through whose life many can live vicariously. There are stories of Viet Kieu scamming the most astute Communist official. There are more stories of kindhearted Viet Kieu who fulfill many an impoverished Vietnamese wish list.

I am mistaken for Santa Claus in Vietnam. A 12-year-old street urchin named Tam nonchalantly asks if I might adopt him and send him to school. A young woman named Phuong, her face deformed by a skin disease, begs for help. "Brother, you could perform a miracle, pay for my operation." And how many times, I wonder, have complete strangers—customs officials, rickshaw drivers, shop owners, ex-Viet Cong guerrillas—offered me their daughters' hands in marriage?

In the old quarters of Hanoi, my aunt's neighbor, a young piano teacher, falls in love with me. That I answered, "Yes, I do like Chopin," was clearly for her a declaration of romance. Chopin's music in due course echoes for hours from next door, riding the humid air to my bedroom window.

In Vietnam as a child, I remember being moved by the

national anthem that emphasized blood sacrifice for the land. I remember feeling inspiration, staring at ripened rice fields. I readily intuited why my mother placed my umbilical cord in an earthen jar and buried it deep in our garden after I was born.

But that was long ago. For me, as well as for many other Vietnamese Americans of my generation, those birth ties were severed and our innocence died when we fled to America.

I have left more than a country behind. Along with Vietnam my ancient agrarian-based assumptions of loyalty and spirituality have disappeared. Vietnam has ceased to claim my soul.

Returning today, a gap opens between my countrymen and me. If I am to them Santa Claus or Odysseus, I feel to myself helpless, overwhelmed by mass misery.

In Saigon a new movie, *People's Love*, claims to have been made both in Vietnam and the United States. In it, a Vietnamese American doctor, disillusioned with American life, returns home to find love and redemption. Such is the predictable government script. It draws few viewers.

I think the untold Vietnamese fantasy is closer to the reverse. Our nation's innocence died 20 years ago with the birth of the Viet Kieu. Vietnamese 21st century romance is not with land, but with borderless life.

No wings sprout from my back. I, nonetheless, have brought a boon back to Vietnam: myself. I am evidence the outside world exists.

Chapter 3
Immigrant Dreams, Survival,
Reflection

We are a country of immigrants, yet we have never gone out of our way to be accommodating to the newcomers in our midst. Not that the immigrants have expected anything else, as most have come from places where life was hard and nothing was handed to them. Some Americans, however, apparently feel that immigrants come largely to feed at the trough of the welfare system. This sentiment led to California's Proposition 187 in 1994, which cut undocumented immigrants off from virtually all of the state's social services and educational opportunities, and to the federal Welfare Reform and Immigration Acts of 1996, which cut even legal immigrants off from welfare benefits. The evidence is clear, however, that few immigrants come to the United States to claim health or welfare benefits. Survey data and other studies show that they come for other reasons: to find work, to rejoin their families and, in some cases, to escape tyranny.

A few immigrants are highly skilled and are recruited specifically to fill critical positions in American business and other institutions. Most, however, must start at the bottom of the ladder, no matter what their skills and job experiences were at home. Many immigrants with advanced degrees start out in the United States driving a cab, washing dishes or working in a motel. Why are they willing to accept such a sharp downward shift in status? Because of their dreams, it appears. The United States is seen as a prosperous nation, full of opportunities where a person may start at the bottom and, with hard work, move up. Or perhaps the dreams are focused on the children; it is not the immigrants who will benefit as much as it will be the next generation.

Some immigrants have low levels of formal education and few job-related skills. In some cases their English is limited or absent. They are relegated to the lowest-level rural and urban jobs, without much hope of upward mobility. They have come here because the wage rate is a multiple of what it is at home—so by working here they can save money to remit to their families, and possibly return home themselves. But many among even the least-prepared immigrants dream that they and their families will eventually participate in a meaningful way in American society.

Immigrants typically do the lowest paying, most unpleasant tasks that the American economy has to offer. They swing hoes, weed fields, harvest vegetables on the nation's farms—and because agricultural work is largely seasonal, they migrate around the country and across national borders. They do unskilled and semi-skilled work in the factories. They do service work in restaurants, hotels and laundries. To the extent that American households can afford to hire personal help for housecleaning, cooking and child care that help is increasingly provided by immigrants.

Some sectors of the economy, particularly in agriculture, services, and some manufacturing, depend upon immigrant labor. This explains why employers often support higher immigration, arguing for a loosening of the restrictions on legal immigration, for less strict enforcement of border controls and for amnesty for undocumented entrants. They know that immigration restrictions would curtail their access to cheap labor.

On the other hand, employers in sectors of the economy that do not depend upon immigrants are largely indifferent to the issue of immigration policy. In this respect, the labor markets of today are vastly different from the labor markets of a century ago, when the great third wave of immigration was at its height. The turn of the twentieth century was the era when large corporations were formed in the United States. In those days there was an almost insatiable demand for strong manual laborers. They were needed to run the mills and the foundries, and to dig the tons of earth for the canals, railroad tracks and roads. Those were the most important economic activities that drove the country to its unprecedented standard of living.

Today, strong backs are less in demand. Factories are filled with sophisticated computerized machines that require skilled operators, not muscle. Construction is performed by increasingly skilled members of crafts trades. Roads and bridges are built with enormous, multipurpose machines and fewer workers than in decades past. The information age has generated many semi-skilled jobs, but these are jobs for people with nimble fingers, not strong backs. While immigrant labor is needed by the U.S. economy, physical labor is not as critical as it once was to the dynamic center of the industrial system. The avenues of opportunity, for Americans and immigrants alike, appear to be narrowing.

The question facing America's new immigrants is whether they will be able to follow the paths forged by earlier generations of immigrants. By committing their energy, their education and their entrepreneurship, will they and their children and their grandchildren be able to move up the social ladder, from menial jobs to skilled jobs, from poor housing to decent housing, from the status of exploitable outsider to valued member of the wider American community? Will their dreams be fulfilled? The path seems harder today than it once was. Immigrants have always had to sacrifice and fight to fulfill their dreams—and the struggles in the twenty-first century may be even harder than those of generations past.

Butterscotch Marble Ice Cream
Cecilia Manguerra Brainard

Cecilia Manguerra Brainard was born and raised in the Philippines and immigrated to the U.S. in 1969. A multi-award winning author, she has written and edited eleven books, including *Acapulco at Sunset and Other Stories* (1995), and the novels *When the Rainbow Goddess Wept (1995)* and *Magdalena* (1995). She teaches Creative Writing at UCLA Extension's Writers Program.

Friday night Mark wanted to go to Swensen's. "I *need* butterscotch marble ice cream," he announced. I was eight months pregnant and wanted to stay home. The night before I hardly slept. I was so big that finding a comfortable position in bed was impossible. Changing position was a major production; getting out of bed was a task. It was depressing; everything was depressing, like the old woman hanging clothes from a line that stretched from one end of the building to the other.

I had seen her earlier that day after I finished scrubbing the thrift-store-bought bassinet with Clorox. The apartment reeked, so I opened the living room window. I spotted her then. She must have been sixty with chin-length white hair whipping around her face. She was leaning out a window—her kitchen window I guessed—and she had some clothespins dangling from her mouth. The way she stopped— or maybe it was her scraggly hair—gave her a defeated look. She hung her laundry then pulled the line towards her, hung some more, and pulled. The entire line rotated slowly and the clothes swayed back and forth rhythmically. Underwear, nightgowns, pants, shirts, and towels wavered in the air; and for some reason they all looked gray. The whole scene looked bleak. As I watched her I had the feeling that years from now I would be doing exactly the same thing, hanging laundry from my fifth-floor apartment in the Mission district of San Francisco.

Our apartment was very small: a bathroom, a walk-in closet, a kitchen, a bedroom, and a living room. Accordion doors separated the living room and bedroom. The bathtub was the free-standing kind with claws for legs; the kitchen had an unused icebox. Mark jokingly called them antiques, but that Friday they appeared simply old to me. Our dream was to buy a Volkswagen bug before the baby was born; Mark had already sold his Kawasaki motorcycle for seed money.

My mother's warning went through my head like a tape-recording. "*Hi ja*, it's easier to marry a Filipino," she had said. "We have our own ways. Why marry someone different? And to live in another country—why leave home? In America they don't even take care of their old people; they put them in homes. What future will you have there?"

For the first time I felt the gravity of my marrying an American and giving up my life in the Philippines.

That Friday, Mark had no idea of the doubts floating through my head. He was happy.

"Aren't you tired?" I asked. He was a senior law student at Hastings. Four nights a week he sorted mail at the post office.

"I feel great!" he said. "Let's go out for ice cream."

"We can't afford it."

"C'mon, don't be a stick-in-the-mud." He put on his coat, grabbed mine, and stood by the door.

"We don't have the money. I wanted to go to Sears to buy T-shirts for the baby, but I only had seven dollars and fifty-five cents."

"I've got a few bucks. Let's go, let's go, they're going to close," he said.

Reluctantly I got up and walked to him. "I wanted to tie-dye the baby's shirts. Elizabeth taught me how. You use rubber bands. That's how you get the pretty rings. You can use several colors. But I didn't have enough money for the shirts and dye."

"Buy them next week, Tuesday's payday."

"I wanted to make them now. I want to get the baby's things ready."

"Move it along, move it along."

"What's more important anyway, the baby or your ice cream?"

"Right now, my ice cream. Everything will be all right."
He grinned encouragingly.

"All right, all right—how can it be all right? We have
cockroaches. Three ran out of the garbage chute. I stepped
on one; there was this loud crunch. It was disgusting. Then
this afternoon, I heard gunshots and an ambulance."

"Firecrackers and a fire truck, that's all." He always
said that even when the next day's news reported some kill-
ing in the Mission District. I wanted to cry. I was so enor-
mous, I waddled. It was cold and my coat wouldn't go over
my stomach. I was still struggling with the first button as
we got on the cable car.

"I want to get the baby's things together, then I'll cook
some food and freeze it for you when I'm in the hospital."

"You worry too much," he said.

That made me even more cross, and I kept quiet. He
went right on about his pinochle game with Chun and Ross
and how Able didn't know demur from demure and Dean
Prosser said, "Young ladies are demure; in law it's demur."

I wanted to tell him to stop. I wanted to tell him how
afraid I was. I was feeling very pregnant; I was feeling very
alone, very foreign in this country; and I felt very uncertain
about my future. Where I came from you knew the cycle of
life; babies were born, they grew up, they courted and got
married; they had children, grandchildren, great-grandchil-
dren, and they died. Everyone knew where everyone's fam-
ily crypts were in the cemetery. You knew where they'd bury
you.

"I hope we're not late," Mark said. "I think they close
at ten."

We hopped off the cable car, hurried to Swensen's and
saw the closed sign.

"Shoot!" Mark said. "It's not even ten yet. I really
wanted butterscotch marble." He paused, shoved both hands
into his pockets and sighed. "Well, c'mon. Let's go. It's foggy
and you didn't really want to go out."

Some of that energy, that optimism faded from his face
and I felt sorry for him. "Isn't there another Swensen's at
Fisherman's Wharf?" I offered.

He smiled gratefully. "Want to try it? How do you feel?"

I rested my hands on top of my stomach—the shelf, he called it. "I'm fine."

Another cable car ride later we were at Fisherman's Wharf, hurrying toward Swensen's. We could see a man at the cash register.

"They're still open," he said hopefully.

"Go on ahead," I said as I tried to keep up with his long strides.

"Just c'mon, move it along. Move those stumps along." I was not very tall, but he was. That night, dressed in my yellow corduroy jumper (one of the two clothes that still fit me), my trench coat that wouldn't close, white knee-high socks and brown loafers. I must have looked like a strange humpty-dumpty.

The man tilted his chin when we entered. "Closed." he said.

Mark and I exchanged glances and moaned.

The man continued counting money. "Sorry, ten o'clock, closing time." He was very serious. I located the clock on the wall. "It's ten," I declared defeated.

Maybe it was my tone, but the man looked at me, his eyes resting briefly on my huge stomach. His expression softened. "You need it bad?"

I realized he thought I was the one who wanted the ice cream. I nodded.

"What kind?"

"Butterscotch marble, a pint please," I said. Mark winked at me.

The man dished out a pint, handed it to me. Mark reached into his pocket for his wallet, but the man shook his head. "It's free. Good luck."

I didn't know what to say. I smiled and committed his face to memory: harried-looking with a dark mustache, pale skin with a bluish tint, the kind that hadn't been under the sun much; he was around my age, twenty-two. "Thanks," I finally said, and we left.

Outside the fog had lifted and the air was no longer damp. As the cable car inched its way up Powell, Mark said,

"What do you know, free butterscotch marble ice cream. All because of this." He stroked my stomach; just then the baby kicked and we both laughed.

Back in the apartment, Mark got two teaspoons and settled in front of the television. *The Hunchback of Notre Dame* was on.

"Wow!" he said, "a classic. Come and watch and have some ice cream."

I shook my head. "I feel fat and ugly."

"You're beautiful," he said. "Besides free butterscotch marble is always low cal."

He ate the ice cream alone while I stood by the window, peering through the darkness to where the woman had been hanging her laundry.

"What are you doing?" he asked.

"Thinking."

"What about?"

My thoughts were still clicking around in my head; they hadn't settled into words yet. All I knew was that life wasn't as bad as it had been earlier that day. I said, "I hope she brought her laundry in."

"Who?"

"Never mind," I said.

The baby kicked once more and I shifted my weight. Something wonderful happened when I did that—the light fell on the window in such a way that I lost sight of the outside darkness and saw Mark's reflection instead. He was sitting on the couch, contentedly eating his ice cream, a gentle happy giant of a man.

I saw in that reflection my future.

Goddess of Learning
Anjali Banerjee

Anjali Banerjee was born in India, raised in Canada, and received degrees in Anthropology and Psychology from the University of California, Berkeley. She is the author of two novels for children, *Maya Running* and *Looking for Bapu*, and two novels for adults, *Invisible* Lives and *Imaginary Men*. Her passion for social issues continues in this short story about a type of racism that is difficult to explain to those who have not experienced it.

"Don't be a party pooper, Divya. Come with me just this once!" Gita, all cleavage, curves and perfume, smacked her red, lipstick-drenched lips in front of the mirror. "They'll even have a DJ at the frat house. You can't stay here and study with Lyle Beanton *again*."

"I can't go with you, Gita. Lyle and I have a marathon night of homework." Divya flopped on her bed and pretended to study her chemistry textbook, but the formulas turned into illegible Sanskrit on the page. A twinge of excitement stole up under her ribs. She longed to break free, to laugh and flirt without fear the way her room-mate, Gita, did, but Divya had heard scary stories about fraternity parties. They could become mob scenes, meat markets where half-naked girls flaunted their assets for drunken frat boys. She was too shy to flaunt anything. But still—

"Homework, shmomework. Being a freshman isn't just about studying," Gita said. "It's about having fun, letting go. If my Ma knew I was wearing this—" she yanked a strapless black dress, tight as a glove, down over her hips, "she'd have a cow and die."

"I'd rather not risk killing my beloved mother in that horrible manner." Divya turned the page in her textbook. Or maybe she *would* take the risk. Her parents lived three hundred miles away. Her father wouldn't pop his head in to make sure she went to sleep by ten. She could party all night. What a thought.

The tiny brass statue of the Hindu elephant-headed god, Ganesh, watched her from the desktop. A gift from her grandmother, Ganesh had helped Divya pass exams and excel in music and writing since her fifth birthday. Could he help her gain the confidence to mingle at a party, to flirt with an Orlando Bloom look-alike?

She peered out the dormitory window. Seven stories below, students moved like toy figures in the courtyard, their voices drifting up in a hum of excitement. The thrill of Friday night merriment swirled around her. She wanted to venture out and mingle, but she wasn't bold like Gita, who knew how to exoticize herself; she'd put a tiny red *bindi* on her forehead and lined her eyes with black kohl. *Guys love it,* she'd said. *You'll see.* Gita had grown up in Berkeley, had never left. She was comfortable here, where ethnic groups blended like oils on a palette. She had never been the only brown kid in school, had never endured little boys taunting *Paki, Chocolate Shit Face. Did you rub your face in shit? Go back to Pakistan!* Divya longed to forget childhood, leave it where it belonged, frozen in snow three thousand miles north.

"You're the World's Most Hopeless Case, Divya." Gita pulled a brush through her silken hair. "You need to have a little fun. Why do you think they put us in the same room? So I could help you loosen up, that's why. You're a babe. Let down your hair, take off your glasses, and you'll be a goddess."

"You make a convincing case. But I think I'm here to keep you in line." Divya glanced at the shadowy reflection of her bespectacled face in the window. Could she be pretty?

Gita leaned one hip and made a pouty, sultry face at herself in the mirror. "I bet whoever assigned us to rooms probably thought we'd be good little Indian nerds, happy discussing our arranged marriages and cooking curry together. Little do they know! We're two wild and crazy girls!" Gita gave Divya an impish grin, and Divya couldn't help grinning back. She *could* have fun. She could be beautiful. Maybe if she lost the specs—after all, she could see without them, as long as nobody stood too close to her face.

Gita turned around, hands on her hips. Her bright, shiny lips turned down in a delicate frown. "It's crazy to hide in here all night. One last time, come with me. You'll look back and wish you'd enjoyed yourself."

Poised on the edge of a decision, Divya opened her mouth just as Lyle popped his head in the door. Lyle Beanton, her best friend, his glasses thick as the Earth's crust. His blond hair stuck out at all angles and dirt speckled his glasses. "You going somewhere, Div?"

"Don't you ever knock?" Gita fluttered her eyelashes at him. "I could've been naked. Don't I look totally beautiful?"

Lyle gave Gita a blank, perfunctory look and then smiled at Divya. Whenever Lyle smiled, his warmth and sincerity burst out all over his face. "I made chicken noodle soup, and I figured out the problem on page 257. What time do you want to study, Div? It's getting late."

The room fell silent, waiting for Divya's reply. This was it. Lyle Beanton, the Nice Nerd of the Seventh Floor, was her best friend. Maybe her only friend. He had startling blue eyes behind those glasses, and if he washed his hair, he could be cute. But nice and cute weren't good enough any more. Divya wanted excitement. The vibrant promise of Friday night made her starry-eyed and restless. Perhaps Lyle wouldn't mind studying alone for just one night. She took a deep breath. "I'm—going to a party. With Gita. I'll catch you when I get back."

Lyle's eyes widened. "A party. You?"

"Don't look so surprised." She sat up and squared her shoulders.

"Does she need your permission to go out?" Gita said.

"No—fine. Div—just knock when you get back." Lyle ducked out without another word. Divya didn't have time for regret, for Gita already danced around her, pulling off her glasses, playing with her hair. "I'm *so* glad you're coming, Div. Just a little make-up, some sexy threads, and you'll be so hot."

***

The deep bass beat pounded through Divya's teeth. Packed with bodies, noise and the smells of perfume and beer, the dance hall shook with exhilaration. Divya had danced and danced, growing hotter and hotter, and now she lifted her hair to let cool air hit the back of her neck. Across the room, a man leaned casually against the wall. He'd been there a while—notable for his height, broad shoulders and striking features.

And he was looking at her.

A little thrill spread through Divya's insides. She *was* beautiful in an elegant mauve dress, imprinted with a paisley print design, its only daring feature a slightly scooped neckline. She'd let her hair down and rimmed her eyes with kohl. So why wouldn't a man stare at her?

She wasn't used to the attention, and half of her wanted to step back and hide in the shadow. She forced herself to stay put. Could the man really *see* her in the dimness? Or maybe he was looking at someone behind her, but there was nobody there, only the wall.

Out on the dance floor, Gita swayed to the music, every motion a provocative suggestion of foreplay. A blocky football-player type flailed in front of her, mesmerized by her beauty. When the song ended she left him standing alone and rushed to Divya. "Little Miss Universe. I see that guy eyeing you over there. You go, girl! I'll get you some punch." Gita glided away, returned with a plastic cup and again disappeared in the crowd.

Divya gulped punch. Liquid burned her throat, sent a rush of heat through her chest. She wasn't much of a drinker, but tonight the cup nestled like a warm companion in her hand.

The tall man had left his post. He was coming over.

Divya broke out in a sweat. Maybe she could dash into the hall, hide in the bathroom. She stood transfixed, heart pounding in time to the rhythm of the music. She tossed her empty cup into the trash. The man loomed a few inches away, stooping as though accustomed to looking down at people. Close up, he smelled of glycerin soap and faint metallic cologne.

"I must've met you in my dreams last night, Miss—?" His voice came out smooth and cultured, its deep baritone vibrating through her system.

"Divya," she whispered, her throat dry.

"Indian name. The best kind to have. I'm Alan McLeod.

At your service, m'lady."

"I don't think I need any—service." Why did she say that? What did he have in mind, exactly? She didn't think *service* meant doing her laundry.

"You never know. A knight in shining armor might come in handy in a crazy place like this." He lips turned up in a slight smile. His irises were flecked, the color of peanut shells. He didn't look anything like Orlando Bloom. He resembled a young Robert Redford

"So you're my knight? Where's your horse?" There, score one point for Divya in the Witty Comeback department.

He glanced at the ceiling. "He's upstairs, in my room. You don't think I'd let my trusty steed stomp all over everyone down here, do you?"

"How do you hide him from the hall monitors?"

"We don't have hall monitors. We're all grown-ups here." He moved closer to her, making her heart beat even faster.

"What's your horse's name?"

"Raja," he said. "That means King in Sanskrit. King of horses. Did you know that?"

"Of course. I have a cousin named Raja."

"Ah, you're Indian. I knew it." He pressed a hand to the wall behind her head.

"I grew up in Canada, though. I was only born in India. I feel—American." Now why did she say that? She'd drawn Alan McLeod to her, and now she had nearly blown it with him.

"How fascinating." He gave her his full attention, and the rest of the room—the noise, laughter, music—fell away. She heard herself talking, the words spilling out one after the other, about her childhood visits to Stanford where her father taught summer classes, about how she'd loved to wander the campus, pick eucalyptus leaves and crush them in her hand so she could sniff the sharp scent of menthol.

"Eucalyptus isn't a native species," Alan said. "Neither are you. I like that about you. You're different from other girls. You have this—unknown element. In your eyes. They're so dark. And your hair—sexy."

Divya's cheeks flushed, and her chest tightened so

much, she could hardly breathe.

Alan laughed, a deep, rumbling sound, and ran long fingers through his hair. "India's such a cool, mysterious country. You're a mysterious woman."

Divya didn't feel like a mysterious woman, she felt like mush about to melt into the floor. She wondered if Alan would ask her to dance, but he didn't. "Come upstairs and see my steed?" he said instead. "You may be disappointed, though. He's not real."

"Somehow, I suspected as much." There, she'd found her voice again.

"But good news—I don't have a room-mate. Being a junior, I get my own room."

Another little thrill raced through her. She could be alone with him, and the prospect did not frighten her. Instead, anticipation grew inside her. She wondered how his arms would feel wrapped around her, how his breath would feel against her cheek, how his lips would feel against hers. Would he try anything more? Would she mind so much if he did?

Like a sleepwalker she followed him upstairs to the end of a narrow, dim hall. The party receded into a muffled roar downstairs, distant and insignificant.

The heavy scent of incense hit her nose before she entered Alan's room. A bedside lamp cast a diffused glow, transporting her to a Bombay bazaar; no Indian home would be cluttered this way. Indian paintings, statues and rugs emerged in the half-light. A brass God Vishnu and sandalwood sculptures encircled the bed—a jungle of bodies intertwined. A black, wide-eyed mask stared from the wall with mouth open, red tongue hanging out. A particular carving caught Divya's eye—a naked couple, the woman leaning back, her legs wrapped around the man's thighs, her face turned up in abandon. Alan wasn't kidding. He really did have an obsession for India. Yet all these mementos had somehow lost their meaning, removed from their original contexts in India.

Alan strode to the desk and flipped through a dog-eared book. His face looked angular in gauzy light—solid, strong, with glittering eyes. Divya's hands grew clammy. She stood in the center of the room, unsure where to sit. Should she try to make more witty conversation, or wait for Alan?

"Have you seen Satyajit Ray's films?" he asked. "The Postmaster?"

She nodded. "A long time ago in India—I hardly remember." In truth, she preferred independent films from France, Germany, and Spain.

"You remind me of the Indian girl with the round eyes. Only you're darker—"

His voice melted into her memory of a dim theater in Bombay, rife with odors of coconut hair oil and sweating bodies. The audience had chattered through the whole show. She hadn't felt like an Indian then; she'd felt like a Canadian irritated by noise, longing for order in chaos. That was how Alan's room felt now: chaotic and unfamiliar.

"I love your black skin," he said. "Were you born in the South? Madras?"

Nobody had ever referred to her skin as black. She was dark, to be sure, but black?

"That's a stereotype," she said. "People with darker skin must be from the South. Indians always think that."

"I didn't mean it like that." He lit an incense stick. "I meant to say I like tanned skin. That's all. No big deal." He stuck the incense in a stand on the windowsill. "Makes you look . . . healthy."

"I'm supposed to be flattered, right?" She thought of Harold, the blond guy who lived on the sixth floor in her dorm. He dated only African-American women. Divya had never considered his choices, but now she wanted to confront him and demand an explanation, not that it was any of her business. People could date whom they wanted to date, couldn't they? She wondered whether Alan had dated other Indian women, whether he complimented all of them on the color of their skin, on their Indian-ness.

"Why don't you have a nose ring?" he asked. "They're so ethnic."

Divya imagined herself as a black cow, Alan tugging her massive nose ring. She nearly burst into laughter at the absurd thought. "Why do I need a nose ring to be who I am?" She picked up a wooden horse. The tail was cold, smooth and smelled of sandalwood.

"Well—Indians wear kurtas, right? Or saris. How many saris do you own?" He wiped ash off the sill.

"I don't mean to be rude, but I don't see what an inventory of my wardrobe has to do with anything—"

"I think Indian clothes are so cool. Really ethnic."

There he went, using that word again. "You're ethnic too," she said. "Everyone has an ethnicity."

"My family was mostly Irish and Scottish—"

"Then why don't you wear a kilt and blow bagpipes?"

"Hey, I'm a mutt, some English and Dutch thrown in, but India is in your bones. You should be proud of your heritage."

"Excuse me? I *am* proud, but my bones are the same as everyone else's." She put down the horse. Her nose clogged with incense smoke and her eyes burned.

"Your name is Indian, your hair is Indian. Your eyes. Even your dress is Indian. Paisley."

"I bought this dress at Macy's." Annoyance bubbled up through her insides, but Alan didn't seem to notice or care. He took his book and sat on the bed. "I want to show you something." His peanut-shell eyes beckoned her, reflected lamp light. She hesitated, then sat next to him, aware of his breathing.

He pointed at the page. His face twitched with excitement. Modeled in marble, the Hindu goddess Sarasvati gazed out from a glossy photograph. Even in stone, her eyes conveyed wisdom and peace. Two tiny consorts kneeled at her feet. Two more stood by, gripping sitars and lyres. "Goddess of learning, music and literature," he said. "You look just like her."

"That's flattering. But . . . I'm not some statue."

"Goddesses always reflect an ideal—"

"I'm not an ideal. Not even close." She felt suddenly as tenuous as incense smoke.

"You have her *shape*." Alan moved closer until his leg touched hers. His breath carried a faint scent of mint toothpaste.

"Okay. You're right. I'm made of ancient stone and my arms have broken off at the elbows." She stood up and turned to face Alan.

"What? Silly. Come here." He grinned and opened his arms as if he expected her to fall into them. Only a few minutes ago, she had wanted to. Oh how had she had longed to fall into his arms, but this was too much. "Maybe I *am* a goddess." She pointed at the book. "Did you know that Sarasvati is just one incarnation of Shakti?"

"I know Hindus pray to her when—"

"When they want to succeed in the arts. But do you know who she really is, what she becomes when she's angry?"

"Sarasvati doesn't get angry. She's serene. Look at her face."

"Oh yes, she does. She gets angry."

"Divya, you're not making sense."

"When Sarasvati sees demons, she gets angry and rises to defend the world," Divya said, gaining confidence. It was as though the essence of the goddess infused her with new power.

"Sarasvati doesn't fight demons. She plays the flute."

"How much do you really know about Hindu mythology?" She strode across the room to the window. She grabbed the incense stick between thumb and forefinger and snuffed it out. "If you make the goddess angry, she'll become Kali, goddess of destruction, the consort of Shiva. She will become the black hag gripping severed heads, dripping blood. Kali, a synonym for *black*." Divya pointed at the black mask of Kali with her mouth open, red tongue hanging out. "That's her. Or didn't you know?"

"I knew it was a ritual mask worn during the Puja— I've gathered many things like that—"

"Am I one of those *things*?" She spun on her heel. "To keep in your room?"

"Of course not."

"How many Indian girls have you dated?"

Alan looked at his fingers. "Do I have to count them?"

"Ha—do you ever date American girls? European girls?"

"They're not that interesting." He shrugged. "Everyone has preferences. Not everyone likes toffee, or chocolate. I like Earl Grey tea. You might like Indian *chai*. What's the difference?"

"It's different when it comes to people," she said. "And maybe you'd better brush up on your Hindu mythology. You don't want to disappoint the next exotic babe who comes to your room." She couldn't believe she was saying these things. Her body trembled, and she could see the shadowy ghosts of the Indian girls who had been here before. How many of them had bought into Alan's obsession with India? It wasn't a real appreciation of her culture—it was a voyeuristic fixation. Had she been wrong to emphasize those elements of herself in her dress, her make-up? No, she thought. She *was* Indian, but not in the way Alan wanted her to be.

A keen disappointment stabbed at her chest as she strode toward the door. She had wanted to be close to Alan, had fantasized about this tall, handsome man only minutes earlier. How quickly the heart could shift. She turned back toward him for a moment, her hand on the door. "Your trusty steed ran away, I see," she said. "And I thought you should know. Just because I'm Indian, I don't have to like *chai*. I drink double tall vanilla lattes."

"Divya, wait—" he called as she left the room and returned downstairs to the party. She lost herself in the crowd, surprised to find the sting of tears behind her eyes. She had wanted the evening to work out, had wanted to get to know Alan, but if she'd shown up in jeans, her hair tied back, would he have given her a second glance? She suspected not.

In a few moments Alan appeared, his body jerking to the music like a rusty robot. He was looking for her, his gaze sweeping the crowd with precision. Then Gita glided toward him until the two touched elbow to elbow. She was the only other Indian woman here. Divya wanted to whisk Gita away and warn her. *He doesn't care who you are, and he doesn't even know it*, but Gita and Alan found each other like ship and beacon in the night. He leaned down, whispered in her ear and Gita threw her head back and laughed.

Her hair brushed his arm. The two stood with gazes locked as the music ended.

Divya swallowed the lump in her throat and threaded her way to the front door. Outside, she started down the sidewalk in a cool, clear evening. Her breath condensed and dissipated in a soft cloud. Maybe Alan would see Gita for who she was, but somehow, Divya doubted it. Gita flaunted her assets. Although Alan would want to dive into her like diving into an exotic, foreign ocean, Gita could take care of herself. She was an expert at handling men.

The moon had risen, outlining elm and oak trees along Divya's path. Shades of mauve and yellow appeared in leaves that had seemed lifeless before. She stepped lightly, freely, buoyed by the goddess inside her.

She picked up the pace, hoping to catch Lyle still awake in his room. Perhaps he still had some chicken soup left, and later they could take a walk to Café Mediterranean for a midnight latte. Perhaps she might take off his glasses and get a better look at those brilliant blue eyes. A friend's eyes. Honest eyes.

Lavender Soap
Irene Zabytko

Irene Zabytko, a past winner of the PEN Syndicated Fiction Award, has taught ESL and English in North America and Eastern Europe. She is the author of *The Sky Unwashed* (2000) and *When Luba Leaves Home: Stories* (2003). "Lavender Soap" expresses the complexities that one Ukrainian World War II work camp survivor faces with her daughter, husband, health, and work.

The thin, black wire loop glowed a bright orange when Slavka held it over the jet flame of the bunson burner. She liked to hear the sizzling sounds of microbes and other impurities destroyed from the quick cleansing power of the fire.

Next, she transferred the sterilized loop and stabbed it into a vial of phlegm that was taken earlier from one of the sicker patients. The loop collected a mere filmy drop of the specimen, but it was enough to breed thousands of colonies of germs. With the loop, she drew perpendicular lines onto the gelatinous surface of the petri plate before burning the loop again, and taking another sample from yet another diseased patient. When she had inoculated enough plates, she stacked the covered dishes and shoved them into a large incubator that took up most of the floor space in her tiny lab. The next day, like a proud baker, she would remove the plates and be amazed to find the oddly-shaped whorls and beads of green, yellow and white slime that the invisible microbes manifested as proof of their existence. Then she would extract small slivers from the best samples and transfer them to slides where the murderous culprits could be enlarged under the microscope for anyone to witness.

Voila! She smiled and imagined herself to be on stage at a carnival sideshow. "Step right up to the magnificent microscope you idiotic humans," she said in Ukrainian. "Step right up to the wonders of the million and one supergerms! Only the lab tech knows the dark secrets of the invisible beasts that cause diphtheria, gonorrhea, syphilis, and yes, the bubonic plague! Watch the manufacturers of scarlet fever multiply, ready to kill off an entire village. See the cholera microbes grow to ravage an entire unsuspecting population! These evil, living things laugh at bombs and guns—they can stop a two-hundred pound human cold!" she giggled and wished she could be so loose and silly when the students came.

It was late. Slavka knew she was exhausted when she laughed to herself that way. The night shift lab techs were clocking in, and the cleaning ladies were already milling around the floor with their mops and plastic gloves. In the morning, a new batch of first year medical students would be ushered into her section of the microbiology lab, where she would be asked by Dr. Barnstadt to "kindly demonstrate pleeze, Missus, what dangers lurk beyond what we zee . . . " He always asked her the same exact thing, in his long drawn-out German accent, or was it Austrian? Actually, he sounded like Victor Borge, who was neither. But after all those years, she still felt nervous in front of the imposing old doctor even though he never failed to treat her with uncommon genteel, old-world courtesy.

The students were another matter. Slavka felt satisfied that she would confidently answer all of their inane questions when they visited her lab. She liked the way the smug-faced young impudents gradually ignored her thick accent and showed her a semblance of respect during one of her involved lectures. She relished the way they humbly thanked her after she was finished and allowed them to glimpse through her microscope as she effortlessly pronounced the deadly names: *"Treponema pallidum, Vibrio cholerae, Corynebacterium diphtheriae . . . "*

The elevator was stuck again. She decided to take the stairway which led to the patient wings of the hospital, where she could catch another elevator. On her way out she passed the busy reception area desk, cluttered with a little plastic Christmas tree. A weary nurse shouted out room numbers to a cluster of visitors carrying bouquets and cellophane fruit baskets as Slavka escaped through the main doors and out into the cold air.

Her rubber soled boots crunched on the icy pavement

as she made her way to the subway. Men on the street corner were sharing a bottle in a brown sack, and yelling out "got spare change" to passersby. She wished Iwan, her husband, could work the same hours as she did so that he could pick her up in the car. Now that Natalka, her daughter, was old enough to drive, she was always too busy and whined whenever she had to act as chauffeur.

"God, she's lucky she has a damn car," Slavka bitterly thought. Growing up, Natalka was a sweet, dutiful child, but Slavka dreaded her daughter's adolescence. Ever since Natalka had started coming home late from parties, Slavka had rifled through her belongings in search of drugs or birth control pills. Once, she found some seeds and scrutinized them under a microscope to see if they were marijuana. The seeds turned out to be the innocent byproduct of a botany class project. Even so, Slavka was in a rage and wrongly accused Natalka of acting like a *hom*, a street-walker, and she defended her right as a mother to search anything she deemed suspicious.

The strained relationship eased up a bit after Slavka's recent operation. Natalka became more aloof and wisely ignored her mother's irrational outbursts. Slavka was amazed at her daughter's reluctance to fight with her anymore, especially after the last time, when she thrashed Natalka with the back of a wooden hairbrush. "You lousy tramp," Slavka yelled at her daughter, hitting her shoulders. "Late again! Who were you with? You're not going to shame me!" Slavka whacked her until she realized that Natalka stood silently with her hands up to her eyes, not defending herself. Finally, Slavka weakened, and threw the brush away. "What am I doing to you, darling? I'm sorry!" she cried to her daughter who continued to hide her face in her hands. "I'm sorry *donichka!* I didn't mean it."

Crazy. Slavka knew it. Her temper was too much of a luxury, and she was aware of how easily her energy dissipated each time she vented her anger. Well, a blessing, she reasoned, less arguments. "Anyway, she's so young," Slavka though out loud. "Why can't I let her have that much? I don't need the car."

Slavka watched the train lurch down the snow-lined tracks. She hated subway trains not so much because weird, dangerous people often rode in them, but because she was claustrophobic on trains of any sort. Back in the old country, she and her family were squeezed into cattle trains during the war. They were part of a work force from Ukraine—the OST[1] people, the Slavic subhumans from the Eastern-bloc countries, who were forced to go to Germany and work in factories as war prisoners. She never forgot the jerkiness of the train crying its siren all night while the crowds of desperate people held on to one another and filled the car with their stench.

She hated thinking about that, but she couldn't shut out the memory whenever she took the subway. Many of her family died in the German labor camp. Others she knew—school friends and teachers—had been sent to Siberia by the Russians, and she never heard from them again. Often, in her dreams she saw their stiff corpses buried in the tundra with their faces frozen, set in grimaces of terror and their eyes were always open, staring without forgiveness.

She hoped that by going later in the evening, after rush hour, the trains wouldn't be so crowded. But it was the holiday season, and the subway cars were packed with Christmas shoppers. Slavka tightly grabbed the overhead strap and tried not to crash against the anonymous bodies wrapped in thick coats.

"Oh, Pani Medvedska!"

Slavka half-turned around. It was Pani Hnatiuk who attended the same church Slavka had gone to before she had to work on Sundays. She nodded hello, and was dismayed when the pushy woman edged her way to Slavka.

"Pani Medvedska, hello. Och, so many people." She switched to Ukrainian. "*Americanski* Christmas. Be careful because the *mooreni* will steal your purse on these trains. My daughter Halya just came back from Europe. Oh, she had such a good time studying art in Italy. You know, I'm glad she studied art, but between you and me, we know that America doesn't care about real art. So poor Halya needs a good job. She wants to marry Orest Pachnewysky, he's graduating from pharmacy school this year. They met at the youth resort last summer. Nice boy. Well, of course art is nice, but you can't get anything in this country. Oh, Pani you have a good job at the hospital. You are a *magister*, almost a doctor from what everyone says. Could you find something *intelligentski* for my daughter? Something that's a clean job, like yours?"

Slavka smile, "Well, I don't know . . . " She wanted to confess that she was a mere technician, not even officially licensed . . .

"Och, here's my stop. Remember the ladies' church raffle next week. We know you're too busy to make anything for the bake sale, but we hope to see you." Pani Hnatiuk pushed her way towards the door yelling, "Out! Out!" until she was gone.

It was Slavka's stop as well, but she decided to stay on the train an extra stop to avoid walking home with Pani Hnatiuk—a sacrifice that made her all the more grateful to be pushed out into the twilight again where a shaft of frosted wind sliced her on the forehead like a benediction. Her head throbbed from the cold air and the smoke of the nearby factory accompanied her on the short walk to her apartment building. She turned the key to her door and entered into the familiar radiator warmth of her kitchen where she took off her woolen coat and thrust it in the closet.

She drank a glass of *vishniac*,[2] and instantly fell asleep at the kitchen table dreaming of snow and trains. She woke with a start. Iwan, her husband, was kissing her forehead and stroking her graying hair that was tightly held back with a clasp.

"Did Natalka come home?" Pani Slavka asked her husband.

"She'll be home soon. Don't worry. She's a good girl."

Slavka retreated into the bedroom and removed her white uniform. It was only a year since the mastectomy and she knew Iwan still could not look at her butchered body. She understood and quietly closed the door. She wasn't used to it either—the absence of the thick, soft flesh that meant humiliation and survival in her life. In the German labor camp, she had to bare her breasts to the German soldiers whenever she begged for extra rations for her mother. The worst of it was having her mother there watching in horror as the soldiers laughed and molested her. Her sickly, peasant mother, thought Slavka with great sorrow. The same woman who had prayed fervently throughout everything the family endured, but who died from hunger anyway; and only then was Slavka able to harden herself against the others who watched while she stripped for the soldiers, sometimes in front of the entire camp. It was because of her coldness toward the inmates more than her actions that she was called the camp whore, even though she never ate any of the extra rations herself and always gave them away to anyone who was hungry.

Slavka put on her old flannel robe before joining Iwan in the kitchen. He was making the evening tea. These days, it was the only thing he did that pleased her. They had little in common as a married couple; he was far beneath her in education and lacked the sensitivity to enjoy the books and art that she loved. Luckily, Iwan had relatives in America who sponsored his arrival after the war. Slavka didn't care about coming to America; she went for the simple reason that he was the only man who had asked her to marry him despite her reputation in the camp.

Still, he was unusually skillful at making a fragrant, mild, glass of old world tea with his huge farmer hands, now stained with factory oil.

"I think Dr. Barnstadt will be bringing more students into my lab again," Slavka said. "I hope they won't ask me anything I'm not sure of." She quietly drank her tea from the steamy glass, expecting no encouraging words from Iwan.

He cut a huge slab of the honey cake he had baked two nights ago, and passed it to his wife. "You know, I don't know these things like you, but I wish you were doing something else. Something not so dangerous." Iwan was convinced that the mysterious radiation and microbes Slavka sometimes described to him were responsible for her cancer. She sighed and welcomed his concern, but kept silent.

Naturally, she also wished she could do safer work, but Slavka would never ask for it. After all, as she so often patiently explained to her husband, there was always a constant flow of newly graduated lab technicians who were given the less dangerous assignments. As usual, every six months, the lab was filled with a new group of silly, giggly American girls who were not expected to do more than the mindless, routine procedures. They never had to struggle as hard as Slavka did for the privilege of working there.

In the old country, Slavka was a pharmacy student. She would have gotten her degree, but then the Germans came. Her mother begged her not to tell anyone she was educated, because most of her professors were shot or taken away to death camps along with the Jews.

In America, she had to start over again. After her arrival in the States, Slavka studied the English language by day and scrubbed hospital toilets at night. Five years later, she found the correct grammar and courage to apply for a position in a Chicago hospital lab. Twenty years later, she was still there.

At first, her resentment towards the giggly American girls grew. She trained them and they would leave for better positions and more money. Several had even become her supervisor. They called her "that foreign lady" or "that Russian." She particularly hated the way they talked to her in a loud voice as though she was deaf, which always made her more conscious of her accent. And she especially hated it when they called her by her first name—Slavka, could you run a test; Slavka, I need these STAT; Slavka, can you work on the holiday—an impertinent American custom that seemed to her disrespectful and vulgar.

Gradually, her resentment melted into an apathetic tolerance. After her operation, she woke up in the dark recovery room to a bouquet of flowers that her co-workers were thoughtful enough to send. Slavka knew it was a token present given to anyone, but she was grateful for the fragrant flowers which helped her to cope with the pungent, medicinal odors effusing from her thickening scar.

"Hi, I'm home." It was Natalka who dutifully came home in time to see her parents huddled in the dimly lit kitchen sipping tea, the last ritual before sleep. "Mamma, you forgot your pills again. I found them sitting on the table after you left this morning. Your pain will get worse if you don't take them." Slavka smiled ruefully at her daughter's inability to roll her "r's" whenever she spoke Ukrainian. Just like an American, Slavka thought. My only child is a foreigner in my own house.

Natalka was losing the resemblance she had to her mother. Her hair wasn't as bushy, her eyes had lost their innocence and had become more sultry with the heavy eye make-up she wore. Natalka could easily pass as an American of Irish or English descent like the girls in Slavka's lab—thin and eager.

Which one was your father, Slavka dreamily had asked herself whenever she studied her daughter. Some Wolfgang, or that short stocky blond one in the camp kitchen. Maybe it was the young man who stuttered, the one who said he was sorry under his breath before he did it to me . . . yes, I think that last one. In the past, whenever Slavka thought about the men in the camp, she broke out in shivers and a rash, or cried in front of people, usually her co-workers, who thought she was strange anyway. She no longer exhibited any outward signs to anyone. Now, whenever the shadowy features of the uniformed men filed past in her mind, she coldly counted each one like inventory items on a shelf and cursed them in silence.

"See what I bought?" Natalka clumsily pulled out several toiletries from a bag with a red and purple logo. "Just some stuff for the girls at school. We're having a Christmas party. For American Christmas, what's called in English a 'grab-bag.' "

Slavka's eyes riveted to a small, gaily wrapped bar of lavender soap. "Can I have this?"

"Sure. Here take more. I've got a lot more. There's bayberry and lemon . . . "

"No. Just give me the lavender one."

Another war memory. In her barracks, the one she

shared with at least forty OST women, Slavka found a piece of lavender soap someone had left on the floor. It might have been a gift for one of them—they were always getting contraband from the OST men who pilfered things like that. The soap she found was almost new and had held its fragrance. She had managed to stash it alongside a crack in one of the bedposts. Every night, after her hard days, and especially after she had been sent out to the guards, she would take out the soap and sniff it as though it was a shaft of air in a cave. Sometimes she had scratched the soap so that bits of it would settle under her fingernails and she could smell the scent privately, by lifting her hand to her nostrils whenever she couldn't sleep.

"What did you say, Ma?"

"Nothing. Thanks for the soap." Slavka calmly sipped her tea. "Your hair looks good . . . "

"You like it?" Natalka said. "I might streak it blonde."

Iwan grunted.

The phone rang. It was Pani Hnatiuk's daughter asking to speak to Slavka. "Oh her . . . I saw the mother on the subway . . . Just tell her I'll talk to her later," Slavka pleaded. She suddenly wanted to be left alone, especially before Iwan and Natalka got into another argument about money as they always did whenever Natalka bought frivolous things. Lately, they were at odds. Iwan would accuse her in his rough peasant grammar which Slavka used to correct but had given up a long time ago, and Natalka would answer back in her disrespectful American slang. Slavka had had enough. She rose and announced that she needed a bath. "I smell like death."

"Death warmed over," Natalka said. "It's an expression."

Slavka smiled. "I like that, it sounds hopeful, like death isn't so cold and horrible. Not bad."

Like a regal woman, she walked into the bathroom, undraped the robe and kicked away the faded corduroy house slippers from her feet. She stepped into the bathtub as it was filling with warm water, and carefully, lovingly lathered every inch of her body with lavender soap. Slavka wanted the scent to linger on her skin and in her breath forever, at least for the time she had left. She sang softly to herself, an old church hymn she knew as a child, and sighed as the soap touched her scar. "Clean my sins and let me go," she said to herself, cupping the suds toward her chest. "Clean my sins."

[1] Ost: east in German. The Oster were the Slavic Eastern Europeans who were shipped to Germany to work in war factories. "OST" was worn on badges to designate the Slavs from other prisoners. The work camps were not as horrific as the concentration camps, but the OST were treated as work slaves and restricted in their civil freedoms. Ironically, the camp survivors who returned to Ukraine after the war were sent to Siberian labor camps by the Communists who punished them for collaborating with the Nazis.

[2] heavy syrup made from cherries, usually mixed with water or strong vodka.

The Lawyer's Story
Victor Triay

Victor Triay is a history professor at Middlesex Community College in Connecticut and author of *Fleeing Castro: Pedro Pan and the Cuban Children's Program* (1999) and *Bay of Pigs: An Oral History of Brigade 2506* (2001). Born and raised in Miami, his parents left Cuba for the United States in the fall of 1960.

6:05 A.M.

Jose Santander's eyes opened as they did every morning at that time, no matter where he was. He glanced at his watch and then across at the girl sleeping next to him. How old was she? Eighteen? Maybe. He rolled out of bed, checked the "Do Not Disturb" sign on the outside doorknob, and went into the bathroom.

While he was shaving, Santander remember he had promised his wife that he would call her that morning. What was it he had told Her? Oh, right, that he would be in Orlando overnight and would be driving back to Miami that morning and going directly to his law office. He decided he would call her at ten o'clock. His thoughts then went to that old shithead Enrique Huerta and his visit to the office a couple of days ago. The old man wanted to have his body exhumed and reburied in Cuba after Castro fell from power! The old bastard had spent almost three decades of his life waiting for the Communists in Cuba just to disappear. Well, Santander thought, that was the way it always had been with his father's old Mustachio-Pete cronies—getting rid of dictators and anticipating the certainty of a messianic era in Cuba. The last one, the Communist, outlived and outsmarted them all though. And what did they get for their efforts? Exile, frustration, and the chance to bother people with bizarre burial arrangements; not to mention what it did to their families, Santander thought, slamming down the shaving cream canister. He should have thrown Huerta out of a window.

"Good morning," came a voice, breaking his concentration. It was the girl.

"Hmmph," he responded.

She leaned against his back, throwing her arms around him. He grimaced and peeled her arms off.

"I'm shaving," he said, "why don't you take a shower?"

"Are we going to breakfast?" she asked.

"No."

"Well, then, could you drop me off at home?"

"No," he said, then after a moment added, "I have to go to the office. I'm already running late. I'll leave you some money for a taxi."

The girl got into the shower without another word. South American trash, Santander thought to himself. Did she really think we'd go off and have a champagne brunch somewhere? Or that we'd go joy-riding? Jesus Christ, I have a family! He shook his head and reached for a towel.

Santander left the hotel room before the girl was out of the shower. He'd see her again when he needed to. It really wasn't prostitution, he thought as he entered his Jaguar a few minutes later in the parking garage. A little wining, a little dining, a little screwing. That was all. Nobody gets hurt. It really wasn't cheating on his wife, either. After all, he wasn't running away or falling in love with the little bitch. He simply had some needs that twenty-five years of marriage couldn't fulfill. He was a better husband and father for it.

As he turned the ignition key, he felt the vibration from the Jaguar's engine roar through his body. He took a deep breath and closed his eyes for a moment. He then pulled out of the parking space and headed out.

6:53 A.M.

It was a bright Miami morning. The February air was pleasant and Santander lowered his window as he made his way across the Rickenbacker Causeway heading out of Key Biscayne. He popped in Bach's *Air* as he did every morning. The subtle, uplifting rhythm helped clear his mind at that hour. On the Rickenbacker's last leg at Bear Cut, he looked across Biscayne Bay, its waters calm and dark. Rising on its banks on the other end was downtown Miami's sprawling skyline. He pondered on how he had witnessed the city's explosion during his adult life, and on how he had seen it grow more prosperous and complex. In a few minutes, he was past the last bridge and on the Miami side of the bay.

Before going to the office, Santander stopped by a coffee window at a Cuban cafeteria. He ordered toast and *cafe con leche*. He ate on his feet, dipping the long rectangular pieces of heavily buttered Cuban bread into the steaming cup. He finished off the *cafe con leche* in one final gulp, and swallowed the bits of bread that had broken off and lay at the bottom of the cup. He did this carefully lest he stain his Armani suit. He grabbed a paper cup from the counter and took water from the cooler. A moment later, he was back in his Jaguar heading toward the office.

7:27 A.M.

The parking garage was empty, as it usually was at that time on a Saturday. Santander checked his watch and saw he still had over two and a half hours before he needed to call his wife and four hours until his client arrived. Thank God the client was up-to-date on his fees. Today was the day Santander would advise him to negotiate with federal authorities. Blow the whistle on your partners and get only six months in a federal prison. Keep your mouth shut and you are looking at ten years. Medicare fraud was clearly on the "outs" in Miami. Anglo government officials had felt the heat and were no longer cooperative. Well, it was good for a while, Santander thought, reflecting on the size of his own cut over the past few years. After he parked his car, he checked himself in the mirror. He ran his fingers through his light brown hair and took off his sunglasses. He looked into his green eyes to make sure they didn't look bloodshot from last night.

Stepping away from the Jaguar, he activated the alarm and stood for a moment to admire his car from a distance. He smiled to himself. God Bless America. He headed for the elevator.

Halfway to the lift, he heard a faint, lusty shriek. Fucking cats, he thought. Didn't they know it was daytime already? He continued walking, then heard the noise again. He shook his head and made a mental note to mention it to the building manager. Pressing the elevator's "up" button, he looked in the direction of the sound. He saw no cat. Then came the noise again. He squinted his eyes and saw a tightly-wrapped bundle lying against one of the round concrete pillars about twenty yards away. It looked too neat and clean to have been there for long. Then he heard the noise again. Were the damned homeless bums raising cats in here now? He shook his head and turned to face the elevator. It finally arrived.

Santander stepped quickly into the lift and pressed the button for the penthouse. Soon, he would be in his sanctuary overlooking Biscayne Bay. He tapped his breast pocket to make sure he had his cigars. Watching the doors close before him, he caught one last glimpse of the well-folded linen bundle. Then, almost instinctively, he thrust his hand between the two doors just before they shut, causing them to reopen. He stepped out and place his briefcase next to the elevator. He went to the bundle.

Santander stopped a few feet before the bundle of linens and, with his hands on his knees, peered at it for a few moments. He thought he saw it move. He stepped closer, half-expecting a mother cat to attack him any moment. It was moving. In one motion he leaned forward, bent down, pulled at the corner of the top sheet, and stepped back. He sighed, relieved that no cat attacked him. Still crouched, he inched forward, ready to turn and run at a moment's notice. He peered inside.

Santander gasped and jumped back. He overcame his first instinct to run away and instead bounced on the balls of his feet, turning his head side to side for several seconds. His scream for help echoed in the empty garage. He finally stopped and took a deep breath. He went back to the bundle slowly, his knees feeling like gelatin. He went down on one knee and looked in once again. He then took off his jacket. Rolling up his sleeves, he lifted the new-born infant with trembling hands.

7:31 A.M.

He made sure not to trip over anything while he walked back to his car. He couldn't remember when he had ever carried a child so young, so new. His wife had always handled their children when they were babies. He remembered something about supporting its head. He disarmed the car alarm and unlocked the door. He then stepped carefully into the driver's seat and held the child in his right arm. The child felt so cold so he started the engine and turned on the heat. Christ, he thought, how do I get myself into these things? He took his cellular telephone and called 911. He told himself that it would all be over in a few minutes.

7:32 A.M.

He held the infant close to his chest. It kept squirming and whining. That was good, he thought to himself. Suddenly, the baby began wailing loudly, forcing Santander to jump slightly and gasp. Courage, he told himself, courage. He felt his heart pounding hard, like someone punching him from the inside.

"Shhh, shhh," he told the child as he began rocking back and forth as best he could in the small seat. Oh, my God, he repeated several times. He looked back to see if he could see a fire rescue or an ambulance. Where the hell were they?

The child quieted finally and resumed squirming and whining. Santander looked at him.

"You poor thing," he said out loud to the child, breathing loudly, "who the hell did this to you?" He looked outside the window again. Suddenly the child began crying loudly once again. Santander felt his own heart-rate skyrocket. My God—oh, my God.

This time the child did not stop. Santander held the child closer, trying to calm him. In his mind he saw the child's mother, probably a young girl, sneaking in here last night, dropping the baby off and running away. Or maybe she drove off with her boyfriend. He looked down again at the shrieking child, and held it still tighter. He felt suddenly over-whelmed by the realization that for the moment he was the only one in the baby's life.

7:33 A.M.

The child kept crying. Santander's body became numb from the unceasing flow of adrenaline. Feeling hot, he turned down the heat and loosened his tie. He brought the child's head up to his face. He kissed its forehead. After a moment, the child stopped and only moaned, his small body shaking uncontrollably. Santander thought the child was dying.

"Come on, come on," he whispered, wishing for the baby to start crying again, his face against the child's. He shut his eyes tight. The specter of death took his thought to Enrique Huerta's burial arrangement and thought of Enrique Huerta made him think of his own father, long dead.

"I know how you feel," he told the baby calmly, "they abandoned me too."

He saw himself suddenly as a twelve-year-old boy in Cuba and how his father had talked to him one day when he was eating lunch.

"Do you understand what is going on in Cuba?" his father had asked.

"Yes," he had answered even though he only had a vague notion about some horrible Communists taking over the country.

"Do you understand that I must stay and fight?"

"Yes."

"You must go away."

"Why?

"Because it's dangerous for you."

"Do I have to go alone?"

"Yes. Other children are leaving too. We'll be together again soon, right here having lunch like usual."

"I'll help you fight."

"You must go."

"I won't mind helping. I could do lots to help. I can run messages, and I could . . . "

"You must go. We'll be together again. Right here."

"You're sending me because you don't love me."

Santander remembered that after he'd said that his father had snatched him up out of his chair, hugged him tight and had begun sobbing. He'd never seen his father in that condition.

Santander recalled his departure from Havana's airport. He remembered being put into a bus when he got to Miami and being taken to a wilderness camp filled with other Cuban children whose parents had sent them away. He remembered how hot it was and how alone he felt and how he had started hating his father for sending him. He remembered being told one day by one of the camp's workers that he would be sent to a town near Chicago and he would live with the McNair family. He remembered the McNairs picking him up at the airport and taking him to their home. They didn't speak Spanish. He recalled the day the social worker came to the McNairs' house and spoke to them privately and how he found out later that night that his brother had been executed and his father given a thirty-year prison sentence and that his mother had taken ill. He remembered how angry he felt, how he hated his father. Doesn't he know I'm here? Doesn't he know I'm waiting for him to come pick me up? Where is my mom?

He didn't remember when he learned to speak English but only that he did and that he graduated high school. Nobody was there to watch him receive his diploma. He had become a problem for the McNairs.

"Shhh, shhh," he said to the child, rocking him slowly, feeling him move less and less. "Don't die little baby, don't die." He kept his face pressed against the baby's.

7:34 A.M.

Santander remembered when his father finally came to Miami. He was let out of the political prison after twenty years, ten years early, for medical reasons. His mother had long since died. He remembered how old and worn his father had looked and how he had barely recognized him. He only made it to one banquet held in his honor, a real hero's welcome. Huerta and the other cronies were all there, making laudatory speeches about his father in their suits and *guayabera* shirts. What a wonderful man, they had said; and what a son, a lawyer like his father. His father died the next week.

"Shhh," he said to the child, "don't worry baby, I won't leave you."

God-damn it, Santander said to himself, wiping his face. His father had barely spoken to him during those days. He had just stared at him all the time, frowning.

"What do you think that was all about?" he asked the baby, kissing its face.

He shut his eyes and saw his father's face and its expression during those last few days. The image was still clear after all these years even though before this morning Santander tried never to think about it. He began to feel the corners of his mouth droop.

"Don't die, baby, please. I'm sorry."

Santander thought of the girl from last night and wondered what her life was like during the day and whether she had ever abandoned a child in a parking lot. He thought about his wife and how she believed that he was out of town on business. He looked around at his car and thought of Medicare fraud. He thought of his children and how he'd heard them brag about him. He shook his head.

"You know better, don't you baby," he said to the child, kissing its forehead yet again. He held the child's forehead against his cheek. "Just don't die."

7:35 A.M.

He heard the sirens a block away. Within seconds he heard the vehicles park behind him and heard the loud echo of doors slamming in the empty garage and the blaring of an emergency vehicle radio. Santander opened his eyes and sat there with the child for another moment. A paramedic opened the door.

"How is he?" the paramedic asked.

Santander shrugged.

"Is he breathing?"

"Yes."

"Hold on."

Santander held on. He looked down at the child, knowing it was only seconds until it was stripped from him. He held it close to his face and kissed its forehead one last time.

"Looks like we didn't let each other down," he said to the child.

The paramedic returned a moment later, as promised.

"All right, let's have him," said the paramedic.

Santander hesitated. He finally leaned toward to the paramedic and slowly passed the child to him. The paramedic took the child in his arms, and Santander held his index finger inside the baby's hand for one last moment. Just before the child was completely in the clutches of the paramedic, Santander felt the baby squeeze his finger. The sensation pulsated through his entire body. The paramedic raced off with the child and climbed into the back doors of the ambulance. As he watched the ambulance doors shut, Santander waved and, still in the driver's seat, buried his face between his hands.

The Great Taco War
José Antonio Burciaga

José Antonio Burciaga, (1940–1996), was a poet, artist, scholar, author, activist, mentor and strong family man. He was the winner of the 1995 National Hispanic Heritage Award for Literature and the 1992 American Book Award for *Undocumented Love*, from the Before Columbus Foundation. Originally from Texas, his other published works include *Drink Cultura*, *Spilling the Beans*, *Weedee Peepo* and *In Few Words*.

In Redwood City, California, the Mexican flag was hoisted over the Taco Bell fast food restaurant and the local Mexican-American business community was angered and the flag was taken down. Taco Bell is determined to make inroads into the Mexican community through its culture and economics.

Tacos have become the hamburger's stiffest competitor as this country's favorite fast food. As of 1990, Taco Bell had already jumped ahead of McDonald's. But forget hamburgers for a couple of minutes. Today Taco Bell has not only infiltrated the *barrios,* but has even opened its first restaurant in, of all places, Mexico City.

A Colonel Sanders' Kentucky Fried Chicken restaurant in Beijing, or a McDonald's in Moscow does not seem as strange as Taco Bell in the capital city of Mexico. I was already aghast at their having built a Taco Bell in San Francisco's Mission District, where Salsa music, bright murals, and traffic lights compete for attention, and where there is at least one *taquería* every two blocks.

In the Mission District, taquerías are San Francisco's nouvelle eating places. Yuppies and business executives from uptown dine elbow-to-elbow with *cholos* and other Latinos on exquisitely prepared designer tacos and burritos made from charbroiled diced beef, chicken, pork, corned beef, tongue, brains, or veggies for vegetarians.

The taquerías are so popular that most customers are veritable connoisseurs of which is the talk o' the town. So it was brazen of Taco Bell to come into the Mission District and sell their mild imitations of the real thing. Even still, they sold tacos to Chicanos and other Latinos in the barrio like they were going out of *estilo.*

¿Que paso? Taco Bell was competing with what some call the best taquerías north of the border. The news was so disturbing that the "Godfather of the Mission District," Rene Yañez, took me to see it. "You gotta write about this," he said.

This fast food restaurant came complete with California mission-style architecture and a yellow plastic bell. It was surrounded by a beauty salon, a Chinese restaurant, a hardware store, and a mattress store. In the morning, the Taco Bell corner serves as an unemployment line for Latinos in search of a day's work.

Taco Bell does brisk business. What seemed like a crowd from the outside was a slow, meandering line, Disneyland-style. This was better than walking into a burger place and wondering which line would move faster, only to get behind the guy ordering twenty Big Macs, ten regular fries, ten large fries, five diet cokes, five regular cokes, ten malts and two coffees for a hungry work crew.

The Taco Bell menu can be a mystery if one is not familiar with the renamed food items. They can even puzzle a bicultural person. What's an Enchirito? "A combination burrito and enchilada," the manager answered, half bored and following his response with a half-accusing glance at my ignorance. I had envisioned a half-burrito, half-enchilada transplant, and felt the heartburn coming on.

They also featured Mexican pizza, which was a flat flour tortilla smothered with refried beans and topped with ground beef, cheese and shredded lettuce. But what were Cinnamon Crispas? They were similar to *buñuelos*, fried flour tortillas generously sprinkled with sugar and cinnamon.

Other items on the menu included the Nachos Bellgrande, Taco Bellgrande, and, of course, the kid's Fiesta Meal, which seemed incomplete without a piñata. They also listed steak Fajitas and chicken Fajitas, complete with the helpful phonetic spelling—"Fa-hee-tahs."

I ordered two tacos prepared with prefabricated hard tortilla shells at room temperature. Rene ordered the

Mexican pizza. The meat was lukewarm and the cheese and shredded lettuce were cold. Halfway through the taco, the shell crumbled between my fingers and landed on my tray. Rene laughed and then I realized the reason for the plastic forks. When I finally got to taste my "taco" it was different and tasty in a funny sort of way. There is something surreal about having to tear a little plastic package with one's teeth in order to get to salsa that is more mild and sweet than hot. Give me a dark green fresh jalapeño to sink my teeth into any day.

Orders were served in under five minutes and placed on a plastic tray with a paper placemat headlined, "The Border Run." It depicts an open highway in the desert leading to a Taco Bell and surrounded by highway signs that tell you to "Crack It, Bust It, Jump It, Snap It or Cross It." This, of course, is a subtle reference to crossing the border illegally or jumping a once-proposed fifteen-mile ditch south of San Diego. The hidden message is that eating at Taco Bell can be not only a treat but a real, live *Indiana Jones* adventure.

And who is the clientele in this Taco Bell in the barrio? Los pobres, poor people, seniors on fixed retirement incomes and immigrants who have "jumped, crossed or beat it" to this side. At 59 cents a taco, where else can a poor family eat for less than ten dollars with free drink refills? Where else can Latino teenagers hang out to socialize? Not at the barrio taquerías where tacos start at $1.50 each.

A typical day will find the outdoor seating of Taco Bell filled with Latinos of various ages. On one occasion a group of *batos locos*, crazy dudes, yelled at each other across the tables using foul *Español*. This didn't faze the older and younger women who kept right on conversing and eating. On a second visit, there was a whole day care nursery of some eighteen small fries, I mean, four, and five-year-old children. Where else could they have afforded lunch?

In other parts of the city you can see the taco price war between Taco Bell and Jack-In-The-Box: 59 cents a taco, 49 cents a taco, 39 cents a taco, three for a dollar . . . There's no end to the sales.

Not to be outdone, the Kentucky Fried Chicken in the Mission District raised a banner selling: "Oven roasted chicken with tortillas and salsa!" But finally the colonel chickened out. The pollo fare was only on a trial basis. Colonel Sanders may have been making a lot of *Yuan* in downtown Beijing, but in the Mission District he was losing *dinero* to tacos. The growing popularity of fast Mexican food in barrios such as the Mission District will be a significant turning point in the national taco war. Our burritos and tacos are not only the real thing but our first line of defense.

The fast food enterprise is cashing in on the unabashed sale of Anglicized and commercialized Mexican food to low-income Latinos, and the message is clear: "Hey! We can't make it as good as you can, but we can sure sell it faster and cheaper than you." Some hard-shelled Chicanos and Mexicanos wouldn't be caught dead in one of these Taco Bells. For others though, an empty stomach and pocketbook do not distinguish the "real" thing.

C/S[*]

[*] See page 259 for C/S: *con safos.*

Those on Bathroom Walls
William Archila

William Archila (desmadrado y desplazado) was born in 1968 in Santa Ana, El Salvador, where he grew up between Catholic school and civil war. He escaped the war in the 1980s, earned an MFA in poetry from the University of Oregon, and now teaches English as a Second Language in Los Angeles.

From a chunk of earth,
From a small cosmos
cracked open, bleeding with broken bones,
From bits of ashes,
From tiny metaphysics
left alone, silent as a skeleton,
From the land of volcanoes and lakes,
From the land of coffee and iguanas,
From a country as small as a paper cut,
From *Cuzcatlán*[1] *Donde Bate La Mar Del Sur*
donde el cielo calla con sabor,
From tiled floors or dirt grounds
From mountain roads
From pale electric light
on foot, bus or airplane,
Those who carry the dead, eating
ashes in the corners of their eyes,
Those who carry M-16s, strapped
across their waist—helmet
aligned to their hollow eyes,
Those who fled through cornfields
with death playing its trumpet,
Those who pierced eyes
and tips of fingers
with ice needles,
in the middle of day,
Those who learned to leave the bed
without a trace in the moon of night,
Those who saw civilians as punchbags
for the M-16s and black eyes,
Those who turned out the lights

with their blood in Morazán[2]—
fading like the stones of Cuzcatlán,
Those who dropped their sickle
for a badge and a gun,
Those who crossed rivers and mountains
to breathe a little easier—
shaking ashes and dust
off their back
Those who wrapped themselves
in the national flag
like the cloth of a bleeding Christ,
—They, my friends and enemies,
who tag each other out
on bathroom walls
all over this L.A. town
are already dead

[1] "land of richness" in Nahuatl, the land of the Pipiles (native people of El Salvador). Today Cuzcatlán is known as El Salvador.
[2] a northeastern province in El Salvador named after the independence leader and patriot Francisco Morazán. In 1981, the Atlacatl Battalion, an elite Salvadoran Army Unit trained by U.S. forces, entered the village of El Mozote, Morazán, and massacred hundreds of men, women and children.

Immigration Blues
William Archila

In Los Angeles where palm trees
        tower over Beverly drive
lazily resting in Griffith Park
giving no fruit nor shade
        but projecting the sun
        and broken clouds
nobody knows the Quetzal[1]
        of my birth
nobody knows the flower-and-song
        of the earth
My skin, like the color
        of the earth
My corner of Central America
where I drew birds and boats
        against the sky
where I learned the dreams
and memories of the past
My boy-hands dispatching
        Coca Cola bottles
in the soft night
Nobody knows of my birth
until the Old American Adam
bombs Chalatenango[2] to preserve the dream
creates dark factory buildings
along *milpas*[3] and *cafetales*[4]
pisses on my flag
and cuffs the minds
of rising flowers
  The Eagle lands:
      Death arrives
and here I pack my bags
with articles of the past
toilet paper, *burros*[5] and rags

In L.A.
where palm trees
sway to muzak
I am a black and red bird
glittering over western skies
flying through orange blossoms and L.A. drives
Cleaning houses of the L.A. dream
Maintaining palm trees on Main Street
but still praying alone with flute and drum
somewhere between north and south
between earth and infinite skies

---

[1] a bird native to the Central American rain forest, known for its beautiful colorful plumage. The quetzal was the sacred bird of the ancient Mayas; today it is the national emblem of Guatemala.

[2] a northwestern province in El Salvador, controlled by the FMLN (Farabundo Marti Front for National Liberation) guerillas during the civil war.

[3] cornfields

[4] coffee fields

[5] (literally donkeys), traditional peasant boots, manufactured by ADOC and worn by the FMLN guerillas during the civil war.

The Rootless People
Quễ-Doãn-Dô

Quễ-Doãn-Dỗ was born in Hadong, Vietnam. He is a graduate of Dalat Military Academy, Saigon Command, General Staff College and Saigon School of Law. A former Lieutenant in the Vietnamese Army and a former Attorney-at-Law, he is a member of the South Vietnamese Bar Association's Board of Governors. This essay first appeared in the San Jose City College Vietnamese Culture Association Newsletter in March, 1996. He has lived in San Jose, California, since 1980.

After managing to flee their countries, some people think it better to forget their origins and try their best to deny their own culture, sometimes even their language, in order to blend into their new surroundings. It seems to these poor people that by doing this they will automatically become nobler and richer.

When denying their own culture, many immigrants act like they are going to a potluck party without bringing anything themselves. Under these circumstances, the participants of the party would look upon them as cheaters or as if they were so poor that they could not afford to contribute anything. I really do not have any proof about it, but I am quite sure that the American people are not very willing to admit empty handed people into their beautiful country.

Putting aside this image of the above-mentioned foreigners, let's see what their behavior would bring to themselves and their children. I have heard some of these people try their best to use pidgin English to talk with their children because they hope that by doing so they would become Americans and their children would learn English faster. They do not know that this practice will have a boomerang effect and harm their children.

First of all, never can *only speaking English*, especially *pidgin English*, make you become an American, because the language cannot change your appearance. Although medical science and technology have made tremendous progess, they are still unable to change a non-white person (Asian, Latino, African, etc.) into a white American. What huge fortunes plastic surgeons would make if this were so!!

Secondly, those people's pidgin English teaches their children inappropriate ways of expressing themselves which can be very harmful to the learning of correct English. Many studies have shown that bilingual children who speak their native language at home make better progress in English than those who speak only one language. It is not difficult to understand this discovery because bilingual children have to learn twice as much as the others to express an idea, making their minds develop more quickly. Speaking two or more languages is for children like working out for an athlete; the more they practice, the more adept they become with language. Given this knowledge, those who deny their culture by not speaking their native language at home not only take their precious heritage away from their children, but also take away an advantageous learning opportunity.

And lastly, there is the emotional side of being rootless. Certainly, denying one's culture does not make immigrants become Americans, but it surely makes them rootless. When they and their children do not and cannot speak their native language anymore, their roots are cut off. Thus not yet being Americans, and no longer being elements of their native communities, these people are like duckweed floating on the surface of the water. They are denied by both societies and keep wondering who they are. Besides producing grave emotional crises, some identity crises can drive foreigners to madness.

One Japanese man who was born in the U.S., from an immigrant family, always considered himself an American until one day when his American friends bluntly told him that they had never taken him for an American. Severely shocked, he went back to Japan, but he could not speak Japanese so he was not accepted by the local population there either. Profoundly humiliated and despondent, this young man nearly committed suicide. Luckily, after an extremely difficult period, he realized what was wrong with him. He understood that the cause of his suffering was that he had denied what was his own in order to seek what he could never reach. What was his own was his being ethnically Japanese, and what he could never reach was being seen as a white American. Even though he spoke fluent English and had not been interested in picking up his parents' Japanese, his appearance remained unchanged. So why did he not admit that in reality he was a Japanese man born in the United States? In this position, he would have had the advantage of being a bridge which could have helped the two countries better understand each other. Why did he deny his culture and language which are among the most beautiful in the world? He then realized that he had to study the Japanese language and culture and reach the highest level possible to be an "inter-comprehension-bridge." He still continues his study today and instead of being dispirited like before, he is very proud of himself and has excellent morale. Immigrants or refugees should not think they will be appreciated if they try to copy the American people. On the contrary, the population of this country will only esteem those who keep their own culture and use it as a contribution to the intellectual power of the United States.

It was said that in the 7th century, when defeated by the Arabians, a group of Parsi* people from the Persian Gulf preferred to flee their country rather than live under their enemy's authority. After a long journey their boats reached the coast of India. There, the local Emperor sent a high-ranking official to the beach to welcome these refugees on his behalf. The boat people asked for asylum, but the Emperor's representative poured some tea in a cup until it was full to the brim and said, "This cup is the image of our country, it is already full of tea; you see by yourself that we cannot admit any more people just as this cup cannot receive any more tea because there is no more room." At this the Parsi boat-people's leader quietly took some grains of sugar and dropped them into the teacup and said, "Just as these grains of sugar which dissolved in your tea and made it sweet, we refugees will not take much space in your country

---

* *Parsi*: A Zoroastrian religious sect in India descended from a group of Persian refugees who fled from the persecutions in the 7th and 8th centuries.

but we will make it stronger, more beautiful and more appealing." The asylum was then granted to the refugees. Let's wonder what would have happened if, instead of sugar, the boat-people's leader only dropped into the cup some insipid grains of sand or more tea of exactly the same kind as that in the cup? Both of these items would not have brought anything new or could not have made it better, so why should they have been admitted?

A displaced tree can only survive and flourish in a new land if it manages to keep its roots intact; otherwise, it will wither and die. Without roots it cannot absorb the nutritive matter of the new land. It is exactly the same for people. If foreigners and refugees keep their language and culture while trying to learn English, they will be able to contribute their culture to the intellectual life of the U.S., make it ever fresh and stronger. That is what Americans want the most and that is also the way immigrants and their families benefit most.

Selections from *Drops of This Story*
Suheir Hammad

Suheir Hammad was born in Jordan and raised in Brooklyn during the rise of crack and Hip Hop culture. She is the author of *Drops of This Story* (1996) and *Born Palestinian, Born Black* (1996). Her poetry has been featured on National Public Radio, BBC World Service, HBO, and on Broadway in *Russell Simmons Def Poetry Jam*. The following excerpts from *Drops of This Story* use water imagery and fluid word pictures to connect her narrative.

My father let me know I was going to get married. Our way, his way. Never mind that at eighteen, I didn't have a way. He tells me that there's a respectable young man who wants to come over and ask for my hand in marriage. This wetness tells of how this fool drank all the drinks my mother offered without thanking her once. Proceeded to burp after every swallow, you guessed it, without excusing his rude self. I should have known. I looked out the window and saw his balding head in the sunlight. He was wearing a pink shirt. A pink shirt. I don't get this arranged marriage business anyway, but the least this fool could've done was wear a suit. He had a belly, a big nasty belly. No butt. I didn't even look.

My mother kept nagging me to put on some makeup, telling me that I should feel complimented to have so many suitors. Like I wanted them. Then my father yelled at me for not wearing a dress. How was I supposed to explain that this was the twentieth century and people didn't do this in New York. In Palestine. Or in hell? I felt like a show horse. This story is lived out too often. Had me worried that I was gonna end up in a dry, unwanted union.

Beads were forming on the wide forehead of this would-be husband. He wasn't the only one either. They all wanted to marry me, and none of them ever talked to me. They went through my father. Never talked to me. They would see me at a wedding, where I'd be all done up, dressed fly and dancing my ass off. All they knew was that I was somewhat tall, said to be smart, drove my own car and had already been poor, so I wouldn't expect too much. This is how people end up holding hands and linking souls even though they know they don't fit right. There was the guy who didn't say a word to me all night and called my dad the next day, talking about how he just had to have me. The one who had a crush on me for two years before his mother let him know I was too educated for him. The one who wanted to test me before making up his mind. The list drips on down the page. Drops on my page.

§ §

Poetry is my life's air. And the air humid with these words. Tell of Flatbush Ave. and the assault of colors, smells, and sounds of the Caribbean in Brooklyn. Dancehall music oozes out of loud speakers like rivers. Men in crushed velvet suits of royal purple or money green, polish their pointy shoes while checking out the women on the street. The women being checked out are rolling their eyes and walking away snapping their gum. Africa is evident in the adornment of the bodies on Flatbush. Round here, however, the hair is adorned with orange and yellow extensions and glued on rhinestones, rather than cowry shells and *geles*. This time, cheap gold decorates black bodies, rather than prayer beads and sacred shells.

I write wet poetry. About Hammad and Sunset Park. On how Palestinians need to get over our internal colonialism. The British taught my mother to hate and to flatten her butt. Taught my father that he wasn't quite white, therefore not quite right. How we need to accept the Asian, the Mediterranean, the Crusader, and the African in us. Accept and deal with it.

§ §

Sing the song of my mother's full day of labor pains. I was born on the 25th day of the 10th month of the year. Five o'clock in the morning. 5th day of the week. The number 5 is supposed to bring blessings and rid evil. I was born fat, a good 10 pounds. My legs clench just thinking about it. Good things don't come easy. My poor mother was in labor for a whole day. Her midwife was an Egyptian woman, and, delirious with pain, my mother told her that if we both lived through this birth, she'd name the baby after her. My mother says the woman was *samra*, like me. Samra means dark. My father says she was pretty. This wet afterbirth is the story of my name.

As this dew forms on the petals of morning flowers, it directs to my name. Suheir. Suheir means someone who likes to stay up late, female. *Lover of the night*. It's derived from an extinct flower that bloomed nocturnally and once fragranced eastern skies. The wind carries the oil of this flower to Brooklyn, to bathe me in its words. My father didn't tell me what my name meant until my first year in college. I wish he would have told me earlier.

I spent a childhood with too many girls named Maria, Tanisha, and Jill. Suheir sounded too much like *Sahara* or *Sue-her-hair* to make my life any easier. The kids were bad, but the teachers were worse. I would hate to get a substitute teacher, 'cause I'd have to go through the same thing all the time. Wait until I knew my name was next to be called, then shout out that I was present before I had to hear another tongue's rendition of my name. How did they read Suheir as *Sharar*? My resentment tells the story of how none of these teachers ever asked me how to pronounce my name, or what it meant, or where it came from. Or the way they read my last name as Mohammad even though it was Hammad. They did that to me at my eighth grade graduation, where I beat out all the ninth graders for a city writing award. The winner was *Shohar Mohammad.*

I love my name now. I love to say it, and to hear it said, correctly. Trying to make things easier for people, I used to answer to Sue. I don't anymore. Why should I? That wasn't the name born to me. How will the spirits know what to call me? I carry the essence of an extinct night flower. Cool. The drops pick my brain and let me know that this flower must have been a desert cactus.

§ § § § § § § § § § § § § § § § §

The sun turns me a deep bronze in the summertime.
My mother was always yelling at me to stay inside. I was
samra enough. With my black hair, thick eyebrows, and little
mustache, I looked foreign enough. Most people can never
guess what language I speak, or which flag I kneel to. Old
Latina women always thought that I was one of them new,
newfangled Puerto Rican girls who didn't speak Spanish.
Hindi women were always talking to me in their curry
tongue, and when I'd let them know I wasn't Indian, they'd
talk to me in Bengali. Anyway, I was supposed to stay out of
the sun. I was dark enough.

The Arab movies my parents brought home were filled with
blonde actresses whose eyes were the color of swimming
pool water. It was in them eyes that this story was floating.
I never understood why all the actresses were blonde when
most of the people I knew were darker. I knew there was
something wrong. Barbie. I saw the swimming eyes on the
Latino station, rap videos, and Hindi musical. This wasn't
just an Arab thing.

The story of self acceptance. Of finally not minding my skin,
my hair, or even my mustache. Needs to be told. The drops
whisper in too many languages, too many tongues. There
are too many girls who think they're ugly, 'cause they can't
swim in their own eyes. Want to look like Barbie. This is
Barbie's obituary. Barbie was decapitated. She's dead.

§ § § § § § § § § § § § § § § §

The Verranzano bridge crossed the mass of these words,
as my family's American dream came true. Their own house
on some land. I still didn't get my own room, but there was
a lot of grass and trees. Actually, there were manicured lawns
and detailed landscapes. Staten Island was, is, a totally new
world. Ordered nature. A nasty, pretty, dry planet. If Brook-
lyn had soaked me in this story, this new suburb of a

borough was now wringing it out of me. If I had ever enter-
tained the notion of being slightly better 'cause I was slightly
lighter, Staten Island let me know that any shades other
than pale winter pink and temporary summer tan weren't
cool. They let me know it with their oh-so-polite questions
regarding what I was. What the hell was I?

*What did you say? Pakistani? Which one of your par-
ents is black? Hablo espanolo? I bet you can dance real good.
Can you rap? Can you cook curry?*

I'm Palestinian. I'd have to point it out on the map (the
region, not the name).

*Oh, you're Israeli! Did any of your family survive the
holocaust?*

Reply that my people were living through their own
holocaust. Teachers would challenge me:

*There's no such place as Palestine. Where is it on the
map? Why do you people make so much trouble? Don't you
know what the Jews have been through?*

That's when the kids would realize what hell I am.

*You're a terrorist. One of those animals that bombed
the marines in Lebanon. Those gypsies who hijack planes
and kidnap athletes. We know about you. Terrorists. Ani-
mals. Murderers.*

Their words dropped on me like air strikes above Beirut.

§ § § § § § § § § § § § § § §

My mother drank this liquid in as it rolled down her
face from swollen eyes. What did she expect from her man?
What can a woman expect from a man who has the open
option of marrying three other wives? This story is about
the too many women who live in abusive marriages, 'cause
it's a bigger shame to be divorced than to be beaten. These
words write about how arranged marriages become deranged
lives. Too many names make up this story. Too many girls
who had to learn patience and obedience. Patience is the
woman's key to heaven. That's what men teach little girl

brides. Them same men figure that they'll slide right through the pearly gates, 'cause all them male prophets got their backs, are looking out for them. Right in, even though they fornicate, abuse, rape, and war. Just get by, riding on the back of little girl brides.

It's not like any culture treats its women any better than another. I write of Yemeni women getting kicked in the neck by husbands not happy with dinner. Latinas getting beat by boyfriends who didn't like the look on some face. Black women getting dogged for their money by junkies and hard up gamblers. White women getting their faces smashed into windows after leaving an abortion clinic. It ain't like anybody can point a broken finger at anybody else. This story is about women, and how patience ain't some damn virtue. It's a threatening chain of socially accepted submission that has got us down for the count. The drops keep counting off.

§ § § § § § § § § § § § § § § §

Pumped out of the bottles of curl sheen. Use the colorful words to polish nails. Spread the meaning of this madness across lips, shinier than any gloss. Don't need blush, even on sallow days. Line eyes with the lines of these pages, ink as kohl. This beauty is of earth, ain't no plastic here.

Kneaded into the skin of beautiful tired women, this wet tried to reduce the visible signs of aging. Smile lines after years of forcing pleasant faces to a world that hated them. Told their value lay in their looks, were sold face creams and youth lotions, as though they were blessings. Selling their souls, these women bought up these prayers in a bottle with food stamps and welfare checks. Bleaching their hides to reach an impossible shade of porcelain, Arab, Latina, and African women compared each other's progress in the fight against their own natural faces.

The story about the acceptance of tired, sad beauty that radiates with the love of mothers and grandmothers. Tired and sad beauty that's more genuine than any poison in any bottle. It don't sell itself, or buy others. These drops travel down the cheeks of women who have forgotten that God held each of their noses in divine hands and shaped them into perfection. This drop falls on to the tips of Semitic noses and quivers, then joins the ink on the page. I write this love song in the name of our mothers' beauty, to let them remind themselves that we were beautiful before there was Revlon.§

What Has Become of Us Here?
Gregory Gumbs

Gregory Gilbert Gumbs was born on Aruba, but grew up on the French/
Dutch Caribbean Island of St. Martin. He first studied Law and Criminology
in Utrecht, The Netherlands. He is now working as a screenwriter in Los
Angeles.

What has become of us Here?
We, the hope of an entire nation
and people
  we, the talented-tenth
with our beautiful dreams
of an even more beautiful future.

What has become of us Here?
some have returned home
in shame, in shame
  they failed in Holland
  an entire family disgraced
 others have fled into
 alcohol or drugs
or the strange comfort of madness
  for here reality is even more cruel
than they could have ever imagined

What has become of us Here?
  some are still trying to realize their
dreams and potential
  others have reached the finish line
 but not without difficulty
 not without difficulty
we, the talented-tenth

What has become of us Here?
We, the hope of an entire nation
and people
  we, who did so well in their schools and universities

when we first arrived from Curacao, Aruba, St. Maarten,
Saba and St. Eustatia, but
the passage of time, the distance, the new environment
has a frightening way of catching up with you
we, the talented-tenth
with our beautiful futures
promised us on our return home to the Caribbean.

What has become of us Here?
those who have been forced
to consider the situation back home
the unacceptable conditions
the necessary changes always
accompanied by nagging feeling
of uncertainty
fracture
and a growing sense of desperation

What has become of us Here?
those who have succeeded at
the cost of closing their eyes
stubbornly looking away
doing their utmost to forget
to forget about who they are
to forget about where they are from
to forget about everything and everyone
and live in the here and now
in the here and now
we, the talented-tenth

What has become of us Here?
the prison-like loneliness which sticks to us
the broken relationships strewn
across the varying landscapes
here and there here and there
the ongoing struggle to remain one
to remain whole
the constant thoughts about suicide

the sad reports every so often
of another successful attempt to end it all
here and now
here and now

What has become of us Here?
 we, the hope of an entire nation
 and people eagerly awaiting our
   contributions towards a better tomorrow for all
 we, the talented-tenth
 with such great dreams
of whom
 so much was expected back home
 What has become of us Here?
 What has become of us Here?

The Immigrant
J Yarrow

J Yarrow is a second-generation Norwegian-American living in Seattle whose work has been published in *Clear Cut: an Anthology of Seattle Writers*. "The Immigrant" revisits her grandfather's pioneer ethic and hope for a better life.

He came, an immigrant, my father's father,
to these lush valleys, marshlands, streams,
the hills glacier-scraped to subsoil
glacier-covered with stones, gravel, and silt.
On land grown over with fir and alder, he found
timber for house and barn, wood for cooking
in the dark mornings and long, dark afternoons
of rainy winters, green and damp as any
Norwegian spring, a paradise.
                                        With work
and luck, a lot of work—and luck is what you make it—
a man could raise a family here, build
a farm to last through all the generations.
No more beatings at the hand of the sea, no more
renting land, no more logging for the bosses.
A wife, children, beds filling room
after room, and neighbors near
enough to help but not to crowd.

                          A man could live a life
and forget how things change beyond calculation:
children grown, and gone, the barn slowly
melting into the earth of its timbers,
family and farm both long altered,
his hard-shelled dreams now gone to weed,
though he'd find traces still of what he planted.

Aide-Memoire

For Czeslaw Milosz
Elisavietta Artamonoff Ritchie

Elisavietta Artamonoff Ritchie, winner of four PEN Syndicated Fiction Awards, is the author of many collections of writing, the most recent of which are *Awaiting Permission to Land* and *Flying Time: Stories & Half Stories.* She has been published in *Poetry, American Scholar, The New York Times* and is the editor of the anthology *The Dolphin's Arc: Endangered Creatures of the Sea.*

The great blue heron skims low
over the soybean field
stripped by the harvester.

The lance of his neck probes wind.
Wide wings flap with languor
as if slowed by December.

He rises above bare hawthorn,
wineberry canes enclosing the pond
like barbed wire. If you saw him

you would recall the storks
on village roofs of your childhood,
your losses would flood over you

like tide in the marsh. The heron soars
over battalions of cattails, to the river,
disappears beyond channel markers,

but flings his shadow on furrows
where dried stalks bristle and
leftover velvet pods still hold seed.

I WORRY...
Sridevi Ramanathan

Sridevi Ramanathan edited *No Explanations, No Apologies* and has been published in *diS-orient* and *Alaska Women Speak*. Trying to find the perfect balance of cultures has been invaluable to her definition of self and to her writings.

I worry . . .
> that I don't know how to read or write *Tamil.*

I worry . . .
> that I won't formally learn my mother's tongue.

I worry . . .
> that I won't know how to interpret the *Panchangam* for religious occasions.

I worry . . .
> that I won't know how to wear a sari by myself.

I worry . . .
> that I won't be able to cook *sambar* or *rassam*.

I worry . . .
> that Indians will think, "She married out, so she wants out."

I worry . . .
> that Mom and Dad will have to use their second language to communicate with their own grand children.

I worry . . .
> that a conservative grandmother will treat my kids as untouchables.

I worry . . .
> that my kids will refuse to know Tamil.

I worry . . .
> that my kids won't say *slogams*.

I worry . . .
> that my kids will call *Thatha's dothi*, a skirt and *Patti's sari*, a drape.

I worry . . .
> that my kids won't eat *sambar* and *rassam*.

I worry . . .
   that my kids won't appreciate the customs.
I worry . . .
   that my kids won't understand our people.
I worry . . .
   that my kids won't like our Indian family.
I worry . . .
   that my kids will think their mother is a freak.

I worry that it'll all end here with this . . .
                                    ring.*

Glossary:
dothi - male dress
Panchangam - astrological almanac
Patti - Grandmother
sambar and rassam - South Indian foods
sari - female dress
slogams - prayers
Tamil - Language of Tamil Nadu, India
Thatha - Grandfather

*Unlike Christian weddings, Hindu marriage ceremonies do not involve an exchange of rings.

My American Reality
Patricia Jabbeh Wesley

Patricia Jabbeh Wesley and her family moved to Michigan in 1991, having survived a year of civil war in their home country of Liberia, West Africa. She grew up and attended college in Liberia, and in the 1980s studied at Indiana University in Bloomington. She is the author of *Becoming Ebony* (2003), and *Before the Palm Could Bloom: Poems of Africa* (1998).

The Pan American Air Liner, a gigantic, crowded Boeing 747 on its first stop from New York, waited in transit at the Roberts' International Airport near Monrovia, Liberia. Seated on the plane was the entire world—America, on a plane. Fifteen years ago that early morning, I met my America. My husband Mlen-too and I found our seats among a multi-ethnic, racial mix. We were African Missionaries working with the International Fellowship of Evangelical Students (IFES), of which America's Inter Varsity Christian Fellowship (IVCF) is a part. We were traveling to Lagos, Nigeria, to attend one of the many training conferences which equipped us to minister across cultures. Looking across the four-row isles of hundreds seated, my blood froze within me. In that electrifying room were Asians, Africans, Europeans, Americans, South East Asians . . . of all shades of colors—out of America. I had never seen such a reality before. Was this a picture of America?

A decade later, I now find myself confronting America, the beautiful, with my prying, questioning eyes. How many others like me have asked this question: *"Is America real for me?"*

Four years ago as I began my adventure as a College Instructor in the American work force, I couldn't help laughing at the stupidity of prejudice. I arrived that morning, my first day at work, to a long line of cars attempting to enter our college grounds. Parking was limited, I assumed, as a uniformed security officer approached my car. "All students must park at the Reformed Church Parking lot," he shouted, signaling me to leave the line so faculty and staff could get the better parking. He had no need to ask if I were staff or faculty. Being an international, I couldn't imagine anyone was that stupid. I therefore patiently explained that I was a faculty member and needed to get to work. But he signaled again that I should leave the line, probably assuming that I had a language problem.

When those behind began honking, I nervously left the line, driving back on to the main campus road. Suddenly, I realized that I was now in America—not in Africa. I was no longer just a person; I was now a *black woman*. That he would never see beyond my blackness—"another *black woman*" was my new reality. I had to circle around the entire campus to get back to where my security *friend* was, separating the *cream* from the *chaff*. This time as I approached, he ran toward my car, angry. "So, you're back? Didn't you understand you must park in the church yard?"

"I'm not a student." I decided that since he was the ignorant one, I needed to be patient.

"Get out of the line, now," he shouted, his face turning blood red.

"Do you speak English?" I asked, but he would not even look me in the eye. He was shouting at me so hard, I had to wind my window halfway up and positioned my car so no one could enter or leave the school grounds. Then I turned off the engine.

"Your car will be towed away if you don't get out of the way!" he shouted.

"Get the tow truck for me," I said above the honking. "You might also need the college president to assist you; but, if faculty parking is on campus, that's where I'll park."

After ten minutes another security officer, a female, arrived at the scene. Maybe a woman would listen. "What's the hold-up?" she cried, as the huge security officer explained that this student wanted to park in the faculty parking. "Ma'am we're letting only faculty in here because of limited parking," she said in that all familiar tone.

"I'm a faculty member, and like everyone else, I don't yet have my parking sticker. If you don't let me in, no one will go in or come out of campus today. The sooner you get the president out here, the better."

She quickly removed the roadblock her coworker had put there for me. "I'm sorry, dear, please drive in," she said, to my relief.

Four year later as I continue to peel away America's layers for myself, the eternal question, "is America real for me," haunts me. To mainstream America, I am the student, a janitor, the one needing, not giving, the other person, one of them, anything, not an Instructor.

I have only to walk into my assigned class for the first time, and suddenly, comfortable feathers are rustled. In the past four years, I have worked part time, teaching courses in Writing and Literature—including African and African-American Literatures at area colleges in Grand Rapids. My latest, most memorable experience happened when I was assigned to teach an off-campus course, "Writing About Literature." My students were employees at the corporate office of a large food-chain in a suburban neighborhood. Two weeks before the beginning of classes, I was interrupted at home one afternoon by a strange phone call. The gentleman who coordinated the program for this company was on the other end of the line. He was agitated and expressed his fears in the coldest voice. "Ms. Wesley, have you ever taught this course before? Are you new at the college? How many times have you taught here?"

Give me a break! Who was he? Did he think the college had employed "another" unqualified, black woman? Did he just arrive from Mars? My mind joggled with my American reality. Since I do not interview on the phone, I referred him to my Department Chair.

A few minutes after that call, the phone rang again. A woman, another cold voice of concern, called from the same office. Like him, she too was concerned about my African accent, and like people around here, she was quick to say, "Oh you have an accent." After confirming their suspicions, they made separate calls to my Dean and Department Chair, frustrated, whining about the problems that would arise if another Instructor was not found.

"You know, she speaks with an accent, and students will have difficulty understanding her. She's new, and students might not like her."

Did they assign this class because no one else would teach it? And did I get it at the last minute? What if students felt uncomfortable and dropped this course? "Oh certainly, there could be someone else . . . ," they whined in that Grand Rapids accent which they believe to be the *universally acceptable accent.*

My Dean, Department Chairperson, and the people who know me, not only by my teaching skills, but also by my talent for writing, took their stand, fighting to show that indeed, I was as qualified as the other white Instructors. My Department Chair argued that students should be grateful to not only have an experienced teacher, but also a poet with a cross-cultural perspective. But was all this defense necessary? Would this have happened if I were a white American?

Their concerns intensified when I walked into the classroom, not only black, but also really African, and indeed, *a woman.* The man on the phone went to the class, one of the coldest people I've ever met, ignoring me as best as he could as he sold textbooks to my students. *Was I really African— with an accent?* Two students dropped immediately—*how dare this college not understand their concerns?* The workload was way too much for them, the callers again complained after reviewing the course syllabus.

This is just an example of what we of an ethnic, nonwhite race with an immigrant background must deal with daily.

Before coming to the U.S., I was an Instructor of English and Literature (African, American and English) at the University of Liberia, my home of origin, for ten years. Even though Liberian students, like students anywhere, complained, there was never a day when my credibility as a qualified Instructor was questioned; especially, by people who had not yet met me. But America is often a different experience for us African immigrants. American students reject us before meeting us, and where our white coworkers have nothing to prove, we must work harder if we must win students' trust.

Is this because many students were brought up in a society that teaches that unless a culture, people, or teaching is white, it has no validity? Or is this simply a paranoia of us newcomers? My American students often confess that I am their first non-white Instructor, and that before taking my African or African-American Literature class, they only read white American or English Literature. Any other literature, many were taught, was just plain nonsense. What are today's teachers doing to change this? Are English Departments at America's institutions really including other literatures, or are these literatures or cultures being marginalized in new ways? I can only say that wherever I've introduced change, I had to struggle my way through muddy waters or get out. During my four years in the American classroom, I have seen that students may tolerate me if I come across as embracing America while condemning Africa. Often, they argue that black Literature is too difficult to understand, and the books, unsuitable.

Is this just a student problem or is it an American problem? How often have we seen news about Africa, South America, the Middle East, Asia and the rest of the world given such ugliness that we shudder in our seats? Can you remember watching African news that was not barbaric, of poverty, starvation or war? To many Americans, Africans must be the most corrupt and uncivilized people, who alone have brought all the diseases to the world. Over and over, Americans are subjected to half stories and half truths by a white media whose aim is difficult to discern.

Does this attitude impact the way other races, cultures, and peoples are accepted or rejected in America? Why not? Don't these African, Asians, South Americans, etc., represent *those barbaric* people of the world? *Why should they bring their cultures to a culture that is already superior?* One of my colleagues puts it like this: "This new trend of multiculturalism now divides our country. What is wrong with the way we used to learn? Why should students study Maya Angelou's novels or Gwendolyn Brooks' poetry when we can study our own literature?" What is *our own literature?*

We immigrants must quickly assimilate, lose our identities, and take on America if we must achieve the American Dream. The question I ask them is how does an African like me assimilate when African-Americans who were here centuries before me have not yet been assimilated into mainstream America? Do I take on America before she fully accepts me?

As a College Instructor, I look at my classroom as my real America. If my students discover that they can accept me even though I also reflect another complex culture, even though I remind them of difference, an American reality—I am grateful. Often I must work hard to earn this, but when they realize I'm not the monster on television or a stereotype from the movie screen they write me little notes of confession. One student from my classes wrote:

Dear Mrs. Wesley,
Thanks for opening my eyes. When you walked into this class, I wanted to drop the course. I had never had a black instructor before, and I hated you before I knew you. But you have touched my life more than any other in the five years I've been at this university. I love your sense of humor, your positive outlook on life, your love for students' well being. You have opened my eyes."

I have discovered that whether I find myself at a private, Christian college, a state university, or a business college, I will have to live with and in my own reality. The reality that I am a black, African woman, whose accent puts roadblocks in my American journey, is a great reality. However, over and over, I have admired myself for being who I am despite the constant stares from America.

Tears wet my cheeks over and over as I read students' notes, numerous scribbles voluntarily written and often snuck into my books, intentionally left on my desk, or inserted into an assignment. As I now read these notes of confession from students this fall ending, I realize that I must photocopy them and open a new file. These notes tell me that America may not now be what many of us want America to be.

One of my American dreams is the dream that cost Dr. Martin Luther King, Jr. his life—that America will one day discover her strength in her diversity and take advantage of it without prejudice. America is certainly not the America I saw on that Pan American Airliner more than a decade ago. America is a reality in which we must live, struggle, overcome our prejudices, accept everyone—whites, blacks, Latin Americans, African-Americans, Native Americans, Asian-Americans, all. America is my classroom in which students must understand that my African blackness, my womanhood, as well as my accent also reflect America. Even if I cling to my cultural heritage for its beauty and strengths, I am worth coming close to, and knowing. I came to America because she is a great reality. I love her diversity and her ability to keep whole her many parts that now include me. I may be different, but I bring strength in my differentness. I too reflect the American reality.

My Story
Marcela Bruno

Marcela Bruno's father was a pioneer journalist in Peru. She has traveled widely and has lived in New York since 1967, where she enjoys a career in publishing. Her advice to new immigrants is to adapt, think positively and have patience. She has two grown sons, Patricio and Marcos, and is married to the poet Marty Sklar.

This is a true story, a true story about the circumstances surrounding my arrival in the United States of America, where now—at the age of fifty-seven and at the bedside of my dying mother—I can tell it with my heart and soul.

If someone had told me forty years ago that I would end up living in the United States and be an American citizen, I wouldn't have believed it. If they had also insinuated that I would be proud of my new nationality, that I would give birth to two boys in a clinic right in the middle of Manhattan and that I would live like a "gringo"—as we call people from the United States in my country of birth—I would have thought it was all a joke.

I was born in 1939, in Arequipa, a picturesque colonial city known as the "white city" for the beauty of its architecture, which is also unique since most of the houses are built of a white rock formed from solidified lava. This city, located in the south of Peru, is surrounded by three majestic volcanoes called Misti, Chachani and Pichu Pichu. Arequipa is also known as "The Lion of the South" because many political leaders were born there. It is the birthplace of poets, novelists and musicians. On the whole, it was a town full of glory whose sons and daughters felt very proud to have been born there.

I have memories of a happy childhood and am grateful to my parents who surrounded me with love. I grew up in an atmosphere of security and was a calm, obedient girl. As an only child, I never lacked for anything. When I was five, as family tradition dictated, I was sent to The Sacred Hearts, one of the most exclusive religious schools, where my mother and maternal grandmother had studied. At the same time I attended a Spanish dance academy and the regional music school where I studied piano. Though my childhood memories are generally pleasant, the sole exception is the overprotectiveness and suffocating affection of my mother. When I finished primary school, my father decided to send me to a public school, the Juan Manuel Polar National Business Institute, for my secondary education. I noticed the difference in the kind of instruction, and although my mother never approved of the change of schools, that was the deciding step in my education, thanks to the efficient teaching I had the good fortune of having there. Immediately after graduating from the institute, I began working with my father at the newspaper El Pueblo, the most important daily in Arequipa. At the same time, I decided to study journalism and got my degree from the University of San Marcos. Without a doubt, the most beautiful memories I have of my life in my native land are those years of my adolescence and youth when I lived all the emotions one experiences in journalism. Under the guidance of the best teacher I could ever have had—my father, who was editor-in-chief—I held various positions: from proofreader I worked my way through reporter, columnist, designer, and finally executive assistant to the publisher of the newspaper. After experiencing several romances of no great importance—except for my first love, a brief and torrid encounter with someone who would play a very important role in my future—at twenty I met the man I would marry. My marriage was everything a young woman in my city could want, and the happiness I felt was complete but brief.

Drama entered my life when my husband died in an accident and, at almost the same time, my father fell victim to cancer.

I was reborn at the age of twenty-seven, after my life almost ended with my widowhood and the death of my father. The leading man of the "brief and torrid encounter" I had had when I was barely sixteen years old was an artist from Argentina with whom I had always maintained correspondence and who had given me support and strength in the tragic times I went through. He had emigrated to New York with his mother and because "where sweet potatoes have roasted, coals remain," the romance was rekindled. Our almost-daily correspondence reached the point where he asked me to become his wife. We became engaged, and that is how I came to the United States where I began a new life.

I arrived in New York on a Sunday in January. I was married the following Friday, and since that day I've lived at a dizzying pace. Everything here has been like a dream, a dream, sometimes a nightmare, with ups and downs, sadness and joy. The beginning in New York was very difficult, without language, without money, without family or friends. I had to face this "concrete jungle" and I did.

I never had time to seriously study the language; however, I did try to learn it, repeating in the beginning like a parrot whatever I heard, often not knowing what I was saying, reading the newspaper but understanding little of what I was reading, listening to the radio but comprehending little, and watching television though barely able to follow what was going on. I would repeat the words I heard and little by little I learned some of them. I never felt ashamed of trying to speak in English. I was aware that I couldn't express myself but I spoke, often nonsense, and kept speaking . . . speaking . . . and speaking, and I often got support from those who listened to me. They made patient efforts to understand me, rarely showing signs of rejection. I remember that one of my first jobs was caring for an adorable little girl on 26th Street in Manhattan. The mother and I communicated almost entirely by signs. One day it was raining, and when I arrived in the morning I told her: "water, sky, water, sky." She looked at me in wonder and then said, "Oh, it is raining." And that's how I learned a new word: raining.

In spite of never having lost my Peruvian identity, my adaptation to this new way of life and my assimilation to the customs and traditions of my new country is complete. From the first day on, I tried to live in accordance with the customs here, to eat food from here, to celebrate the holidays here, enjoy the music here and above all to feel like a native of this place, defending the customs and interests of this country where I was reborn.

Before coming, I had savored professional success, but upon arriving here, I had to begin from scratch. At the beginning, I would do any kind of work, from childcare to cleaning houses and working in factories. I won't deny that those were difficult times; for many years I had to hold two jobs at once, and my greatest disadvantage was always language.

It is very common to listen to immigrants talk about discrimination at work. Personally I never felt discriminated against: I simply couldn't compete with those who had the advantage of English mastery. Today I feel satisfied with having been able to survive and having struggled tirelessly to perform different jobs. I consider myself fortunate to have forged my own path little by little until I arrived at the place where I find myself now.

The greatest danger for immigrants is that they may either completely forget their roots or simply live an almost fake life, trying to ignore the customs and traditions of the place in which they find themselves. An equilibrium is very difficult to attain. I cannot criticize the hundreds of immigrants who, although they live in the United States, continue to act and think as they did before emigrating; that means they are neither here nor there. Their resistance to assimilation makes their adaptation even more difficult, and as a result they feel frustrated. On the other hand, it isn't healthy to try to forget one's own roots and the country one comes from. The ideal is to attain a middle ground, a balance, so that being aware of our origins, we can manage to adapt to this new life.

Two boys, two sons—they are mine and they were born here. Since they were young, I have instilled in them the idea that they are Americans. Although their father is Argentinean and their mother Peruvian, they are Americans, period. It is most important that their identity be very clear to them, because without it they will lack that pride and that patriotism necessary to every human being. Similarly, my sons' social development is more positive since, no matter what their race, they were born here, they were educated here and they are a part of this place. For them the future will offer better prospects that it did for their parents, and they have all the opportunities of those native to this land, with the great advantage of being totally bilingual. It is a pleasure to hear them speak perfectly in Spanish. My family was surprised to listen to them speak when I took them to visit the land of my birth, where I still keep a house.

I return now to the beginning of my story: My mother continues her deathbed struggle; after working all my life, I am about to lose my job because my contract is ending and there are no new projects on the horizon. However, this is nothing new for me, since I have had to start over more than once. But now I have a lot of experience and, although I still have language limitations, I have always carried out important tasks. Currently I am an editorial coordinator at one of the most important publishing companies in the country. I had previously worked as a production coordinator at a translation company, as head of the word processing department of some of the best-known advertising firms, and as a Spanish editor in the production of an encyclopedia. I have successfully held many jobs. Although I gave up my journalism career in my native country, here I have still managed to do work that has allowed me to support my family and given me personal satisfaction.

My emotional life has been like a whirlwind of good fortune, pleasure, struggle and pain. The first years of my second marriage were happy, and the arrival of my first son was the culmination of that good fortune which was repeated three years later with the arrival of my second son. My mother came to live with me before the birth of the first, and it was she who helped me care for my children since I hardly stopped working for a single day.

Unfortunately, my second marriage began experiencing problems that would result in separation after almost twenty years. It was a sad and tense period. With only my mother, I was left to face life in New York with two teenagers. The older one just graduated with his bachelor's degree in biology. He works at the university and wants to be a doctor. The younger one will graduate next year in economics and has his own plans for the future. Both are engaged to young women who are also first-generation Americans whose parents were originally from Argentina. Seeing one's children become successful is the best reward a mother can receive. My emotional life at present is like a beautiful dream. Six years after my husband and I separated, and when I hadn't the least expectation of a new romance, I found this autumn love that arrived unexpectedly and unsought. If love at fifteen is pink, and at twenty-five is synonymous with having arrived, after fifty it is a combination of the two, added to the serenity and peace one attains only with the years and experience life brings. My husband is a real North American, but not simply that; he is a poet and editor of great artistic sensitivity. This is true love and crowns my life with happiness. If sometimes I have lost and many other times I have lost heart, it has been worth the effort since the profits have been greater and I have never regretted having immigrated to the promised land.

To those recently arrived immigrants and those who have been here but cannot accustom themselves or are unhappy, I can only say to them that the secret is in trying to adapt, to see how many good thing we have here, to think positively and, above all, have patience, lots of patience, because patience will get you to heaven.

Yellow Leaves
María de Los Ríos

María de los Rios, born in Cuba and raised in Venezuela, is a creative writer, storyteller, and folklorist. Her writing, which explores the impact of Third World industrialization on women's lives, has been published in *Conmocion, Esto No Tiene Nombre, Across the Abyss, Pearls of the Past, and Revista Mujeres*. She lives in Tucson, Arizona where she is a member of the Latina writers group *Mujeres que Escriben*.

Okaloosa County, Florida, Feb. 14, 1995

Here I am on four limbs over a carpet of yellow leaves. My thoughts no longer linger in scattered confusion. My eyes watch the oncoming traffic, attentive through thick protective glasses. I have placed a concrete nail and washer in the right spot. The hammer in my right hand is ready to strike the head of the nail, force its body through layer upon layer of asphalt on that white band that marks the edge between the world and the earth. I look up. The sun makes my tired eyes twinkle. In the distance, the honk of a double wide truck brings me to my feet. I ebb to the shoulder of the road for refuge. Then I go back to perform my task. That is what a regular day is all about—getting on my knees and jumping up. If I think of the speed of those trucks passing by, I know that my plastic yellow helmet and my thin orange jacket that waves like a flag in the wind are not going to save me. If I think of the facts that I have no insurance, that I have to work under the rain, through cold days, under inclement weather, to breathe the fumes of technology, listen to my runaway thoughts . . . that I am here in this foreign margin, terribly alone, disjointed from my own culture, my own people, my own values, I would quiver to hear the rumbling voice of the poet Pablo Neruda thunder my depths, asking me "Why do the leaves kill themselves as soon as they feel yellow?/¿Por que se suicidan las hojas cuando se sienten amarillas?"[*]

I recall the image of a lonely yellow leaf during the fall. In that vision, the ruthless cold wind blows over her vulnerable body. She clenches fiercely to a tree branch, not wanting to let go. I used to see my face on every single yellow leaf. A long time ago this image would shatter my soul into pieces. It doesn't matter anymore. *Mater amabilis. Ora pro nobis.*

Like the yellow leaf, I fight many battles, ultimately surrender that inner struggle, and fall with dignity aware of natural cycles. There is no end and no beginning. There is no separate reality, only a place where all parts, like pieces of a giant puzzle, eventually come to meet. For all I knew then and all I know now, there is an army of strong women working on the margins of these roads of progress to nowhere. The head of the nail reaches the paved surface. I stand on the earth and observe that wound that is the edge of the world. I pick up the measurement wheel, set it to zero, walk parallel to the world, spray a cross of red fluorescent paint on the white band every one hundred feet. Red splotches on this regular road are like pools of blood. I have learned to keep on walking, keep on moving.

I measure the depth of the site, from the red cross at the margins to the litter catch point, the mowline, the hedge, sometimes a fence. I force a metal rod on the grass, string the area, and survey the green rectangle. One beer can, one smashed plastic soda bottle, one baby diaper with contents, one snack, one cigarette pack, one tire piece, one plastic film canister, one cardboard fast food box, one polystyrene cup. My recorder listens attentively. I measure how much we have trespassed on the earth by literally counting trash. Litter is one terrible habit and the county has hired me to study it as a temporary worker. To drop things out the window shows how little we care about our home.

After the day is over, in the temple of my room, I close the door behind me, lay in my bed, stare at the ceiling crack and hear the voices of my land. The place my soul chose to return to this life, the sanctuary where my roots await. What is a tree without a strong and deep root system?

In this new land, I grow under planned controls. My hopes, dreams and aspirations are constantly trimmed like a small bonsai. I urge to grow like a huge, strong tree. I long to return. With time, I have learned of my strength. I roam the surface of the earth with the hunger of a lion.

But I am also content to be in this country. I no longer yearn for a piece of land, a piece of crumb, a piece of dream, a piece of pie. The world is an abstract and an absurd surreal painting. As in dreams, I wake everyday to a mural of injustices that await me outside my door. I grab the doorknob and walk through the opening, my thoughts like jackals. Like a cold, still life, this canvas that is the immigrant's experience, devoid of opportunities and overfed with boundaries and limits swallows my body in like a vampire. I move cautiously through its sharp edges, longing, yearning, burning to belong. The earth, on the contrary, embraces me and provides me with sustenance to endure my journey. Wherever my feet stand, I reclaim as my land because I know who I am. I belong to the land. If I give up what I believe, I fall on my knees terribly alone and empty handed.

My worker's boots step again over the brittle carpet of dry leaves. I imagine Neruda's vision at the sight of falling leaves, and I keep on walking, waiting for a new spring.

---

* "Why do the leaves kill themselves as soon as they feel yellow?/¿Por que se suicidan las hojas cuando se sienten amarillas?" from Pablo Neruda's *Late and Posthumous Poems: 1968–1974*, Edited and translated by Ben Belitt. Binlingual Edition. Fundación Pablo Neruda. New York: Grove Press, 1988.

The Passport Office
Melissa Aranzamendez

Melissa Aranzamendez was born in Manila, Philippines, and immigrated to the U.S. at the age of fourteen. Her work has appeared in *Contemporary Fiction by Filipinos in America*. She is currently writing a novel.

There were already several lines inside the passport office when Rosario took her place as she waited behind the information counter. There were nine people ahead of her. She surveyed the Filipinos who were both standing around or sitting on the bright orange plastic chairs, each clutching a stub which indicated the order at which everyone was to be serviced. Many glanced at their watches; some kept their gaze at the red digital display on the wall, hoping that it would finally exhibit the number on their stub. Rosario noticed a heavily made-up woman in a trench coat who was making small talk and handing out leaflets, which at first Rosario thought contained political propaganda literature, but turned out to be advertising fliers for a courier business. Someone should ask the lady to leave, Rosario thought, since the woman was taking up precious seats, and the people left standing were confusing those who were on line for the information window.

Everyone seemed to be flying back home for the holidays. As soon as the climate turned cold, Filipino Americans always felt compelled to take a trip back home, and the passport office would be packed with homesick *balikbayans*[1] anxious for *misa de gallo*[2] and some *noche buena*.[3] Rosario counted herself amongst the Filipino immigrants who spent considerable sums of money on immigration lawyers and endless hours on line at the American embassy in Manila, but who could not wait to hop on the next flight back once their visa was granted and they've settled in the States. The only difference was that it took Rosario a good six years to save up for her round-trip airfare. She looked forward to the authentic *kare-kare*[4] and the *pancit malabon*[5] that would be waiting for her during Christmas dinner in Blumentritt. Neither the Filipino eateries in town nor her own attempts to replicate the dishes satisfied her, and Christmas in New York was not as festive, although she did her best to keep up with the Filipino holiday traditions that she observed as a little girl. Inside her apartment window, a twenty-four-inch red star made of slender sticks and shiny red cellophane hung five floors above 32nd Avenue in Queens. She had insisted on a *parol* to hang; and her American boyfriend searched every Filipino American store in the tri-state area, to no avail. She ended up making it herself, with her boyfriend helping to wire the object so that it would light up, although its makeshift appearance and its scarlet glare only led unknowing passersby to assume immoral activities inside.

Finally, Rosario was next in line at the counter. Although quite annoyed that it took almost half an hour, she was glad that she took her mother's advice and put in a full vacation day for this task. Apparently, the same person who was servicing the information desk was also the cashier, and he had to switch counters every now and then, and of course his main priority was getting money. During her wait the crowd seemed to get noisier and noisier, and Rosario heard the English language mixed with every imaginable Filipino dialect. One Ilocano couple spoke of the current political situation, and another described how hot it was during their last trip back. Two teenage sisters, who spoke English perfectly, kept complaining of the wait but entertained themselves by telling funny jokes about how inefficient the process was and how amusing Filipinos in general were. Most of those present were quite visibly irked by the long wait and silently shook their heads in disapproval. Everyone seemed curious as to which part of the Philippines another person was from. Then they'd ask each other where in the area they resided, and exchange information on which Fil-Am Stores stocked the hard-to-get items.

Then a young woman carrying a manila envelope and accompanied by a Caucasian man walked directly to the information window, bypassing everyone in line, including Rosario. The crowd stared at the round, olive-skinned face framed by a lion's mane of blond highlights. Beneath the blue contact lenses, the woman's eyes stared accusingly at the man behind the counter as she threw the envelope under the window.

"I had to miss half a day of work to get this, so you better give me my passport now," the blond woman demanded. The clerk took a look at the envelope's contents, which included the woman's income tax returns for the past five years, an old, expired Filipino passport, and her passport application, completed the day before. The old passport showed a picture of a scrawny ten-year-old child, one front tooth missing, yet all smiles. Rosario, who was a step away from the window, glanced at the documents on the counter and found nothing in common between the black-and-white photo in the old passport and the contemptuous face confronting the clerk.

"The name on your application is different from the name on your old passport. Is your first name Ellen or Elena?" the clerk inquired, his pen poised for correction.

"On my social security card, it's Elena. Listen, how much longer is this going to take?" the blond woman asked, while her friend wandered toward the bulletin board and read about the latest calamities in the Philippines. The clerk quickly took some white-out and corrected the handwritten name on the passport application.

"Would you take a seat, please?" the clerk asked, although it was more an instruction than a request. He then took his place at a nearby desk, filled out additional notes and data on the applications, and added up some figures on a calculator. The blond woman rolled her eyes, shook her head and stood where she was. She waited by the window and motioned for her friend to come and keep her company.

"As soon as we return from Aruba, I'm calling my lawyer and I'm applying for citizenship. This is such crap!" Rosario heard the woman say.

Rosario had met Filipino Americans who had seemed ill at ease with other Filipinos, but nobody she had met compared with the blond woman standing nearby. Sure, she had encountered Filipinos who always insisted on speaking

English to her (even though she made it known that she spoke her native tongue fluently), always confusing the p's with their f's and their v's with their b's revealing their heavy Tagalog accents. There were those who claimed never to eat rice, or stayed out of the sun's rays to appear lighter-skinned, or had their noses surgically narrowed, or their eyes deeper-set. Rosario attributed those western inclinations to the three-and-a-half centuries of colonial subjugation. But by her appearance alone, the blond woman renounced everything Filipino, and her deprecating attitude confirmed her embarrassment.

The clerk returned to the window with a smirk. "Excuse me, miss?" I think you made a mistake on your application." He pointed to the entry for eye color, which the blond woman had printed "BLUE." "I believe in your old passport, they're dark brown. We don't consider contact lenses, ma'am."

Fuming, the blond woman replied, "Just get me my passport."

The clerk used the desk calculator again and asked the blond woman to come to the cashier's window. "Ma'am? We'll need you to make out a check for $1,496."

The blond woman's grayish-blue eyes popped open. "What the hell are you talking about?"

"As a citizen of the Philippines, you are required to report your income and to pay taxes to the Filipino government. The sum I have added up is the equivalent of the money you owe the Filipino government while you have been taking residence here in the United States. I'm sorry I can't issue you a passport until the amount is paid."

The blond woman made a spectacle of herself, screaming and banging her fist against the window. "Why are you doing this to me? I don't even remember that God-forsaken country, and now you're telling me that I can't have my vacation because I owe you a thousand bucks? For what? So that some chinky-eyed ex-beauty queen can take office and spend my money on shoes? That country is a joke, and you people subservient martyrs who don't even share a common language! Has that country ever done anything for me?

Absolutely not! And now you want to rob me of my holiday? If anything happens so that I miss my vacation, I'm suing you and the entire Philippine government! And I'm never paying you a cent! I haven't been there for over ten years and I have no intention of returning! I'm not leaving without a passport!"

Then she burst into tears. Her friend tried to calm her down while the clerk called the supervisor. She glimpsed at the crowd that was now anxiously waiting for the supervisor's arrival, obviously entertained by the aberration in front of them. Somehow, Rosario knew that the blond woman would not be able to make the trip to Aruba, and Rosario felt a twinge of guilt in gaining satisfaction from someone else's aggravation. She looked around and saw anger and disdain expressed in the brown faces of the people about her. The women whispered amongst themselves. Some older Filipino man kept eyeing the blond woman lasciviously. Although they tried to be discreet, the two teenagers snickered. The clerk motioned for Rosario to step up to the window, but went to gossip with another clerk before actually assisting her.

The blond woman was eventually told that the supervisor was out to lunch, and that she would have to wait until 2:00 p.m. if she wanted to speak to her. Exasperated, the crying blond woman bolted out of the passport office with her man.

After having waited on line for the copy machine, the photographer, the income tax calculation, and the cashier, Rosario finally received her passport. She did not, however, head home. Instead, she hurried out to Newark and went on another line—at the Immigration and Naturalization building for an application for American citizenship.

[1] an immigrant who returns to his/her native town or country.
[2] midnight mass which is celebrated on Christmas eve.
[3] The Filipino dinner which traditionally follows misa de gallo.
[4] a Filipino stew made with peanut sauce, oxtail, and green vegetables.
[5] a Filipino dish made of thick noodles and seafood gravy, originating from the town of Malabon.

Chapter 4
First Generation
Language, Identity, Achievement

The four great waves of immigration into the United States originated for the most part in different regions of the world—the first wave in Britain and Africa, the second in Ireland and Germany, the third in Southern and Eastern Europe and the fourth in Latin America and Asia. This results in the extraordinary diversity that characterizes the American population at the turn of the twenty-first century; with each passing year, the face of the country more nearly resembles the face of the entire world. While many exceptions exist, most Americans of European and African descent trace their ancestry in this country back many generations, while many people of Latin American and Asian descent are much closer to the experience of immigration.

One of the questions that confronts a student of today's immigration is whether new immigrants in the United States are simply beginning the same trajectory that other immigrant groups followed. Will the first generation begin to merge into the mainstream economy and society, perhaps retaining an ethnic identity but participating at the center of American life on equal terms with other groups, or will it stay more separate?

The burden of this question rests heavily on the first generation. A child born in the United States is not Mexican, Korean, or Vietnamese, at least according to internationally recognized citizenship laws. He or she is an American citizen, by virtue of the Fourteenth Amendment to the United States Constitution, adopted in 1868. The amendment begins, "All persons born or naturalized in the United States, and subject to the jurisdiction thereof, are citizens of the United States." The amendment was adopted after the Civil War, in order to give citizenship to newly freed African Americans. While it has come under attack in recent years from people who believe that the American-born children of undocumented immigrants should not be citizens, there is little chance that it will be amended. Everyone born here is American.

They are also, however, Mexican, Korean or Vietnamese. They were born into families whose culture and language were formed in those countries, and their ethnicity is central to their identity. How the first generation works out these tensions—between the new country and the old, between the new culture and the old—is the central life theme of the first generation.

No single pattern predominates; the responses are legion. Some in the first generation adopt a stronger affinity for the home country than even their parents hold. In some Mexican immigrant households, the parents encourage the children to speak English, and sometimes even forbid them to use Spanish, in order to help them succeed in their new country. But the children may cling to Spanish, and may regard the use of English as a mark of betrayal. In other Mexican American households, the children of the first generation grow up speaking Spanish, yet because the language is not reinforced in the schools or in the wider culture they may not learn it well.

The first generation grows up in America. They are different from their parents and often feel a vast gulf between them. Both generations feel the gulf, framed by the issues of language and culture, and by the ease with which the children feel themselves drawn to a part of the powerful non-immigrant world in which they participate. It is a gulf often unanticipated by the immigrant parents. They came to America to find work and to offer more opportunities to their children, but rare is the parent who anticipated that his or her child would be drawn into a new, inaccessible culture and away from them. Sometimes the new culture is frightening. Often first generation children become the guides that their parents need, helping them navigate the unfamiliar shoals of the English language and the American bureaucracies. Sometimes the child, who has made the transition to the new country more easily, becomes the parent to the parent, with emotional costs to be born by both sides.

First generation Americans are pulled in both directions: both American and, let us say, Iranian—yet neither completely and easily American, nor completely Iranian. It is from that tension that the defining problems of the first generation arise—but also their creativity and insights, as the passages in this section show.

The Immigrant Story
Grace Paley

Grace Paley was born in New York City in 1922. She received the literary award for short story writing from the National Institute of Arts and Letters in 1970 and was elected to the American Academy and Institute of Arts and Letters in 1980. Her short story collections include *The Little Disturbances of Man* (1959), *Enormous Changes at the Last Minute* (1974), and *Later the Same Day* (1985). Her highly acclaimed, legendary fiction has been published in *The New Yorker, The Atlantic* and *Esquire*. With acerbic wit and clarity, "The Immigrant Story" sketches the emotional position of many first-generation Americans.

Jack asked me, Isn't it a terrible thing to grow up in the shadow of another person's sorrow?

I suppose so, I answered. As you know, I grew up in the summer sunlight of upward mobility. This leached out a lot of that dark ancestral grief.

He went on with *his* life. It's not your fault if that's the case. Your bad disposition is not your fault. Yet you're always angry. No way out but continuous rage of the nuthouse.

What if this sorrow is all due to history? I asked.

The cruel history of Europe, he said. In this way he showed ironic respect to one of my known themes.

The whole world ought to be opposed to Europe for its cruel history, Jack, and yet in favor of it because after about a thousand years it many have learned some sense.

Nonsense, he said objectively, a thousand years of outgoing persistent imperial cruelty tends to make enemies and if all you have to deal with these enemies is good sense, what then?

My dear, no one knows the power of good sense. It hasn't been built up or experimented with sufficiently.

I'm trying to tell you something, he said. Listen. One day I woke up and my father was asleep in the crib.

I wonder why, I said.

My mother made him sleep in the crib.

All the time?

That time anyway. That time I saw him.

I wonder why, I said.

Because she didn't want him to fuck her, he said.

No, I don't believe that. Who told you that?

I know it! He pointed his finger at me.

I don't believe it, I said. Unless she's had five babies all in a row or they have to get up at 6 a.m. or they both hate each other, most people like their husbands to do that.

Bullshit! She was trying to make him feel guilty. Where were his balls?

I will never respond to that question. Asked In a worried way again and again, it may become responsible for the destruction of the entire world. I gave it two minutes of silence.

He said, Misery misery misery. Grayness. I see it all very very gray. My mother approaches the crib. Shmul, she says, get up. Run down to the corner and get me half a pound of pot cheese. Then run over the drugstore and get a few ounces cod-liver oil. My father, scrunched like an old gray fetus, looks up and smiles smiles smiles at the bitch.

How do *you* know what was going on? I asked. You were five years old.

What do you think was going on?

I'll tell you. It's not so hard. Any dope who's had a normal life could tell you. Anyone whose head hasn't been fermenting with the compost of ten years of gluttonous analysis. Anyone could tell you.

Tell me what? he screamed.

The reason your father was sleeping in the crib was that you and your sister who usually slept in the crib had scarlet fever and needed decent beds and more room to sweat, come to a fever crisis, and either get well or die.

Who told you that? He lunged at me as though I was an enemy.

You fucking enemy, he said. You always see things in a rosy light. You have a rotten rosy temperament. You were like that in sixth grade. One day you brought three American flags to school.

That was true. I made an announcement to the sixth-grade assembly thirty years ago. I said: I thank God every day that I'm not in Europe. I thank God I'm American-born and live on East 172nd Street where there is a grocery store, a candy store, and a drugstore on one corner and on the same block a shul and two doctors' offices.

One Hundred and Seventy-second Street was a pile of shit, he said. Everyone was on relief except you. Thirty people had t.b. Citizens and noncitizens alike starving until the war. Thank God capitalism has a war it can pull out of the old feed bag every now and then or we'd all be dead. Ha ha.

I'm glad that you're not totally brainwashed by stocks, bonds, and cash. I'm glad to hear you still mention capitalism from time to time.

Because of poverty, brilliance, and the early appearance of lots of soft hair on face and crotch, my friend Jack was a noticeable Marxist and Freudian by the morning of his twelfth birthday.

In fact, his mind thickened with ideas. I continued to put out more flags. There were twenty-eight flags aflutter in different rooms and windows. I had one tattooed onto my arm. It has gotten dimmer but a lot wider because of middle age.

I am probably more radical than you are nowadays, I said.

Since I was not wiped out of my profession during the McCarthy inquisitions, I therefore did not have to go into business for myself and make a fortune. (Naturally many have remained wiped out to this day, gifted engineers and affectionate teachers . . . This makes me think often of courage and loyalty.)

I believe I see the world as clearly as you do, I said. Rosiness is not a worse windowpane than gloomy gray when viewing the world.

Yes yes yes yes yes yes yes, he said. Do you mind? Just listen:

My mother and father came from a small town in Poland. They had three sons. My father decided to go to America, to 1. stay out of the army, 2. stay out of jail, 3. save his children from everyday wars and ordinary pogroms. He was helped by the savings of parents, uncles, grandmothers and set off like hundreds of thousands of others in that year. In America, New York City, he lived a hard but hopeful life. Sometimes he walked on Delancey Street. Sometimes like a bachelor he went to the theater on Second Avenue. Mostly he put his money away for the day he could bring his wife and sons to this place. Meanwhile, in Poland famine struck. Not hunger which all Americans suffer six, seven times a day but Famine which tells the body to consume itself. First the fat, then the meat, the muscle, then the blood. Famine ate up the bodies of the little boys pretty quickly. My father met my mother at the boat. He looked at her face, her hands. There was no baby in her arms, no children dragging at her skirt. She was not wearing her hair in two long black braids. There was a kerchief over a dark wiry wig. She had shaved her head, like a backward Orthodox bride, though they had been serious advanced socialists like most of the youth of their town. He took her by the hand and brought her home. They never went anywhere alone, except to work or to the grocer's. They held each other's hand when they sat down at the table, even at breakfast. Sometimes he patted her hand, sometimes she patted his. He read the paper to her every night.

They are sitting at the edge of their chairs. He's leaning forward reading to her in that old bulb light. Sometimes she smiles just a little. Then he puts the paper down and takes both her hands in his as though they needed warmth. He continues to read. Just beyond the table and their heads, there is the darkness of the kitchen, the bedroom, the dining room, the shadowy darkness where as a child I ate my supper, did my homework and went to bed.

Funny-Sounding Names
Dan Georgakas

Widely published as a social historian and film critic, Dan Georgakas is a contributing editor to *The GreekAmerican,* a weekly newspaper, and the *Journal of the Hellenic Diaspora.* He is the coeditor of *Detroit: I Do Mind Dying* and *The Immigrant Left in the United States.*

We were Armento, Cammarata, Grillo, Spilko, Trajchevich, Szychmenski, Shammas, Aboud, Saed, Koukios, Georgakas, Peponis: the people with the funny-sounding names. We did not suffer the kind of ethnic discrimination our parents endured in the prewar years, nor the rabid hostility blacks endured, but we knew we were not regarded as favorably as the Kettners, Allens, and Sandersons with whom we went to school. Oddly enough, there were fewer snubs from our classmates than from their parents and other adults. These snubs were often quite subtle and we could only wonder if they were the tip of a still considerable hidden iceberg of animosity or the last flotsam of a large, melted intolerance.

At a friend's house, we might hear a parent explaining over the phone that her child was playing "with that Greek boy down the street." We might be warily queried on how we could be Christians if we were neither Protestant nor Catholic. Our foods came under stern scrutiny as well. Yogurt seemed a horrible thing to do to milk in those pre-health food days, oregano was a suspicious powder, olive oil something only greaseballs would cook with, and garlic's major civilized function was to ward off vampires.

The most unexpected place where we got the cold shoulder was in some of the classrooms of the public-school system. At that time, the Detroit schools were in the final stages of a system a century old. Most of our junior high and elementary school teachers were unwed, had only two years of higher education at a "normal" school and had limited experience of the world. They had been cloistered in a system which allowed them to teach the same subjects in the same neighborhood schools for decades. They regarded themselves as guardians of the American way. Their white heads, like yellow dandelions gone to wispy seed, were not responsive to the glows of the new entertainment called television and they were not attuned to a world beginning to move to a rock-and-roll beat.

Some of the old guard were wonderful teachers and quickly came to see our virtues, but a considerable number literally could not get past our names. That became evident the first day of a new semester when they read the class roll. Coming upon an unfamiliar constellation of letters, they would spit out a garbled version as if it were totally irrelevant whether their rendering was correct or not. Some would even announce that a particular name was too difficult for normal people to pronounce and as a consequence they were going to refer to the student by first name only. Such teachers never asked to hear the name spoken so they might try to mimic the correct inflections and they never apologized for their verbal butcheries.

I remember them well: Miss Field, Miss Weber, Miss King, Miss Burns. We dubbed them the Pig, the Owl, Hitler, and Pie Face. Mostly, there was an armed truce between us with our differences left unarticulated. On occasion, however, there were skirmishes. The most volatile situation for me involved Miss Cummings, the hated music teacher at Jackson Junior High. She had a shock of natural red hair that had sufficiently thinned for us to call her Old Baldie. She was not particularly old and I suspect she had once thought of having a stage career. Early in our first session with her, she said that she didn't expect much from people with funny-sounding names. Before sitting at the piano to play a light classical piece, she stated that she knew we would not appreciate or understand the music she was about to expose us to, but she expected we would have enough self-control to remain quiet. When she got around to teaching us songs, she often picked patriotic or religious tunes that she thought would be uplifting to our morals.

Cummings generated the teacher's nightmare: the smart kids leading a general revolt against authority. Under leadership of the long names, the class managed to sing slightly off key just as she was getting warmed up. We would have coughing spells. We would drop pencils from our desk at one-minute intervals. We asked incredibly stupid questions in the most polite manner and after her earnest response, we would rephrase the same question so that she would have to repeat herself. If she had pulled the window shade down so the sunlight would not disrupt her playing, we would pull them up. We opened windows so there would be a draft and a new round of coughing. We developed chronic bowel problems, causing us to ask to be excused to go to the bathroom. Whether or not the request was granted was irrelevant as long as she was annoyed, which she was.

Midway through the semester, our harassments caused her to lose her temper and lash out at Ted Lindsey, the class hood, who she mistakenly thought was the ringleader. Teddy, who always wore a leather jacket, was not a vicious person by Detroit standards, but he was tough enough for us. He carried a knife and told of occasional fights. We often did his homework for him to keep him out of trouble and earn his good will. Lindsey's approach to school was not to bother the teacher if the teacher didn't bother him. He thought our music-room revolt was juvenile. He did not participate but gave us his moral support.

One day, Cummings shouted that she wanted Lindsey to sing. When he did not comply, she called him a bum. He responded that she had no right to talk to him like that, but Cummings answered she would speak to him as she wished and would slap his face if he was insolent. Lindsey's honor was suddenly at stake. He rose and beckoned with his hands for her to come slap him. We were stunned, hoping she would not push the issue but wondering how he would react if she headed toward him. Doug Armento saved the day by faking a convulsive coughing attack. The boy behind him rose and slapped him on the back to resort normal breathing. Others of us began to cough and our friends got into the back-slapping mode immediately. John Ellers sneezed and asked for tissue to clean his nose. Cummings grabbed a small baton she sometimes used but dared not strike at any individual. The bell rang and we all surrounded Lindsey and escorted him from the room. On the way out, one of us managed to stick a wad of gum on her desk chair and another smeared gum on the lock to the room. Cummings complained to our homeroom teacher, but we all vouched for Lindsey's innocence and said the gum was surely the work of the class which succeeded us.

The following week Cummings was ready for us. I had managed to come in a full ten minutes late with a pass from the previous class excusing my tardiness. Following up the success of interrupting her lecture, I made a lot of noise lumbering to my seat, complained loudly that I didn't have a music book and made a general nuisance of myself. When we started to sing, I hit a false note hard. This was easy for me as I didn't have much musical ability to begin with. She shouted at me, and I complained that the room was too cold. I got up to close a window and managed to knock my book to the floor. She must have been having a bad day for she spun on her stool and shouted, "I have had enough of your nonsense, you young man with the impossible name." She grabbed her baton and lurched in my direction. I thought she was going to give me the slap or poke she had intended for Lindsey. I ducked and shoved my mobile desk forward to block her. Her skirt caught in the legs of the desk and as she tumbled to the floor, the class cheered and whistled. I jumped to my feet and ran down to the counselor's office.

I realize now that Cummings' xenophobia must have been an embarrassment to the administration. If I had complained to my parents about the ethnic insults, she would have been in trouble. But we had not been trained in those kinds of responses and even if we had known about them, our parents would have been too respectful of teachers as a group to press the issue effectively. The counselor, knowing I was one of the top students in the school, took an easy way out by asking if I would like to have a library class instead of music. I thought this was a great idea. I could finish my homework during the extra free time and then read Sherlock Holmes stories when I was done. The tumult in the music room continued in my absence. Armento and Ellers were soon assigned to library as well.

Cummings had at least been honest about her feelings. More often, we were not aware that people with funny-sounding names were being bypassed for one or another consideration. We rarely got the major roles in the senior play or nominations for the scholarships to the better colleges. Much of what we missed did not actually slow our momentum; it was just that each step forward was primarily due to our own analysis and effort. Some of the missed frills might have been wasted on us anyway as our parents had huge lists of prohibited activities, especially for women. The values of the all-American high school often clashed with the values and attitudes we found at home.

At Wayne State University, I encountered the funny-name syndrome in its velvet-glove aspect. I was forced to take a class in recreational leadership as part of my teacher training. One day, a coach called me out to lead a game. He asked my name and as I stepped forward, I gagged from nervousness and my voice was just a whisper. The coach put his arm around me and ever so kindly, ever so condescendingly advised me, "You shouldn't be ashamed of your name." I was offended. Never in my life had I been ashamed of my background, and I thought it contemptible that he should assume otherwise.

But the name pressure never ceased. Everyone understood that even in the most liberal environments, a difficult name made for awkward introductions and raised ethnic issues that might interfere with a smooth business transaction or professional interchange. Many of us Greeks Americanized to names like Karras, Syros, and Kappas and a few achieved Anglo-apotheosis by transforming Liakonis to Lincoln and Androcopoulos to Andrews. My mother had tendencies in that direction. When giving our name for a laundry ticket she often identified herself as Georgans or Jorgas and she occasionally mentioned that some of our relatives had cut their last name to George. One time when she was on the phone, a merchant thought she had said Jackson rather than Georgakas. She liked that and wondered if it might not help my teaching ambitions to have the name of an American president.

My grandfather, a maverick to the core, thought American names were ugly and let the matter rest there. I quickly learned never to be offended by a mispronunciation as long as the effort was sincere. I just pronounced correctly and told people that it was easier to name me correctly if they did not look at the spelling. I was not a genuine purist either, for my father had allowed American to transform the soft Greek *g* into a hard Anglo *g*. I would explain that, too, if the occasion was appropriate and restoring the soft g was the only change I seriously contemplated. Given my own direction in life, I decided that having a distinctive name could be an advantage. Among learned people I would say that Georgakas was a name like Dostoyevsky. Once you heard it, you were not likely to forget it.

Queen of the West Indies
Mary McLaughlin Slechta

Mary McLaughlin Slechta is a poet and fiction writer whose father emigrated from Jamaica. She is the author of *Wreckage on a Watery Moon* and *Buried Bones*. Her other writing has appeared in *Forkroads: A Journal of Ethnic-American Literature, Many Mountains Moving,* and *IKON*. Also a teacher of English as a foreign language to children, she lives in New York with her husband and sons.

She had good hair, she had fair skin and she was only moments away from being crowned Miss West Indies of 1968. The moment had finally come—and she was on stage. She refused to even consider the number of tickets her father had had to buy for the pageant. It was an unspoken asset to any beauty queen, an asset with mutual beneficiaries: The West Indian Social Club needed contributors to the busing fund and its daughters needed a stage to display their beauty. There was, of course, the spring cotillion, but the queen of this contest had the singular honor of leading the Independence Day parade down Main Street, Hartford.

In preceding summers Olive Campbell had watched the parade go by from an uncomfortable seat on the reviewing stand. She suffered the sweltering Connecticut humidity like a soldier in full battle gear. Neither a hair-sprayed strand dared spring out of place nor a drop of sweat penetrate her well-powdered face. Only her hollow stomach complained.

She expected no comfort from the furious face of mother to the right, swatting flies and cursing the lateness of "colored people's time," or from the flushed face of father to the left, waving weakly like a deposed king.

Instead Olive steeled herself with memories of the one triumphant year she'd ridden the parade route beside her father. How different he'd appeared then: light skin glowing with excitement, grey eyes darting across the crowd sometimes ten-deep along the streets, straight black hair shiny and parted to the side like a Cuban. It was the West Indian Independence Day parade, with many islands and

American blacks represented, but everyone knew the Jamaicans, originators like her father, were the big shots in the Cadillac and Lincoln convertibles.

"Thump! Thump! Thump-thump!"—the drums of the Bellevue Square Marching Patrol, the highlight of the parade for the city people, rolled and tumbled inside her chest. Girls and boys exploded onto the street, shaking and hooting their approval. Olive felt her father slow down to put more distance between their borrowed black Lincoln and the marchers, now swallowed up inside the ecstatic crowd. "Wave, Olive," he reminded her as the calypso music behind them could once more be heard. She lifted her tiny gloved hand above the windshield and saw the mothers and fathers pointing her out to their children. Boosted on pillows, she was keenly aware of brown pipecurls ringing her face and layer upon layer of white lace nestling her prettily oiled arms and legs.

The pungent smells of barbecue and rotis began to fill the air as they approached the end of the hour-long route. Suddenly hungry, Olive was disappointed to see the "Closed" sign on Mr. Vernon's variety shop. She often accompanied her father to the cramped little shop where Mr. Vernon, in his bulging tropical shirt, would pull a smuggled can of ackee from beneath the counter. Each week elicited a new story on how the price had fluctuated and why the U.S. customs— "never them Canadian customs boys, mind you"—had banned the Jamaican fruit: "One fool-fool person drop dead from eatin' unripe ackee and the whole world gon suffer so." Grinning at Olive, Mr. Vernon silently indicated the candy shelf with his pooched out lips, and on cue she'd remind her father to buy a treat. "How about a nice pear," Mr. Campbell teased, holding up a giant-sized avocado. As proud as she was of her father, however, nothing about the Jamaican foods and smells appealed to her. Ginger beer burned her throat and coconut drops scratched it. The poisonous ackee was entirely out of the question. She wanted only candy bars and chips and Archie comic books.

As Olive and her father approached the reviewing stand, some fifty very well-dressed ladies and gentlemen of the club and their prodded children rose in applause. Officiating over the festivities in a dignified black suit. Mr. Vernon fiercely pumped the hand of a balding white man. "The Mayor of Hartford himself," her father whispered. "Wave, Olive. Wave!"

For a wonderful while it seemed the entire reviewing stand and the street crowd had eyes only for Olive and her father. Then, hearing a shout from behind, Olive tilted her head around and remembered the queen and her court whom they'd been escorting all the while. From atop a mountainous float of red and white carnations, the young people swung to the rolling calypso rhythm and waved to the crowd.

"How's the little girl?" a gentle female voice asked. Olive opened her eyes to the most lovely woman she'd ever seen. Later when the Queen of the West Indies slipped her gloved hand inside Olive's and they posed for pictures in front of the Lincoln, Olive imagined herself a real princess.

In subsequent summers, other little girls and their fathers escorted the queen's float. Olive and her father were relegated to the reviewing stand with her mother and the flies. As her sixteenth birthday approached, however, Olive began to strategize her ascension to the throne.

The first project was the lightening and smoothing of her elbows and knees. Following Granny's advice, she scrubbed her skin with lemon slices and, to hasten the process, applied brightening cream lifted from a cousin's drawer. At bedtime, she oiled her scalp with pink *Wonder Hair Grower* from Mr. Vernon's store and brushed one hundred strokes. She slept in a silk hairnet and cotton gloves, and refused any cleaning chore, including dishes, that might potentially roughen her hands. When her mother protested, as she regularly did, it was easy enough to produce an awful red rash for her father.

Despite Olive's rigorous efforts, however, disappointment followed disappointment. The first year, she'd lost because her father, insisting she was the most beautiful girl in the *world*, refused to play by the rules: he'd bought only two tickets! The second year, he'd purchased more tickets than he had friends, but still had been outspent: the parents of *that* year's queen sold high-priced real estate in Bloomfield and Windsor. This year promised to be different. Despite every objection her mother raised, nothing seemed to obstruct Olive's path to victory. Her father secretly agreed to purchase double the number of tickets, and, based on his increased hours at the factory, Olive was confident he could.

On the morning of her third pageant, Olive stayed in bed until the last possible moment. She listened to her parents rising noisily in the next room. Her mother still sounded angry about the gown.

The entire week before the pageant, Olive had worried over the length of her powder blue chiffon gown and placement of some decorative flowers. Finally on the night before the pageant, she'd taken scissors and managed to botch up the hemline. Her mother, finding her weeping over the mangled dress, threatened to "call off the whole damn business."

Her mother's threats frightened her into bed where she huddled under a pink blanket, too afraid to move. When the door creaked open again, she peeked through the weave and watched her mother silently come in and take away the dress. An hour later her mother returned the dress just as quietly. It had been neatly repaired and ironed.

But this morning, through the wall, her mother still sounded angry. "No more," she shouted to Olive's father, and then some whispered complaints which Olive could recite from memory.

The complaints only began with "Olive's lazy ways" and "the waste of time and money on foolish vanity." Somewhere in the middle they crossed the unfairness of the Ladies Auxiliary: "One hundred percent fool's labor for fifty-percent membership—that's what we women get!" But the complaining wasn't through until Jamaica itself was unrolled like a map on the kitchen table. Every West Indian success was tossed back at her father as scraping and bowing to the white man.

"I was born in this country," her mother fired back at any objection, "and we still don't have freedom to this day."

Her mother's sympathy for the militants who were inciting civil disobedience and riots caused a bitter consternation among the West Indian businessmen and their wives of the Ladies Auxiliary. Born in the rural South, Mrs. Campbell could not contain her opinions when "Burn Baby Burn" became a reality in many cities during the summer. Fortunately for Olive and her father, who knew better, sober minds among the Club membership attributed Mrs. Campbell's outbursts to the devilish powers of over-proof rum, especially on a woman.

"Fool-fool," her father muttered quietly about her mother's attitude. "Law-abiding idiots," her mother muttered less quietly. "Thank God, you favor your father," Granny wrote from Jamaica. "Don't listen to those ignorant people," her mother countered after visits from her father's side: "All stuck on color and hair." Olive didn't like thinking about who was right and who was wrong. She didn't want it to have anything to do with her.

But now Olive was up on the stage. Her proud moment had finally come and she reminded herself to smile because the runners-up were about to be called. She and the remaining girls hugged closer together to fill in the gaps made as one by one they were led offstage with a bouquet. The choice finally came down to herself or Dolly MacFarlane, a dark-skinned girl in a flaming red dress. Olive had never considered Dolly a serious competitor. Dolly kept her hair cut short in one of the new Afro styles. Like somebody right off the boat, she clattered and clanked in gold loop earrings and an armful of variously shaped bangles. Olive wore only modest pearl posts and a pair of delicate silver bangles against her light wrist. A little pomade highlighted the dozen golden strands among her brownish, corn-silk hair.

She felt a sudden urge to run a hand through her hair, but her mother's disapproval of public displays seemed to leer at her from the audience below. So instead she put both arms around Dolly's waist and pulled the two of them as close together as possible. She ran her tongue across her teeth and smiled more prettily then ever. Dolly stood solid as a cow, alternately chewing on her lower lip. Night and day, Olive has been dreaming of this honor for a long time; she knew she was finer than all the other girls. Now they would have to look up to her.

The emcee, a well-known personality up from Brooklyn, strutted to center stage, waving his arms and making quick little turns that sent the tails of his tuxedo twirling. He told some silly joke about Joe and his thirsty donkey; he rhapsodized on the beauty of island women; and finally he relented to the cries of the hecklers at the far end of the room who demanded he finish up the whole business and let them move on to the drinking and dancing to follow.

"A drum roll, please," he said. No one laughed. Olive silently prayed he might yet topple from the stage. He pretended to open an envelope, took a deep breath, smiled and announced, "The first runner-up is . . . Miss Olive Campbell. The winner and next Queen of the West Indies is the beautiful Miss Dolly MacFarlane!

Olive's thin, pale knees shivered under her powder blue gown. She still hung onto Dolly's waist, but found herself being embraced now in return.

Dolly's fleshy wet cheek burned against her own, seemed to collapse against her own like chocolate left too long in the heat. In a moment somebody broke them apart and hustled Olive offstage with flowers. She turned in the wings to watch Jackie McKinley, the previous year's queen, set the crown on Dolly's head. The sparkling rhinestones winked from the top of the pitch black Afro, and Dolly grinned. She waved one gloved hand, high and slow.

The standing latecomers and hecklers at the back were already pressing out of the cramped room into the bar and lobby. Quicker than people could rise from their sticky seats, boys were folding chairs in order to make room for the dancing. One of the organizers came by the dressing room and barked at the girls to hurry it along so the band could set up. There was a frantic search for clothes and shoes, and a number of quarrels broke out over missing items. A makeup mirror shattered on the floor. Olive, having already shoved the flowers into the waste can, grabbed up her belongings without bothering to change. She went straight off to the kitchen to share her outrage with her mother.

Mrs. Campbell threw her hands in the air when she looked up over a pot of curried goat and saw her daughter storm through the door.

"I'm up half the night slaving on this dress," she shouted, "and Miss Fancy Pants here wears it to the kitchen!"

At that moment Olive could detect not one shred of rancor between her mother and rest of the Ladies Auxiliary. The other women, faces wet from sweat and steam, glared at her from their pots and platters.

"Well, Missy," her mother continued, "come put those fine hands to work."

Olive was made to change in the pantry. She'd barely put a toe out before one of her mother's friends had tied an apron around her waist while another handed her a stack of plates. When she stepped back into the outer room, the dizzying calypso and swinging couples made her wonder if the pageant had really happened.

"Over here, Olive-gal!" her father shouted.

She froze. At one of the round tables that now ringed a dance floor, her father reclined in front of rum, Coke and glasses. Dolly, still dressed in her red flounces, bows, and crown, sat grinning beside him. Mr. Campbell's right arm hung casually around Dolly's neck. When he took a sip from the glass in his right hand, their two heads met, his balding and grey, hers managing to keep the captured crown steady. And Dolly grinned. She grinned so hard that Olive could see her white, chapped lips pulled back against her black gums. A man slapped her father on the back, nearly upsetting his drink. "A real black gal gon represent us now, man," he shouted above the steel drums.

Chuck Pehlivanian
David Kherdian

Armenian-American poet, novelist and essayist David Kherdian has produced many poetry collections, including *Letters to my Father* (2005), *Beat Voices* (1995), plus a memoir, *I Called it Home* (1997). His awards include a Newbery Honor Book, The Jane Addams Peace Award, the Friends of the American Writers Award, and a nomination for The American Book Award.

We had certain lunacies in common,
but the one I remember best was the
idea of digging our own fish pond
in your family's backyard. We went
so far as to consult Old Man Cook,
who ran the bait shack by the pier.

He wasn't the first one to laugh at us,
but he was the only one who took the
trouble to explain why it wouldn't work:
no running water meant no oxygen, and
even if the fish survived they'd soon
be swimming in their own shit.

Never mind. We decided to build a boat
instead. At this point our mothers
brought our fathers into the act.
Your dad had a car—very unusual—
and together they took us fishing.
We supplied the gear and enthusiasm,
they got to supply everything else.

None of us knew where to go or what
to do once we got there. I think they
figured we couldn't all fish out of
one boat without at least three of us
drowning. And so, not finding a place
to fish at Brown's Lake, we worked our
way back towards town, finally settling
for a tiny pond at Johnson's Park.

There was this big concern over the minnows
that kept splashing onto the floor in back.
First one of our dads, and then the other
would turn around and say, "Watch it out
the minnets," or "Be careful, don't spill
it, the winnets." Neither one of them
could speak English worth a damn.

They dropped us off and went searching
for grape leaves, figuring we'd only
get wet, and maybe decide to quit.
The pond wasn't deep enough to drown
a good sized fish. We made a game of
throwing first the winnets and then the
minnets into the pond, imitating their
accents, and then cracking up and falling
to the ground.

We didn't catch a single fish, and they
didn't do much better with grape leaves.
We were wet and miserable driving home,
and they were sad and disgusted—but also
relieved to have it done. We drove back
in silence, staring out our private windows,
filling the landscape with our different
dreams and losses.

Your father broke the silence with a sigh,
saying, simply, "Where we are, where we are,"
meaning, not this ordinary day with its
ordinary losses, but the time of his life,
that had taken him all the way here,
America, from all the way there, Armenia,
the bewildering and inexplicable passage
of our mysterious life on earth.

From *Letters to My Father*
David Kherdian

It must have been 1950. Racine, Wisconsin. Was
I nineteen. Was my father sixty, or sixty one—
the age I am now.
It must have been my first car, a Plymouth.
My father never drove, nor my mother.
Only one Armenian family,
as I remember, owned a car back then.

It is evening and I am driving him
to the Veteran's Building for some event
or meeting that he is attending.
We are downtown before I realize that
he is uncertain of the address.
He is used to walking everywhere,
and has become disoriented in my car
(but I don't realize any of this
at the time). I am being impatient
with him. I don't like being his chauffeur,
I want to get on with *my* life, not
be a helpmate in his.

Pull over, he says, reading my thoughts.
Which I do, feeling a little
uneasy, my conscience fighting
with my impatience. But I
pull over. He gets out
and quickly begins his hurried walk—
the walk I will always know
him by, and that I will always remember
when I think of him and think of myself.

He gets out in front of Woolworth's.
It is dark out, but the street lights
are not on, and I am there, alone

in the semi-darkness,
unable to move, my car stationed at the curb.

And I am there still, watching,
staring at his back as he moves away,
knowing the Veteran's building
is just three blocks away.
I would call if he could hear me
but he is on his own and alone
as I am
with whatever this is that I am.

Our Life With the Windsors, 1953–1990
Valerie Miner

Valerie Miner is an artist-in-residence and professor at Stanford University. She is an award-winning author of twelve books, the most recent of which are *After Eden, Range of Light, and The Low Road: A Scottish Family Memoir*. Her mother immigrated to the U.S. from Scotland at the age of 20 in 1930.

I always thought Mother looked like Queen Elizabeth. The Second. Attractive, although not pretty in that clean-scrubbed, long-nosed way. Both were small figures with swept-back hair. Open-faced, no-nonsense. The kind of woman who enjoyed giving directions, but would say straight out if she didn't know where you were going. My best friend from the fifth grade, Carol, told me this summer thirty-seven years after the fact that she used to think my family was rich because my mother made such large ham sandwiches for lunch.

I liked to think Queen Elizabeth was also generous with her subjects. As I grew older, I came to see it was the other way around. They stocked *her* larder. And in recent years I've been disappointed by the Queen's petulance about paying taxes. Time for the twentieth century to catch up with her, after all. There have been other disappointments: the Corgis, truly ugly dogs; those boring horses and horse-faced children; and some of the hats, after all. Still, over the years, I've felt a twisted filial pride in Elizabeth's dignified but pleasant dresses (both she and my mother look good in blue); her low-key, powdered-nose presence at state events; and the unflustered way she responded to the intruder she found sitting by her bed in Buckingham Palace (I would have screamed). So fond have I become of her in this strange projection that I'm always horrified when she opens her mouth and seems to be talking in that pinched, upper-class English accent.

Our connection is first revealed to me at age six in late May, 1953, a week before the Coronation of ER II. A package arrives in our New Jersey home from Aunt Bella, a Canadian cutout book with cardboard models of Princess Elizabeth and the Duke of Edinburgh as well as beautifully colored facsimiles of the royal carriages. I remember those best—body by Fisher—impressed that this was the same firm that constructed our neighbor's car. Mom regards the gift with shifting emotions—delight, disturbance, humor, as if Aunt Bella has sent pornography through the international mails. OK, she says finally, I can look through the book, but cannot cut out the figures until the actual Coronation day. This will be televised on our new Magnavox, which has recently shown us pictures of Edmund Hillary climbing Mount Everest and the American government testing nuclear bombs.

Anticipation thickens by day. Like Christmas, this Coronation reveals that our family is more than my brothers, my parents, Grandma and myself. As Mom and I bake cinnamon cookies for the big event, she reminisces about Scotland, that Protestant place she is from, where Aunt Bella is also from. This is the first time I hear about the new aunt who lives in Canada, where we might visit one day. Canada, Mom explains, is not as far away as Scotland. And it is in a different direction—a Northern place that's very cold.

I wonder if Aunt Bella is pretty. My mother isn't pretty and I'm just coming to terms with this. In fact, I am getting preoccupied by prettiness. Recently I decided that since God is fair, He would make me pretty as I grow older to compensate for my extreme ugliness at age six. I propose this logic to my mother who smiles and shakes her head. "But you're a very pretty little girl. And you'll be a stunner when you grow up." This isn't true: I am pudgy and freckled and my new front teeth are coming in at a 45 degree angle.

Perhaps I am obsessed by beauty because of the TV actresses now streaming into our house or the omnipresence of Virgin Mary statues—another lady who looks nice in blue—at Church and school. Perhaps it's those young nuns' pink faces, plucked forward by their wimples, the holy card visages of clear, piercing eyes and turned-up noses. Most likely it's the comparison I make between my thin, formal mater and the mother of my best friend Gerry Kliemisch. Mrs. Kliemisch is as pretty as the nuns, but also warmer, looser. She smells of vanilla or pickles or hot chocolate while my mother smells of cigarettes and Tide. She washes the dishes in Tide because it's silly to waste time on two kinds of detergent. Mrs. K.—who is always smiling in the kitchen with one of her seven children pulling at her skirt—seems the ideal, pretty mother and for an entire week, every night, I kneel down beside my bed and pray that God will give me a pretty, Catholic mother.

Suddenly one morning when I am home sick from school, perhaps overwrought by the frenzy of Coronation preparation, I realize that if God gives me a pretty mother, I will lose Mom, whom I love, in spite of everything. I don't want another mother after all. Will God let me take back my prayers? I become obsessed that He won't. From everything I hear in school, He is a make-up-your-mind-kind-of-guy. What have I done? There are two people I can ask— Sister Margaret and Mom. But I'm too sick to ask Sister Margaret and this heavy burden won't wait until I get well. Anything could happen by then.

And so, although I know this could hurt my mother's feelings, I confess what may happen to me, to us. She is sitting on my bed, blowing on the Campbell's tomato soup to cool it down for me. Slowly, she explains, as she often does, that I shouldn't fret so much. God isn't going to trade her in for another mother. Everything will be fine. She offers me a spoonful of the bloody soup.

I am sobbing. "I'm sorry. I'm sorry." I swallow some soup and moan, not knowing whether my sin has been insult or betrayal, but understanding my sin has been against her, not against God.

"Don't fret," she says again. "I know you love me and you'd never do anything to hurt me."

I have recovered by Tuesday, 2 June, the Big Day. Mom has got me excused early from school for this historical event.

We've set the cookies and a large bottle of Pepsi on the living-room table, our stubby altar in front of the hallowed television tabernacle.

Grandma retires upstairs: as an Irishwoman who'll have no part of this sacrilegious tripe. Still, I don't know if her objections are religious or political—or for her whether this is an important distinction. Her room is right above the parlor and soon we hear the familiar, almost comforting sound of her manic rocking and muttering. Praying, Mom tries to persuade me Grandma is praying, but I know the difference.

Together Mom and I open Aunt Bella's book and leaf through every page before I pick up the scissors. Where should I start? The spectacular vestments? The bouffant silk dresses? The gleaming jewels? The fur-lined robes?

"It's not a happy life," Mom warns me as if I'm in danger of running off to marry a prince.

I watch her carefully because I have come to know that if my mother isn't a pretty mother, she is a very smart one.

"There are so many duties."

Again, the ornate carriages catch my attention and I wonder what progress the automobile represents. Who would choose one of those smelly, dirty, oversized bowling balls when you could ride in an airy, gilded vehicle pulled by sensuous grey horses?

"Our milk was delivered by horsedrawn carriage when I was a little girl," my mother muses.

I laugh, thinking of Mr. Munson's white dairy truck turned into a cart.

Mom is taken aback, then notes it's almost time for the ceremony to begin. Not wanting to miss a moment, we watch five minutes of test pattern before an image of Westminster Abbey appears.

"That's where Mary Queen of Scots is buried," my mother murmurs.

Because I can't tell if she's talking to me or herself, because I know nothing about this particular saint, I peer at the screen, waiting for Princess Elizabeth in the newsreel footage.

Her size is disappointing. I have hoped for something more magical—or majestic—or miraculous in front of our altar of home-baked treats. Maybe I expected her to pop out of the television. I am painfully conscious of the royals as miniatures in the rectangular box.

The first shots, of course, are background. Even a six-year-old knows this isn't the main event. We watch Princess Elizabeth in her diamond wedding tiara with the dark sash across her strapless formal. The tall, handsome Duke of Edinburgh hovers nearby. Then shots of the princesses together—the reserved, alert Elizabeth and the sultry-eyed Margaret—with their sweet-faced pigeonbodied mother. Charles is my brother's age, but looks both younger and better dressed. Anne, with her golden curls and inquisitive eyes, reminds me of Rosemary, my favorite doll. Altogether, a family a six-year-old can identify with.

Aware of the strange silence (TV noise was becoming crucial to family conversations, as if we would talk only with a witness in the room), I notice my mother studying the screen like a difficult book. Usually she maintains detached curiosity about TV and the Catholic Church.

Suddenly the screen is transformed with the Coronation Day fanfare. All of London has turned out to catch a glimpse of royal metamorphosis. Half the world has joined them: heads of state from Europe, Africa, Asia. Mother points out Nehru and Menzies and Churchill.

My favorite is Queen Salote of Tonga, who rides smiling through the rain in an open-air carriage. At six foot three inches, she is the world's tallest queen. Her confident smile is cherubic in a triumphal, archangel way—as if all the traffic and cheering and cameras are for her.

Mom nudges me when the McKenzie Highlanders appear, thrumming and piping down the street in their funny kilts. "Ah, look, they're wearing our dress tartan. It's too bad you can't see the colors, such a lovely mix of blue and red."

I am puzzled. The plaid picnic blanket takes on new meaning.

"We're McKenzies. That's my maiden name. Those men

are Scots, see their kilts?" She is disappointed I haven't picked up nationality by osmosis, one more unmentioned or unmentionable thing that I'm supposed to have intuited. Yes, of course, I understand that a long time ago, my mother came from Scotland. She still talks so fondly of the Royal Mile and Princess Street. I nod enthusiastically, trying to warm to the sound of drums and whining pipes.

The announcer describes thousands of people lined along the Mall, Piccadilly, Trafalgar Square to see the world leaders and beautiful carriages. London is festooned with images of crowns and other salutes to the new monarch. I have already made up my mind one day to live in London.

Up the streets march other bands and with each one Mom recalls a different sibling. Uncle Alec in New Zealand, Colin in Australia, Johnny gone to India, but now back in Scotland. With the RCMP salute, Mom remember Bella in Victoria and Chrissie in Toronto.

"I thought Aunt Chrissie lived in Maine," I say.

"It's another Aunt Chrissie, dear, in Toronto. And I guess you have a third Aunt Chrissie if you count Danny's wife in Cleveland." She says this matter-of-factly, in a that's-the-end-of-that voice.

Recklessly, I persist. "How many brothers and sisters did you have?"

Her faces fixes on the screen. The royal coach is pulling up to Westminster Abbey.

"How many?"

"Oh, about twelve, " she says. "Don't ask so many questions. Watch this, you'll learn something."

It is now that I recognize the resemblance between my mother and the new Queen of England. Such parallels in coloring and features, but an even deeper connection in the strained dignity of expression, that serious, worried look, even when their faces are meant to be in repose. You couldn't call Elizabeth a pretty woman.

So like a wedding: The Abbey is crowded with expectant people. As Elizabeth walks up the aisle, ladies follow, each gripping her elaborate train, as if assisting a wounded, giant bird. The old Archbishop of Canterbury looks like a Catholic priest, but Mom explains this is a Protestant Church, that the Coronation occurs here because the monarch is the head of the Church of England.

Here I know something is wrong. Very wrong. I am in serious training for my First Communion and I fear that watching this ceremony is some kind of heretical complicity against the First Commandment, which prohibits attending services outside the One True Church. Is this why Grandma went upstairs?

Perhaps because I'm preoccupied with the state of my immortal soul—at best this is a near occasion of sin—I grow distracted from the long, elaborate ceremony in what sounds like a cold, hard foreign language. When the comely Duke of Edinburgh kneels down to pledge his faith and trust to Elizabeth, my romantic impulses are roused again. But this is too brief. And all that liturgical raising and lowering of crowns makes me nervous. People are droning on and on and on. Blessings, Vows, Boring commentary. My attention is drawn back to the cut-outs of Aunt Bella's handsome Windsor Grey horses, the little men in black-visored hats, the amazing crown of diamonds and rubies and other jewels frothing around a lush, purple pillow.

When I look up again, it's almost over. She is leaving Westminster Abbey, fancy ladies following her train in the opposite direction. Cameras pan over throngs of ordinary bystanders, people like my aunts and uncles who have returned from corners of the empire to witness the Coronation. The announcer tells us that the crown weighs four-and-a-half pounds, then, at the risk of being indelicate, compliments the young queen's neck muscles. Elizabeth is concentrating hard to do it all correctly and again I see my mother's worried expression. Looking from Mom to the Queen and back again, the family resemblance is all there. Elizabeth is carrying a scepter and orb just like the ones in my book. These, apparently, are also heavy and I think of my mother's admonition. "It's not a happy life."

I understand I am meant to aim for something between the lives of Elizabeth II, queen, and Mary Gill McKenzie

Miner, waitress, toward some happy medium.

This is when my life with the Windsors begins.

Many years later, we recall the Coronation while we are on a train or bus or auto trip. My mother and I often travel together: movement is in our blood. And we have our best talks in transit, as if leaving home frees us from our history and secrets and the damn resilient web of daily lies that holds our family together in my mother's imaginative optimism. Only when Mom and I leave home, it seems, do we enter the real world together. Perhaps while we're on the road, the material pressures of negotiating gasoline levels and road directions and room prices stimulate direct, honest talk. At any rate, it's on one of these trips that she suddenly says:

"You know. I left Scotland because of the King. People should be ruled by vote, by democracy."

"Really," I say, surprised because she has suddenly swerved from the topic of my brother's wife. Surprised, too, because it seems she had more pressing economic and emotional reasons to immigrate. "Doesn't Parliament run things?" I ask. "Isn't the monarch just a figurehead?"

"The Scots don't need an English figurehead."

What can I say to this? Still—perhaps because I've always harbored this long, semi-conscious affection for the Queen, I say, "Well, why did we watch the Coronation, then?"

She smiles, "You remember that."

"Oh, yes," I tell her. "The Pepsi, the cut-outs, the two of us visiting Westminster Abbey for the first time."

Her face softens as she thinks. One thing I enjoy about my mother is how often I find her thinking. This thoughtfulness lends itself to a certain old-fashioned sincerity.

Her voice is serious. "We watched because it was an historical event."

I laugh. Mom fed us historical events the way some mothers prepare fresh fruit and vegetables.

She smiles back. "Besides I've always loved a parade."

I see the procession of all my aunts and uncles. I think about the day I learned about the three Aunt Chrissies.

"Remember the Queen of Tonga?" She asks.

I nod, "Six feet, three inches."

She is laughing, that fine, merry, pretty mother laugh and I hope that Queen Elizabeth, despite her uneasy life, has moments like this.

A Secret Language
Chen Lin

Chen Lin emigrated with his family in 1977 from Taipei, Taiwan, when he was six. His stories have appeared in *Disorient Journalzine* and the *Asian Pacific American Journal*. He is a graduate of the University of Southern California's Professional Writing Program. While on the surface "A Secret Language" may seem lighthearted, the author is aware that there will be penalties if his secret is discovered.

It's after dinner and we're watching "Breakfast in Tokyo" on the International Channel. My father and older brother are relaxing in the living room; I'm in the kitchen washing dishes, but I can see the TV from here. Mother died years ago, and it's just us guys at home, so there's no question who inherited her chores: Me, the youngest.

Father translates bits and pieces of the TV show from Japanese to Taiwanese for Brother and me—Taiwanese because his English is limited. I remember how he and Mother used to speak Japanese whenever they needed to talk freely and didn't want us kids to know what they were discussing. It was their secret language, to protect their privacy. Ironically, during the Japanese Occupation, Taiwanese was the secret language. A punishable thing, it was used—in whispers—only when necessary. If caught, the transgressors would be beaten, their homes ransacked for evidence of cultural dissent such as old school books, Taoist scrolls.

A sleepy-faced woman is on TV making breakfast while her husband and children are still snoozing. She smiles and bows perfunctorily at the camera which keeps getting in her way. Her tired, pinched eyes show just a glimmer of annoyance which she cannot hide behind the acts of courtesy. I think the show's host and camera-men barged in on her without warning, but I'm not sure. Father doesn't say.

The phone rings. I rinse the suds from my hands and answer it. It's my friend.

"Hey, girl! We're going dancing tonight. Can you come?"

"Great! What time?" I say.

On TV a group of Japanese drag-queens gather around a table inside a cabaret. They pose in their seats while waiting to be served. "Hey! Drag-queens!" I talk about them loudly to my friend—such glorious ensembles and giddy, grand gestures! All the while I stare at the back of my brother's head, knowing he can hear me.

Though speaking excitedly, I'm careful about my words. Brother doesn't know yet, but I'm planning to tell him. The strategy is to feed him full of hints and suggestions until he bursts out asking. Or I'll just tell him when the time is right. Either way, he won't be able to say that he didn't have a clue.

Father can hear, but I doubt he understands. My slang-slick English to him is like Japanese to me.

Brother is shocked at how beautiful the drag-queens are, how convincing. He asks Father if they're performers at the cabaret or just customers.

"Yes, performers," Father says. "Women born as men."

Brother doesn't respond, just quietly receives the answer. Perhaps he's been piecing together the evidence, like my fascination with the drag-queens, and feels uncomfortable acknowledging Father's response. Oh, wishful thinking. I hang up, finish the dishes, and go to the living room to watch the show. Plenty of time to shower and dress before I go out.

We watch a bride-to-be who is too nervous to eat on the morning of her wedding day. She is stoically coy, though sadness pulls at the corners of her mouth. Father sucks his teeth and belches. "What kind of girl you marry?" he asks me.

Why is he asking me this? Did I let something slip, say something obvious? Did my voice rise beyond the masculine register?

Brother interrupts my moment of shock. "He'll probably bring home a black girl," he says.

I laugh, surprised by his answer. He's sensed that I will not fulfill their expectations, though the truth will prove more astonishing than their imagined possibilities.

Concerned, Father instructs. "Marry a good girl," he says. "Someone who cook, clean, take care of you."

In a grand gesture of defiance, I shake my head and declare, "I'll marry a princess."

Barely Audible
Nahid Rachlin

Nahid Rachlin, born in Iran, came to the U.S. at 17 to attend college. She married an American and stayed on. Her most recent books include *Persian Girls*, a memoir; *Veils*, a collection of short stories; *Jumping Over Fire, Foreigner, Married to a Stranger*, and *The Heart's Desire*, all novels. Her many awards for fiction include a National Endowment for the Arts grant, a Wallace Stegner Fellowship, and a PEN Syndicated Fiction Project award. In "Barely Audible," Pari is painfully aware of the differences that keep her from being "free" like other American women.

In this production company we dub various videos from English to Farsi and Arabic. My job now is office manager—doing the bookkeeping, answering the phone, typing, putting ads for our videos in Farsi newspapers and television and radio stations. Occasionally they let me translate a script from English to Farsi for dubbing. A glamorous sounding job but there's a lot wrong with it, mainly the poor pay and the bad office politics.

Aside from myself, there are two other employees in this office—Sheila Harrington, the director, and Latifeh Behbahani, who does a variety of tasks, selecting actors to do the dubbing, among many who come and audition for the parts, seeing that they get everything right, dealing with customers.

The office on the eleventh floor of an almost all-glass highrise building in Century City has a magnificent view of Los Angeles. Its decor, selected by Sheila Harrington, is bright and glossy—with shiny stars on the ceiling, the walls, sky blue, the furniture, a dizzying mixture of red, blue, purple, black. And colorful movie star posters are everywhere.

Sheila Harrington came in this morning, straight from her therapist, still lost in herself. She believes in self-knowledge, self-analysis like a religion. She sings, when she lies on her therapist's couch, tunes from her childhood. Sometimes the urgency of her memories does not allow her to sing and she weeps instead. She has had two marriages, one broken by death and the other by divorce. She is alienated

from her teenage children who are both in boarding schools.
She wonders if her first husband's suicide was her fault.
Was it an accident that he was driving his car so fast com-
ing home from work not long after he had caught her in an
embrace with a friend of theirs on the beach? She wonders
if she also could have prevented the death of her twin sister
who fell out of the window of the house in Del Mar.

Leaning back in her chair, she talked for a long time on
the phone. "Of course, my dear, I'd never do that. She's still
my friend." Talking to Peter, David? It does not matter to
her as long as they listen. I kept staring at her turquoise
Mexican rings, the kind of jewelry she wears a lot of, the
huge bright lips on her tee shirt, as if they were real lips
about to speak to me, her hand rubbing on her tight black
skirt, her shoes tapping the floor. She was smiling a little.
She often has that self-absorbed smile on her face. It makes
her seem unfeeling. I have been tempted to ask, "What are
you smiling about?" But I already know the answer. She is
thinking about a clever remark she is going to make to some-
one or is recalling a flattering sexual memory.

I needed her signature on a letter I had to mail off to
one of our clients, but I was really waiting for the right
moment to ask her for a raise that I feel has long been due
me. I got up and stood before her with the letter in my hand.
Finally she looked up at me. "What is it?" she asked, cover-
ing the mouthpiece with her hand.

"I need your signature."

After a cursory glance at the letter, she signed it and
resumed talking on the phone. A part of her skirt was pushed
aside, revealing her thighs. She is careless that way. She
has a youthful figure for a forty-five-year-old-woman—slen-
der legs, a narrow waist. She always dresses in bright col-
ors, makes up her face lightly and wears her blond hair long
and casual, not bothering to hide the gray coming in. She
finally hung up but then she jumped up and said, "I have to
run, I have a dentist's appointment."

She picked up her purse and dashed out of the office.

I am alone here now. Latifeh called in sick this morn-
ing. I go to Sheila Harrington's desk and try to work there,

since her corner has the best view. The desk is in a terrible mess, cluttered with transcripts, memos, and then, a box of condom—condoms on her desk in bright daylight! I pick up the box and hide it in her desk. My eyes catch a letter in her handwriting. I cannot help it—I begin to read it. It is to a boyfriend, an ex-boyfriend. She rambles on about how she had to break up with him because their relationship had come to a standstill. She always talks like that, claiming she has to do certain things. The letter is full of ambiguities and vague references. The phone rings. I jump, a little startled, I have been so absorbed.

"Pari." It is her. "I have a favor to ask. I forgot to take my folder with all the work I meant to do today. Do you think you could bring it to my house?"

"Sure." She often asks me to do errands for her. I enjoy them. They give me a chance to leave the office for a few hours.

It's mid-October and, after a terrible heat wave, the weather is mild, the sky is a mellow blue and masses of flowers are visible everywhere, a contrast to the grayness of my mood. I get into my car and drive toward Brentwood where she lives. Wilshire Boulevard is swarming with young people, mainly students, the girls with book bags slung over their shoulders, some bicycling, some on foot. Girls, younger versions of Sheila Harrington, with the same air of being on top of things, free spirits. I wish I had a little of that. Though I am seventeen years younger than Sheila Harrington, I feel older.

As I approach her house, in a cul-de-sac, which holds six other houses, I am full of a strange anticipation. Am I going to be able to have that talk with her about the raise? Is she going to brush me off somehow?

I ring the bell. Bougainvilleas with masses of purple flowers on them stream down the walls on both sides of the driveway. The water in the heart-shaped pool is shimmering under the sunlight and the tall flowers planted around it glow in vivid colors.

Her maid, a middle-aged Mexican woman, answers the door. "Yes."

"This is for Mrs. Harrington, is she home yet?"

"No."

I give her the folder, disappointed. The maid says goodbye sullenly and shuts the doors.

I sit by the window of my room in our modest apartment, one among many in rows of all-alike apartment buildings—the banal sameness extends to the whole neighborhood which is filled with Iranian families—and try to do some work I have brought home with me. But my thoughts are on Sheila Harrington, how hard she makes it for me to talk to her about the raise and how little understanding she has of hardship.

I deserve a better life than this, I think, bitterness rising in my throat. At the least I should have my own apartment and in a different neighborhood rather than living with my mother here. I want to be a part of this culture, not sheltered with other Iranians in our own alcove. After all I have been here since I was seven years old. What is it that holds me back, lack of confidence, lack of a firm voice? My room is much the same as it was when I was still in high school. There has been little alteration in the whole apartment, for that matter. I did not even go away to college. I lived at home and went to the two-year community college nearby. I had to do that partly because Mother couldn't afford sending me away and partly because she believed I was too young to be on my own. When my father disappeared we immigrated to America, and the money she had in Iran shrank in the exchange from *toomans* to dollars. Mother, Uncle, and I came together—mainly for them to get away from traumas they had had in Iran. But then Uncle died from a heart attack. "From all the stress," Mother always says. In Iran he had been forced to leave the newspaper he was working for because of having written some critical articles about the Shah's secret police. At least he was not murdered, as my father probably was, for saying the wrong thing.

At the beginning when we moved to America, Mother made a bare living for us working in a beauty parlor (what she still does). Hairdressing is among the few jobs she can do with her poor knowledge of English—though she has been here for years she has only a small vocabulary.

I hear her in the kitchen, preparing supper, and at the same time watching the Farsi speaking channel on a small TV she keeps on the counter. She is a gentle woman with a delicate figure and face. I look different from her—I am tall with large bone structure and more prominent features. I could do things I suppose to make myself look sexier, like Sheila Harrington—wear different clothes, dye my hair.

Mother has a "friend." He comes over frequently to take her out. Before he come she dresses up and puts powder on her cheeks and bright red lipstick, which livens up her normally prim appearance. I wonder about the nature of their relationship. Mother has always said to me, "Sex is only for marriage." Whatever their relationship, I find his presence in our house nearly unbearable. Something about his dominant, arrogant personality chokes the very air. Still, it is good for her to have him; he has pulled her somewhat out of her depression. He came from Iran to America years ago also and the two of them reminisce about the good old days. Something is missing from everything in America, the way they see it. People, food, even the stars and the moon were better at home.

Every week they go to the "Persian Night," at the San Fernando Valley nightclub, where Iranian pop singers and musicians in gaudy clothes perform, and where the audience is almost all Iranian.

It is dusk. The street lights go on. Windows light from the inside. Cars pull into driveways. Children run out to greet their fathers or mothers.

A window opens in the building across the street and Mary Parsipoor looks out. She doesn't seem to see me. We went to high school together. She is married, has two children. We have little in common anymore—she is absorbed in her marriage, children, domestic chores.

"Pari, Pari," Mother is calling me, in her thin, high voice. "Dinner is ready."

In the office Sheila Harrington and Latifeh are carrying on a conversation while I compose a letter about the raise. Maybe I will get better results by writing her. I will put it on my desk and she will have to read it and think about it.

"... We must have a talk. I spend hours every day organizing this office which is always in danger of sinking into chaos. Isn't it time for me to have a raise ... ?"

I read it over. It sounds too angry. I tear it up, thinking I would be better off speaking to her about it after all.

I stare at the bouquet of yellow roses on my desk, which Jahan brought over for me, but the sight of it, the thought of Jahan himself, only makes me more depressed. Lately something, a spark, has been missing between us. Our romance reached a peak within the first few months and then began to dim slowly. In fact, after a frustrating evening together last week, he said to me, laughing, "Have you forgotten how to kiss?"

He is one of our distributors and one afternoon when I was alone here and he came in we talked for a long time. Then we started going out. When we had just met he said to me, "I came from Iran to L.A. to see Marilyn Monroe and Ava Gardner, but got here too late. They're all dead."

Sheila Harrington and Latifeh are still talking on and on, oblivious of what I am thinking, doing. Latifeh has a superior manner. She is obsessed by her appearance. Her purse has to be exactly the same shade of color as her shoes, her hair perfectly in place, her face made up just as perfectly. She thinks she is devastatingly beautiful, though she in only eye-catching, with her long jet-black hair and black eyes.

"Back when everyone was doing drugs in college," Sheila Harrington is saying, as if it is something to brag about, "I pretended it was day when it was night and night when it was day."

They both laugh. I had heard Sheila Harrington say before that she had once committed herself to a treatment center for a month to straighten up. She has also told us in vivid detail about the first boy she ever kissed, the first cigarette she smoked, the night she drank so much that she passed out.

Morning is getting on. An ambulance shrieks outside. The footsteps in the hall sound urgent. Soon it is going to be lunch time. That is always a hassle. Who will eat first? Who is getting Sheila Harrington's lunch? Latifeh says to her, "Can I get you something to eat? I say, "I'm going to the Bakery, do you want me to get you some cookies?" Which one of us might she invite to eat out with her? Latifeh and I compete to do favors for her.

The two of them get up and start to leave together, without a word of explanation to me. Yesterday I overheard Latifeh saying to her, "She's uptight." I was coming into the office, carrying a cup of coffee for myself. I went straight to my desk and pretended I had not heard anything.

It is dawn. A dream woke me up. In the dream I was running barefooted through a vast grassy field. I was wearing a white, full-skirted dress and a ribbon pinned on my hair which was loose and wind-blown. Someone—it seemed it was my mother—was shouting after me, "Stop, your feet are going to bleed," but I kept on running, full of an inexplicable happiness. My footsteps were light as if I were running in air.

Then I remember what happened last night. It started with my leaving the office late in the afternoon, very tired and irritable. The slightest noise made me jump. Even the drive back home seemed like a nightmare. Out of desperation I thought I would go to Jahan's office, which was not far from ours, and see if he was in. Most of the stores were still open and I walked slowly, looking at shops carrying ultra-modern merchandise, the kinds of things Sheila Harrington and Latifeh like. I paused in front of one shop, looking at the outlandish silver earrings in its window. I heard a shuffle behind me and then Jahan's voice, "Pari, what are you doing here?"

"Oh, I was going to drop in on you."

"Oh, good. I haven't eaten, are you hungry?"

"I could eat a little."

"Shall we go to our usual place?"

He meant The Dive, with its ocean sights and sounds, giving an underwater impression. "I guess so."

"Is something wrong?" he asked as we walked back to my car which was parked closer than his.

"Things have got to get better at work."

"One thing good about my work is that I can be on my own most of the time."

In The Dive, we sat by the window and each ordered cheese melts with raspberry and cherry, and vodka drinks served in tall glasses.

After we finished eating, he said, "Shall we go somewhere else? El Paso?"

So we went to the nightclub, and watched stars, mainly the ones long dead, being impersonated. Marilyn Monroe, Joan Crawford, Gregory Peck. I could see how deeply enveloped Jahan was in the glow of the glamour the whole place projected, what had brought him to Los Angeles to begin with. He kept ordering drinks and I kept drinking mine quickly, something I am not used to.

At the break between impersonations a pale young man with dark curls of hair hanging on his forehead sat on stage and played the banjo and sang. Looking at him made me wistful for a real romance, not what my relationship with Jahan had become. I closed my eyes and tried to remember . . . I was fourteen, being kissed by Nancy's older brother, Eric, in the dark hallway of their house, a surreptitious, quick kiss. This was before he withdrew from me and before I heard him say to someone at school, "She's from a different culture." I was twenty and was kissing Kim, a boy I had a crush on in the junior college . . . One night he said to me, "You're a strange girl, you know that? You're always holding something back." Then he stopped calling. I know I can't let go of myself, though I wish, yearn to be light, feathery, quick to laughter, the type of person who breaks dates easily, who is usually late to appointments. Like Sheila Harrington. All my dissatisfactions began to crowd my mind. The fact that I am just a glorified secretary, still living at home with my mother, that I haven't seen the world like

Sheila Harrington, that I am undereducated, underpaid, undervalued . . . The banjo player was singing, "Oh, dark night I'm waiting for rays of light to open up, to reveal what you hold in your depths."

An urge, an irresistible impulse came over me. "Let's go and see Sheila Harrington," I said to Jahan.

"It's eleven o'clock."

"She won't mind. She's an open person."

He paid and we left. "Let's go to my apartment."

"Not until I've talked to her."

"Are you out of your mind?"

"I'll go by myself." I started walking rapidly, almost running, to my car. Most of the shops were closed now. In the shadowy doorways prostitutes were lurking, showing their long naked legs and thighs.

I got into my car before Jahan reached me. As I drove away I saw him shaking his head. People and cars wavered before my eyes. . . Then I was standing in front of her house and ringing the bell. She answered the door herself. A shadow erased her feature and I could not see her reaction.

"Pari, is that you? I was wondering who it could be at this hour?"

"I thought I'd drop in to have a talk."

"God, you sound drunk, I didn't know you drink. Come in."

She led me into the living room. She turned on the light and just stood there. The house was furnished tastefully with touches from all over the world, a Grecian rug on the floor, a Mexican lamp hanging over a table, and American silk-covered chairs and sofas. The house struck me, for the first time, as very carefully worked on to appear casual. Then I wondered how much of her absent-minded attitude was a cultivated front also.

"Were you out drinking?" she asked. She must have been asleep. She was in her nightgown, her hair was tousled, her eyelids a little puffy. She kept yawning, it was as though she could not wait until she got back into bed. Clearly she was not in a mood to talk.

"Yes, with Jahan."

"So, you're still going out with him." Was it scorn I detected in her tone? "Why don't you sleep on the couch, there're sheets in that closet." She started going up the steps.

"I must talk to you."

"About what, at this hour of the night?" She paused in the middle of the stairway.

"I want to settle some things." My voice was trembling.

"Settle some things?" She was a little flushed now, impatient.

"About the raise . . . "

"You come here drunk, late at night . . . " She resumed walking up the stairs in a rapid, irritable way.

"I tried many times . . . "

But she was no longer in sight.

A chain of memories from my childhood flashed at me. Going to visit my aunt and uncle I always had to pass a wobbly, wooden bridge set on a wide stream. Every time I was terrified that the bridge would cave in or I would slip and fall into the water, my head hitting the dark stones at its bottom, and be carried away, my body finally lost.

Everybody's Business
Fran DeVenuto

Fran DeVenuto's family immigrated to the U.S. from a small town in Italy.

"He had to go through the whole village with his pants leg ripped."

The younger woman stared at the stout, older one in disbelief.

"Why, Mama? It doesn't make sense."

"That's the way it was then, that's all."

The younger woman looked puzzled.

"Do they still do that?" she asked.

"Luisa, how should I know? I haven't been back there in years. Probably."

"But Mama, why a ripped pants leg?"

The older woman, her fat torso encased in black, sighed.

"I guess it was kind of like a flag, so the whole village would know . . . "

"Why did the whole village need to know? Why was it any of their business?"

"Because, Luisa, it was everybody's business."

"And then what happened?"

"What do you mean, then what happened?"

"Did they stay married, or what?"

"Stay married? Are you kidding? It was a disgrace, a horrible disgrace for the bride's family. They could never raise their heads again, and they had to take their daughter back. Of course, no good family would ever want her . . ."

"But Mama, how did anybody find out?"

"Find out what? The old woman yawned, then pulled her dark shawl tightly around her shoulders.

"Find out she wasn't a . . ."

"A virgin? They knew because the next morning the village priest and the mother-in-law went over to check the sheets."

"Check the sheets?" the young woman was stunned.

"For blood, Luisa, what do you think?"

"Well, what if she didn't bleed?" Luisa felt angry now, and she didn't understand why.

"What about her husband? How did they know if he was a virgin? How did the village priest check that?"

"What garbage talk is this? Lucky your papa's not alive to hear it."

They stood in silence for a few minutes, waiting in the drizzle for the bus.

"Mama, did the bride's family always take her back?"

The balding old woman shrugged, "Sometimes yes, sometimes no. Like Maria di Angeli. Her family took her back, and her father beat her all the time. Finally, she killed herself."

Luisa shivered; the old woman blew her nose and continued talking.

"Some girls ran off and became prostitutes, some married foreign men, some killed themselves. Now, where is that bus? We're going to be late for Mass."

Dad
Abby Bogomolny

Abby Bogomolny's paternal grandfather came to the U.S. to avoid being sent to the front in the Russo-Japanese War. Her last name means "one who prays to God" in Russian. While she was born and raised in Brooklyn, she lives in California where she is an English Instructor at Santa Rosa Junior College. This selection is taken from her collection of poetry, *People Who Do Not Exist* (1997).

deep inside your bones a mysterious agenda
to me you confide "I don't understand
what is happening to my body."
medical reality: needle based profit, analytical brokers
power drugs, cold as an examining table,
kind doctors lost to insurance,
hospitals and nursing homes crack the continent,
the feelings of families are open and bleeding
health care proxies, i.v. to the vein of intelligence.

the kindness of your past, dear father
draws the suburban nieces and nephews
into the city to see you,
with mother and me at your side.

you always gave me
a handful of dimes and quarters, so I could have change
told me what I needed to know,
who were friends to the Jews during the war,
you had the list:
not Ford, don't buy their cars, those *antiShimityn*,
you screamed at the TV
how you were hit by a streetcar, running after your sister
at age five and saved by a free clinic on Henry Street,
how you walked blocks and blocks in the snow
to school on Blake Avenue
after setting up the wood for your mother's pushcart,
how the only line you heard
in Russian as a child was "don't hit him,"
how you were 13 when you first saw big homes,

another part of the city where grass grew,
not like Brownsville, Harlem or the Lower East Side
where you grew up in tenements and laundries,
how you went to the same doctor
from the clinic that saved you twenty years before
because you had a rash
and he told you "to get married,"
how your father told you that those sent to Siberia
saved themselves by sucking on raw onions,
how you cared for your father for so long
and finally had to have your own life,
how during the depression you were chosen
from hundreds to work in Jersey as a cutter,
how it doesn't matter how much your job pays,
as long as it's steady,
how important it is to have a pension,
how we can always talk with God,
how everyone turned their backs on the Jews in 1938.

I am an impression stamped from you
I am the daughter and the son, the oldest and the youngest
the fulfillment of your future, the failure of your wishes
who could have expected this wild card?
you did your best to be kind.

Finally...My Two Dads
Marie G. Lee

Marie G. Lee was born and raised in Hibbing, Minnesota. She is the author of the novels *Finding My Voice, Night of the Chupacabra, If It Hadn't Been for Yoon Jun, Saying Goodbye,* and *Necessary Roughness.* Her work has appeared in the *New York Times, The American Voice,* and *the Kenyon Review.*

I am a first-generation Korean-American. On my first trip to Korea at age twenty-six, I found that I had two fathers. One was the Dad I'd always known, but the second was a Korean father I'd never seen before—one surprising and familiar at the same time, like my homeland.

I was born and raised in the Midwest, and to me, my Dad was like anyone else's. He taught my brothers to play baseball, fixed the garage door, and pushed the snowblower on chilly February mornings. If there was anything different about him, to my child's eyes, it was that he was a doctor.

Growing up, my siblings and I rarely came into contact with our Korean heritage. Mom and Dad spoke Korean only when they didn't want us to know what they were saying. We didn't observe Korean customs, except for not wearing shoes in the house, which I always assumed was plain common sense. I'd once seen a photograph of Dad in a traditional Korean costume, and I remember thinking how odd those clothes made him look.

With my parents' tacit encouragement, I "forgot" that I was Korean. I loved pizza and macaroni and cheese, but I had never so much as touched a slice of kimchi. All my friends, including my boyfriend, were Caucasian. And while I could explain in detail everything I thought was wrong with Ronald Reagan's policies, I had to strain to remember the name of Korea's president.

Attempting to learn the Korean language, *hangukmal,* a few years ago was a first step in atoning for my past indifference. I went into it feeling smug because of my fluency in French and German, but learning Korean knocked me for a loop. This was a language shaped by Confucian rules of reverence, where the speaker states her position (humble, equal, superior) in relation to the person she is addressing. Simultaneously humbling myself and revering the person with whom I was speaking seemed like a painful game of verbal Twister. To further complicate the process, I found there are myriad titles of reverence, starting with the highest, *sansengnim*, which loosely means "teacher/doctor," down to the ultra-specific, such as *waysukmo*, "wife of mother's brother."

Armed, then, with a year's worth of extension-school classes, a list of polite phrases and titles, and a Berlitz tape in my Walkman, I was as ready as I'd ever be to travel with my family to Korea last year.

When we arrived at Kimpo Airport in Seoul, smiling relatives funneled us into the customs line for *wayguksalam*, "foreigners." I was almost jealous watching our Korean flight attendants breeze through the line for *hanguksalam*, "Korean nationals." With whom did I identify more—the flight attendants or the retired white couple behind us, with their Bermuda shorts and Midwestern accent? My American passport stamped me as an alien in a land where everyone looked like me.

I got my first glimpse of my second father when we began trying to hail cabs in downtown Seoul. Because the government enforces low taxi fares, the drivers have developed their own system of picking up only individual passengers, then packing more in, to increase the per-trip profit. The streets are clogged not only with traffic but also with desperately gesticulating pedestrians and empty taxis.

Even my mother was stymied by the cab-hailing competition. When Mom and I traveled alone, cabs zoomed blithely past us. When we finally got one, the driver would shut off his meter, brazenly charge us triple the usual fare, and ignominiously dump us somewhere not very close to our destination.

But traveling with Dad was different. He would somehow stop a taxi with ease, chitchat with the driver (using very polite language), then shovel us all in. Not only would the cabbie take us where we wanted to go, but some of the usually-taciturn drivers would turn into garrulous philosophers.

I began to perceive the transformation of my father from American dad to functioning urban Korean. When we met with relatives, I noticed how Dad's conversational Korean moved easily between the respect he gave his older sister to the joviality with which he addressed Mom's younger cousin. My bother Len and I and our Korean cousins, however, stared shyly and mutely at each other.

Keeping company with relatives eased my disorientation, but not my alienation. Korea is the world's most racially and culturally homogenous country, and although I was of the right race, I felt culturally shut out. It seemed to me that Koreans were pushy, even in church. When they ate, they slurped and inhaled their food so violently that at least once during every meal, someone would have a sputtering fit of coughing.

Watching my father "turn Korean" helped me as I tried to embrace the culture. Drinking *soju* in a restaurant in the somewhat seedy Namdaemun area, he suddenly lit into a story of the time when Communists from North Korea confiscated his parents' assets. Subsequently, he became a medical student in Seoul, where each day he ate a sparse breakfast at his sister's house, trekked across towering Namsan Mountain (visible from our room in the Hilton), and studied at Seoul National University until night, when he would grab a few hours of sleep in the borrowed bed of a friend who worked the night shift.

I have always lived in nice houses, gone on trips, and never lacked for pizza money. But as my father talked, I could almost taste the millet-and-water gruel he subsisted on while hiding for months in cellars during the North Korean invasion of Seoul. Suddenly, I was able to feel the pain of the Korean people, enduring one hardship after another. Japanese colonial rule, North Korean aggression, and dependence on American military force. For a brief moment, I discerned the origins of the noble, sometimes harsh, Korean character. Those wizened women who pushed past me at church were there only because they had fought their way to old age. The noises people made while eating began to sound more celebratory than rude.

And there were other things I saw and was proud of. When we visited a cemetery, I noticed that the headstones were small and unadorned, except for a few with small, pagoda-shaped "hats" on them. The hats (*chinsa*), Dad told me, were from a time when the country's leaders awarded "national Ph.Ds," the highest civilian honor.

"Your great grandfather has one of those on his grave," Dad mentioned casually. I began to admire a people who place such a high value on hard work and scholarship. Even television commercials generally don't promote leisure pursuits, such as vacations or Nintendo, but instead proclaim the merits of "super duper vitamin pills" to help you study longer and work harder.

After two weeks, as we prepared to return to the U.S., I still in many ways felt like a stranger in Korea. While I looked the part of a native, my textbook Korean was robotic, and the phrases I was taught—such as, "Don't take me for a five-won plane ride"—were apparently very dated. I tried to tell my Korean cousins an amusing anecdote: in the Lotte department store in Seoul, I asked for directions to the restroom and was directed instead to the stereo section. But the story, related once in English and once in halting Korean, became hopelessly lost in the translation.

Dad decided he would spend an extra week in Korea, savoring a culture I would never fully know, even if I took every Berlitz course I could afford. When I said good-bye to him, I saw my Korean father; but I knew that come February, my American dad would be back out in our driveway, stirring up a froth of snow with his big yellow snowblower.

Una Carta a Puerto Rico / A Letter to Puerto Rico
Lola Rodríguez

Lola Rodríguez was chosen by Los Angeles' *Latin Beat Magazine* as one of the most important women in the arts today. Both a performer and writer, her work is featured in *The Coffeehouse Poetry Anthology* and *Poets and Painters*. She is a several-time recipient of the Lila Acheson Wallace Reader's Digest Foundation Grant, and lives in New York City.

Querida Borinquen,[1]
    I am not *Lola Rodriguez de Tió*[2]
    The national heroine
    Whose black hair cascaded into black print
    In praise of your beauty.

I am the Lola Rodriguez of myself
With my own history and music.
From snow and skyscrapers
I create palm trees, turquoise seas, and mountains.
I see you when I close my eyes
When I send postcards I can hear
Your *bomba y plena.*[3]
I burn like the vivid *flamboyán.*[4]

I am writing, dear island
To thank you for what you have given me,
A past and a future that only I can understand.
You invite me but I cannot be with you.
    Today, I have become someone else.
    A stranger.
This is between you and me, dear island
    My Spanish is not so good,
    I eat frozen Goya dinners.
    My eyes are dark green with golden centers and
    I am yellow and pale
But we shall not forsake one another.

Although I was not born in San Germán, Like Lola,
I will sing your praises *con la letra y musa de mi
añoranza,*[5]
For I too, am Lola de América
   La patria llevo conmigo[6]

[1] *Querida Borinquen:* dear, beloved Puerto Rico.

[2] *Lola Rodriguez de Tío:* distinguished poet, scholar, and freedom
fighter who designed the island's flag and wrote the national anthem of
Puerto Rico.

[3] *bomba y plena:* Puerto Rican folkloric dances rooted in Africa.

[4] *flamboyán:* flame-colored tropical tree.

[5] *con la letra y musa de mi añoranza:* with the words and music of my
nostalgic longing.

[6] *La patria llevo conmigo:* I carry my country within (A quote from
Julia de Burgos).

Dakota Thunderstorm
Laurence Snydal

Laurence Snydal is the son of immigrant Norwegians and Icelanders. He has published over 30 poems in magazines and anthologies and has helped raise two sons. He teaches cooking and makes music. Though a resident of California, Dakota is still dear to him.

Paling from black to bruise blue, granite grey,
Clouds like soiled pillows pile to heaven's blunt brow
From the bluffs where bison died. I see how
This storm pelts the prairie. I know the way
Wet weather works. I see how quickly day
Descends to dark, how pressure pulls its plow
Through shocked air, how grain and grass will bend, bow,
And bend when the storm comes marching. I stay
In. The sun sinks. Water walks on baled hay.
Light links low and high. Light links here and now.
Light leads loud down to where my ears allow
Its entrance. Then at last the rain will lay
Its hard hand on the roof and I stand under
Lightning's neat knife, hammer blows of thunder.

Mama
Joey Garcia

Joey Garcia was born in Belize and now lives in Cameron Park, California. She writes a weekly newspaper advice column and lectures on spirituality. Her awards include Honorable Mention in the 1995 Randall Jarrell Poetry Competition for "Mama" and a Fellowship from Writers Conferences and Festivals.

I. Lips
Mama frowned at photos of me,
as far back as I can remember.
"Gal, your lips are thick," she'd say,
head wagging,
tongue clicking punctuation.
"Don't smile so big, you look like you're grinnin'."

Locked in the bathroom
for hours,
I practiced curling my lips over my teeth
        just so
she would be happy.

II. Hair
Mama sends me for Afrosheen and magazines
on Black hair care
in neighborhoods where we do not live.
Waiting outside, engine running.

"At least you got good hair," she'd sigh Saturdays,
mixing chemicals, heating up the straightening comb,
trying to make her kinky hair look like a bad perm
so she could pass for white
or at least Mexican.

Her hair fell out one Saturday.
I glued the woolly black clumps to my rubber swim cap,
pulling it over my straight black hair,

so I could see the African in me.
She cut my hair the next week,
said she was fixing to make a wig.
"It's long as a horsetail, anyhow," she said.
"You're young, it'll grow back."

Draping the hair across her arms
she took to her bed
and lost hours combing it
lost hours pleased with her "good hair."

III. Nose
After the happily-ever ending
of bedtime tales
came the exercise:
thumb, forefinger stationed at the bridge,
sharp pull down the nose,
like molding a beak.

"Do it right or I'll get a nose minimizer, hear?" mama'd
say
threatening to send me home to Belize
for a hinged metal plate to screw over my nose,
keep it from spreading wide.

Fearful, my fingers flew
until the light went out.
Then I'd flare my nostrils,
like the bull in my picture books
sucking in air like it was love.

Choosing Camps
Joey Garcia

In my California school I heard tales of men,
women, children lying on the earth,
sparrow arms tucked into flannel sacks,
wagging heads lulled to slumber. I asked
my immigrant father if I, too, could bed beneath the stars,
silent as a stone
      inhaling luminosity.

He laughed as deep and thick
as the Belizean jungles, where he had labored
as a logger for a dollar a day to surpass
palmetto hut poverty. He laughed at North Americans
with roofs and Macy's mattresses who slept instead
on the rigid earth, pebbles caught in spines, trying
to call it vacation. He laughed at their dog noses and
damp clothing.

      Then he painted

a galaxy on the ceiling over
my four-poster bed. Tucking me in,
he pointed out jaguar spirits and monkey gods.

     When I was sure he was asleep

      I slipped away

to plunge my head into the liquid night
and pretend I was a stone.

Drink
Miriam Sachs Martín

Miriam R. Sachs Martín, born in East San Jose, is of mixed ethnicity and
mixed class background. She is currently working on a performance art piece
about being fierce. Says Martín, "Doy mil gracias to all the other Cuban
Jews out there, also to my mother, my girl Heather, and my cat Georgia
Brown. Peace."

Everybody drinks in my family

rare night that I come home and not find wineglass left
out, red stains on the starched tablecloth

I live with my mama, like a good unmarried Cuban girl (if
you ignore a few certain tidbits, at least I keep the door
closed and the noise level down), and we alternately
harangue each other about drinking too much and sit at
the table and drink together—laughing uproariously and
fighting bitterly

    i drink alone, too

come home after ten-hour shifts at the battered women's
shelter, come home hunched over from carrying around
the pain it is my job to witness, and down beers until it is
time to go to bed, and down sweet numbness, sweet relief,
until it is time to get up and go back to work

    my aunt is a drunkard

although not one for the bottle you can see her blood
rushing you can see her sweet numb skin singing as she
goes for her children with curses and hands, schoolteacher
teetotaler she used to punch my cousin for gettin "C's" on
her report card

    my abuelito used to drink but now
    my abuelita won't let him

he can't drink, can't smoke cigars, can't sip the bitter
lifeblood of Cuban coffee, he's too blind to dance and too
broken as well; he's reduced to shouting at my grand-
mother to come aim his dick while he pisses and to crying
inadvertently for his own hidden reasons, or if one of us
just mentions the magic incantation: 'Cuba,' the furious
tears will start rolling down his wrinkled face

> everybody drinks in my family
> and I don't know why.

could it be the anguish of being landlocked, of missing
sweet island breezes? I have been there, I have borne
witness (as I know so well how to do) my family in Cuba
does not drink, does not swell and crest on heady ebbs of
power and wine, they are solemn, non-violent, and live
with their pain instead of drowning it out. The humidity
strokes their serious faces, they walk to work and school,
and come home to think it all out in brightly colored
houses decorated with wrought-iron lacework (far con-
trast to drinking six-packs in a cardboard cut-out condos).
Maybe they would drink if they could, but they can, they
can, for the revolution has brought us cheap rum in 10
gallon laundry buckets y a nadie le necesita hacer falta

> went to see my cousin the other day

she offered me an almost empty bottle of something called
"aftershock" a vile red drink made with cinnamon candy
booze. Try some, it's good, it makes you feel good, she said.
We ended up polishing off a gallon bottle of wine instead
and passing out on the couch

> my family immigrated from Cuba in 1952

supporters of the democratically elected Carlos Prios, they
fled severe political oppression from dictator Juan
Bautista. They fled poverty, worms, not having shoes

my mother being thrown in jail at age eleven because of
who her family supported. They went to New Jersey and
tried to pass, white is right in my family, and were thrown
out of apartment after apartment after they were discov-
ered speaking Spanish, my grandfather was a union
organizer, in Cuba he once killed a man in the boxing
ring, my abuelita was eleven years his junior, she was
poor as cheap dirt which is why she married him, he
chews his mouth and cries all day, she waits on him hand
and foot and curses him bitterly from morning to night,
they worked all their lives to be rotting away in a South-
ern California suburb thousands of miles away from the
rumba-washed air that could make life meaningful—it is
no wonder we all drink in my family—we have too much
of what we don't need and not enough of what really counts.

> everybody drinks in my family
> and no one wants to talk about it

what are you talking about, they say as telltale flushes
darken their faces and eyes, we don't have a problem, we
don't drink, we don't like to talk about it. My mother's two
day pre-adolescent stint in jail is one of my favorite topics,
my mother the brave childhood revolutionary, my mother
the burning coal of Latino fire, my mother my unwilling
hero

> she hates it,

alternately asks nicely that it not be mentioned and then
says that it's all a lie my father made up. Don't talk about
it. Jesus Christ but the roadmap I have made of my body
disgusts and frightens my family—flag of Cuba on my
forearm, dove of peace on my leg and interlocking
woman symbols etched in rainbow fire on my scalp, don't
talk about it, White is right—how could you? I scorn
makeup and instead am decorated with indelible ink, I
am symbolized to the outside world, I am out, I am proud,
I wear my identity like a badge of honor—how could you?

Hide the bottle, hide the glass, hide the bruises, we are a proud people, they say, dress to the teeth keep your back straight and a distant smile on your proud face, everybody drinks but we don't talk about it, and to me, the walking microphone, they ask—"How could you?"

i bought a bottle of aftershock today

seventeen dollars, which is two hours worth of work at the shelter. It tastes both divine and disgusting; could be a metaphor for my life. I sip it, typing, as I try to figure out how to begin to bear witness to sobriety of intention and ethic while honoring my hereditary borrachera of spirit. How to bear witness to my proud culture and not disgrace my people while doing so. Cuba beats hard and fast in my blood as I down sweet anesthetic. Mi cubita linda, will you still make me curse and swell with sensuous pride when I scorn the drugs that invoke your memory? Anger, after-shock, and wine, you have nothing on sun-blessed sea scented air, I say, as I pour myself another drink.

Bungalow People
Charles Fishman

Charles Fishman created the Visiting Writers Program at the State University of New York at Farmingdale and served as its director until 1997. His books include *Chopin's Piano* (2005), *Country of Memory* (2004) *The Firewalkers* (1996) and *Blood to Remember: American Poets on the Holocaust* (1991). His volume of poems on the Holocaust, *The Death Mazurka* (1989) was nominated for the Pulitzer Prize in Poetry.

Bungalow people
Old-World-aged
other-tongued
stare
from scabbing porches,
kibitz, knit—
perpetually—
emblems of desire:
shawls to mourn in,
bibs for the newly born.

When I walk past them
to pluck
the sacred mushroom
curiosity
they sigh audibly
and knit faster.

I feel their angry wind
butt my legs
like a goat:
nothing scares me
like their death-
scratched voices.

Nothing muffles the horn
in my side
blowing pain.

I can't get away
from the burning porches,
from their white-hot
needles
weaving up the sun:
the more sweat I pour
into leaving
the nearer they come.

Spanglish
Rebeca Gutierrez

Rebeca Gutierrez wrote this essay when she was a student at Cabrillo College in Aptos, California. Spanglish is her first language.

I see Spanglish as an art, a beautiful, talented language that only Chicanos know. Why, you may ask? Because it's the way we express ourselves, the way we show the world who we are, much like painters do. I know it may sound kind of corny, even ridiculous, but it has become our language; ¡nos guste ó no!/like it or not for those non Spanglish-speaking people.

In all of my English classes, I have had trouble expressing my thoughts and putting them down on paper. I'll tell you why, by telling a little bit of my pasado/past. When I was in elementary school, my mother put me in bilingual classes, but had the teacher instruct me only in Spanish. When I would ask why I was the only one not learning how to read and write in English, my mother said, "Para que no seas igual de pendeja a tus hermanos y le sepas bien el español/so that you won't be as slow as your ungrateful siblings and know proper Spanish." It was a good explanation, I thought, at the time and I did not ask her again until I transferred to junior high school. Suddenly all my classes were in English. Yo no sabía que hacer/I didn't know what to do.

My counselor in school put me in a small RSP class where they helped me one on one with my illiteracy in English. In high school I stayed in RSP to help with my spelling and to transition to a new school. However, my second year of high school, I transferred to normal classes taught in English. Como no estaba satisfecha con mi spelling/since I wasn't satisfied with my spelling, I applied myself to the readings and the class discussions to get my grades, embarrassed by the fact that I was not as good a speller as my compas/classmates.

Ever since I can remember I have used Spanish and

English in the same sentence; even before I knew it was called Spanglish. I never really thought about Spanglish but it has always been a part of my everyday life. It's not something that I even think about before using it—like when a person has a really annoying voice and he/she can't do anything about it to change it. It's the same way with Spanglish speaking people; we can't help but to talk the way we do. Even if we tried, sooner or later we would start with our Spanglish again.

My father always says, "If you're going to speak, speak right so that everybody understands. It doesn't matter what language you're speaking in, as long as you speak clearly and one at a time; don't mix languages together. If you're going to speak Spanish, speak Spanish and if you're going to speak English, speak English. No léagan al pendejo," he says in an upset voice.

"We can't help it," I say, "no lo pensamos." I mean we think about what we are going to say, but we don't think about which language we are going to say it in. It doesn't really matter which language we use, as long as the other person understands. It's not like we go around speaking Spanglish to English-speaking people; we aren't that unconscious—just to the people who we know will understand us, like friends and family. But the result of using too much Spanglish is that we have trouble finding the words we need to express ourselves.

Both of my parents speak "broken" English and all my siblings and friends speak a language of their own—Spanglish. So, we use both languages incorrectly, según los gringos and according to my parents. "Which isn't helping any of us get ahead in life," says my father.

Gifts for the Dead
Jennifer Lagier

Jennifer Lagier is former co-chair of the National Writer's Union, Local 7. She has published work in *Unsettling America: An Anthology of Contemporary Multicultural Poetry, La Bella Figura: A Choice, Voices in Italian Americana, The Dream book: An Anthology of Writings by Italian-American Women,* and *Poeti Italo-Americani e Italo-Canadesi.*

I do it
for the women
of my bloodline,
the ones unable
to make independent decisions
or see any way beyond prayer
out of miserable lives.

Every day I purchase
a little more
of my family's freedom,
pull on education and credentials,
begin a forced march
up my own career ladder
on their behalf.

I see cheated Italian girls
with a chance
within the mirror of my
aging and frustrated mother's
still-angry stories.

For those quiet and obedient saints
who died before me
I earn the dreams
their tradition denied.

Both Sides of the Border
Cathy Ruiz

Cathy Ruiz is a freelance writer born in Seattle, Washington. She has published poetry in *Through the Eye of the Deer: An Anthology of Native American Women Writers*, the *Raven Chronicles*, and *Gatherings: The En'owkin Journal of First North American Peoples*. She holds a B.A. from the University of Washington, but considers world travel her greatest source of knowledge.

First of all,
I'm from both sides of the border.
That is, my mother is Canadian, Cree Indian
and
my father is Mexican-American.
So I don't check neatly into any one of those little
ethnic group boxes,
and
have found it frustrating all of my adult life
to be asked to choose.
And, if I,
let's say,
Track down a member of a certain Native American
professional group and
say,
"I'd like to join,"
and she says, "What tribe are you?"
and I say, "My mother's Cree from Canada, but I'm also
part Mexican and prefer
to recognize all of my background,"
she glances at me coolly and says,
"We'll send you an application in the mail."
Then,
there's the Mexican-American professional group
whose member sees my last name and
addresses me in Spanish with the steady roll of a bilingual tongue.
But when I say,
"Please, repeat it again, slowly,"

She glances at me coolly and says,
"Here's an application. It costs $50 to join."
You see, I never grew up with any one culture.
We were a culture in ourselves,
a mixed culture
that my parents plopped down in the middle of all-white
communities
because their common language was English
and they had high hopes of blending in.
But we stood out.
Oh yes we did
my two sisters
and I,
with our short-cropped
near-black hair
and shy, dark faces
a mean little boy
down the street called
"dirty."
We were a flock of geese that flew in our own pattern,
with our Sunday dinners
of flat, round loaves of bannock, a Cree bread staple
and moose-meat from the wilds of Manitoba
served with pinto beans cooked whole, south-of-the-border
style.
My father used a belt
with the tyranny of a
conquistador
when
we wronged, but
told us to,
"Stand tall and face off your name-callers,"
at school.
Only
we weren't boys
so
he told stories about the Mexican gangs in his native
Chicago,
of their admiration for Pancho Villa and how

we should be revolutionaries too.
My mother swore in Cree
when she was angry at my father for being too harsh
but would pour her ancient recipe for love
into our empty cups while
dancing the jig with us in the living room when my father
was away at work.
She spoke proudly of
my late grandfather's Scottish heritage and
tried to forget the
Indian
but there was her accent and my grandmother from
Canada
who insisted, "Speak Cree!" and
who would stay for weeks, until the nasty woman next
door
began to gossip,
"Margaret's a chief's daughter."
"Ignorant!" my mother called her over the backyard fence,
"If I were a chief's daughter, I wouldn't be living next door
to you!"
and they never spoke again.
Spanish? I'm still trying to learn it.
Cree? I can swear in it.
I can't write for one ethnic group but,
if they'll let me, I can write for two
otherwise,
I'll just keep walking,
outside of the boxes
on both sides of the border.

Chapter 5
Second Generation
Assimilation and Amnesia

The grandchildren of immigrants are American, not just legally but in their heads and possibly their hearts as well. They are not Mexicans, Chinese or Irish; they are Americans. But—and here lies one of the great ambiguities of American life—they may be "ethnic Americans." The identity of Mexican, Chinese or Irish means something important for some Americans, particularly those who are two generations removed from immigration. For some the distance from an immigrant past makes the ethnic identity less meaningful, while others retain it ever more tightly.

Ethnicity matters in America, for some in a completely involuntary way, for others as a matter of choice. By the second generation, the descendants of the original immigrants have assimilated into American society—but it is not a uniform community, not the America of the "melting pot" myth. It is a society of many divisions: many ethnicities as well as classes, religions, sexual preferences and ideologies. These divisions provide the occasion not only for our identities, but for our friendships, social relationships, career opportunities and even our political activity.

The divisions are most acute when they are reinforced by race. The second generation can assimilate into the American culture, but their place in that culture is defined at least partly by their race. The children and grandchildren of Irish, Italian and Norwegian immigrants can merge, if they wish, into the dominant white culture. They will face all of the problems that white Americans typically face, but they will not confront the racism and prejudice that has marbled U.S. history. Americans of Latino, Arab, African, and Asian descent face a more complicated life.

For each group the situation is different. Immigrant families from the Caribbean and Africa are shocked to discover a culture that embroils them in the struggle of American Blacks. Arab Americans cannot avoid the opprobrium that comes from America's partisanship in the struggles of the modern Middle East. Many Asian Americans find themselves in a deeply uncomfortable position, for while they are perceived as not quite genuine Americans, they are held to a super-achiever stereotype. Latinos are often in a particularly ambiguous situation. As the Census Bureau is tireless in reminding us, "Hispanic" is not a race. Consequently, according to the official American statistical system, Latinos can be white, black, Asian or Indigenous. But most Americans do not abide by the Census Bureau's taxonomy; in present-day American culture, Latino is a race.

While only fifty years ago classified advertising and signs in public places could legally say "No Jews need apply," Jewish Americans have seen overt anti-Semitism wane. Religious discrimination still exists, compounded by calls for school prayer and other measures that weaken our nation's separation of church and state.

It is the second generation that feels the diverse pulls more strongly. The second generation is, for the most part, close to its grandparents but they generally do not speak their language. If they do speak it, it is often as an act of will; it was learned as a second language. Second generation Americans are in contact with the old culture, but they can feel it slipping away. If it is to be preserved, it will be done self-consciously, not automatically.

The patterns are numerous. Much depends upon whether the grandchildren continue to live in an ethnically homogeneous community—be it Irish in Boston, Jewish in Brooklyn, Mexican in East Los Angeles or Chinese in San Francisco—or whether they have moved into a more heterogeneous area. The processes are different, but in many cases the grandchildren frequently find meaning in their lives by returning to the cultures of their family.

The return is seldom easy, however, because the second

generation is pulled to the center as well. It turns out that Americans of all backgrounds share things in common, including for many the culture of blue jeans, baseball, rock music, Hollywood movies, TV soaps, and perhaps even an allegiance to U.S. democracy. Most Americans have the experience of a public school education where they share a curriculum which is, if not uniform across the country, at least fairly similar in many respects. Although Americans are divided in many ways, the country does have a dominant culture, a culture from which some are excluded but in which many find ways of participating.

That participation is deeply ambiguous, however. The melting pot of American life, so celebrated by some in the first half of the twentieth century, worked, to the extent that it worked at all, only for white Americans. Those on the bottom of the social order in Europe eventually became first class citizens when they arrived here. The United States is not, however, a white, melting pot country. The United States has been multicultural since Africans labored in the fields, Chinese worked on the transcontinental railroad and Mexican ranchos dotted the Southwest. Since the arrival of the first settlers on American shores, it has been a country of many races and many cultures.

Americans are typically pulled, therefore, in many directions: by the dominant culture, by ethnic cultures and by other forces as well. While some among us claim that only some of those directions represent the "true" America— America is a Christian nation, they claim, or European, or exclusively heterosexual—in fact they all form part of the American mosaic. Jews observe the High Holidays, Passover and Hanukkah, yet some put up a tree and exchange gifts at Christmas as well. Mexican American children observe the Day of the Dead, but dress up for trick or treating at Halloween too. Chinese Americans celebrate two new years in close succession. And to make the situation more complex, many Americans of other backgrounds join them in their ethnic observations, so Jewish, Mexican and Chinese customs, among others, have become part of mainstream American culture. Add to that the ethnic foods—the hummus, the burritos, the egg rolls—and one begins to get a sense of the centrifugal and centripetal forces that combine to make our America.

Ellis Island
Vincent Corvino

Vincent Corvino was born in the Bronx, New York, in 1972 to parents of Italian descent. His stories have appeared in *New Letters, Suffusion, The Purchase Review* and *The Quarterly*. He teaches English and Creative Writing at Plainedge High School in Massapequa, New York.

Everyone has something to say in New York.

After promising he'd exclusively use Cunningham's Car Service, Anthony Greco changed to plain old Checkered, because the drivers were mostly Pakistani and kept their advice and their Gods to themselves. Two weeks before this, while driving Anthony from the Federal Records Center in Bayonne, New Jersey,, back to his place in Brooklyn Heights, a Cunningham's driver named Marco asked, "You hear about that actor, Reeves? Fell off his horse?"

"Yes. Unbelievable," said Anthony. "A man like that. And he might be paralyzed . . ."

"Aah, happens."

"Happens?"

"Whatta you think?"

"Seems a little uncommon to me."

"That's what most people think. You'd be surprised. Most people I ask say the same thing you just said there. But I mean, a horse's a thousand pound animal, you gotta think about that." He jabbed his finger at his temple, covered, partially, by a pretty bad toupee. "It takes the slightest thing . . . ," he smacked the steering wheel, "and you're fucked."

Anthony hunkered down in his seat. He hadn't expected such a strong rebuttal. "You've got a point." If Marco had spoken out of his hat like most wash-ups Anthony ran into at the gym or in the neighborhood bar, he would've called him on it, and gotten into what little he knew about jockeys and thoroughbreds. Usually just some Sunday-knowledge on a subject could dethrone a guy like Marco.

Anthony knew better than to talk about things he didn't completely understand. There'd been no room for stupidity when he was growing up. His old man once broke a hairbrush over his leg for mouthing off in front of company. His old man was a plumber because he had to, and an intellectual because he wanted to, and he'd told Anthony that the Greco name was riding on him.

Anthony loosened his tie and looked to the side of the turnpike for that great view of Ellis Island. He liked the idea of getting chauffeured past the spot where his grandfather had arrived a stowaway.

"See, I had a horse once," Marco said. "I'm going back twenty years now. I was livin' in Colorado at the time. Me and a friend rented one. We wanted to buy her. Five bills. Guy wouldn't sell. Sharp." He poked at his head, again. "Knew he could get more rentin. Story of my life . . . so what's your line of work?" He fumbled for change as they approached the toll.

"I'm an attorney."

"No kiddin," Marco said. He thanked the toll collector. "Big shot, huh? I'm gonna leave the window open. Is that a problem? If it is, just say so."

"My old man always said don't trust anyone who's always cold."

"Yeah, mine said some things too . . . an attorney, huh? That's interestin. I've been meaning to ask someone about this thing. About this thing that happened to me. You mind?"

A good diplomat knows that if you really don't want to talk to someone, the best way is to just say so. No one likes being led around to his own tail. Anthony checked his watch.

"No problem," Marco said. "I understand. Guys like you got a lot to do. A lot on your minds. Don't need guys like me and our problems."

"It's not that, it's just—"

"Hey! I said it's okay, guy. Don't need to beat a dead horse. Get it? Dead horse?"

Anthony smirked. It was five o'clock and all he was thinking about was slipping into his robe and having a martini. Guys like Marco. What did they go home to? Hot dogs and beer, probably. Guys like this were always dipping into porn shops on Times Square. No class or self-respect.

Anthony's old man had never let him hang with kids on their way to becoming Marcos, kids who ditched their books and rebuilt Camaros. Five years after graduation, you'd catch them in old station wagons hauling painting supplies or auto parts.

Marco watched Anthony through the rearview mirror. "Actually, I was gonna be a jockey but, you know, it didn't work out. Had a kid and then who had the time? Once you have a kid . . . know what I'm sayin?"

"I don't have kids."

"Planning on them?"

"Well, maybe . . . right now—"

"Yeah, I know, career man, unless you're . . . never mind. Sorry, I meant no offense."

Anthony shifted in his seat, annoyed, and said, "I do have plans."

"I'm sure you do. Really, no offense. You know, after the jockey thing, I got into carpentry. I happen to be a professional carpenter. I know—'Whatta you doin drivin a cab?' Can't tell you that. See, that gets into the area I already know you don't wanna talk about."

Then Marco was quiet. Anthony wondered how Marco had known to "drop a grenade and leave the shrapnel hanging around," as one of Anthony's favorite professors had called it. Sometimes, the best thing you can do to get your way is to nag silently. If at first you fail to press your issue, wait a while and bring it up again. Then, pull back. Let your words spin around the other person's head—there's nothing as unnerving as quiet, especially to big city people. Sometimes guys like Marco could surprise you with their street smarts. But Anthony's old man had always said, "Street smarts are at best reactionary, a slick way of worming out of something. There's a big difference between men of action and men of reaction." It was something he'd read in Nietzsche. Sometimes, around the office Anthony like to mention that his father had read Nietzsche.

Anthony told Marco, "It's not that I don't want to help you out—"

"Hey," Marco said, "no explanation needed, guy."

The ride through lower Manhattan and over the Brooklyn Bridge was conversation-free. Marco slowed down considerably as he entered Anthony's neighborhood. The leaves were just beginning to turn and to drop gracefully along the promenade. "Over here, on the left." Anthony grabbed the handle of his briefcase as Marco pulled up to the curb. "What do I owe you?"

"Thirty-five."

Anthony handed him fifty. "Give me three back."

"Nah, guy, that's a big tip—"

"I always tip well, I'm Italian . . . like you. Ever hear the one about why Italians give so much at church?"

"Nah," Marco sifted through a wad of singles.

"Because they think they're tipping the Pope."

Marco laughed. "Y'know you don't hear many Italians makin jokes about themselves. Me? I could give a shit. Life's short. Look, by the way, remember this name, Lucky Stars. Got the word on that horse. She'll double your money."

"Lucky Stars," Anthony mumbled to himself. Marco reached over the seat and gave him his change. So that was why he drove a cab. Pissed all his money away at the track. Anthony had forgotten to include OTB* as another magnet for guys like Marco.

"Am I writing you a receipt?"

"Yes. But, make it out for forty-seven," Anthony said. "The firm reimburses me."

"Oh, guy, I can't do that," Marco shook his head, "ride's in the book as thirty-five dollars. I can't do a thing like that."

"What do you mean? How else am I supposed to give you a healthy tip?

"You can take it back. I don't mind."

"What's the matter?"

"Nothin. I'm Catholic like you." He crossed himself. "I gotta be able to sleep at night."

---

* OTB: Off Track Betting

***

Even though it was no big deal, the incident followed Anthony through his martini and into his few groggy moments before sleep. He stared at the ceiling as though it were a new page in his legal pad. His mind put questions there, jotted down key points, loopholes. That's no way to be, gambling and praying. Then to come off like some holy-roller and make a person feel like dirt for a little perk he took advantage of now and then. You couldn't even call it a sin. The firm encouraged it. They wanted you to eat up your expense account. They wrote it off on their taxes.

Anthony had been about to slam Marco's door, when Marco had said, "Look, guy, no hard feelins, all right? It's just the way I operate. Everybody's got a right. I tell you what. I got a pager. Any time you need a ride back from Jersey, you page me." He searched the glove box for his wallet. He pulled out a Cunningham's business card and wrote the pager number on the back. "Here." He handed it to Anthony through the passenger side window. "From now on, anytime you ride with me, it's a twenty-five dollar ride. Good enough?"

***

"Did you take my advice?" Marco asked, a week later.

"What advice?" Anthony had forgotten as much as he could about their first ride. He didn't like bringing pieces of his workday home.

"Lucky Stars."

"I don't play the horses."

"It's a good thing. I took a bath on that one."

Anthony leaned forward. "What does your wife say when you lose money like that?"

"I don't live with my wife anymore. We're separated three years now."

"Because of the gambling?" Anthony felt bold enough.

"Nah, you kidding me? We used to go to Atlantic City all the time. I could leave Helen at the slot machines all night. She'd walk away dizzy. You could see the lemons in her eyes. Nah, it had to do with that problem of mine. But I'm not gonna bother you with it."

"Go ahead," Anthony sighed.

"Nah, really, I don't wanna put you out or—"

"Go ahead." What kind of attorney would Anthony be if he couldn't admire and even reward such a salesman? He could say what he wanted to about Marco, but the guy had put together a sob-story of the quality that gets guilty men off. He'd have you believe he was nothing more than a good Catholic whose ship had never come in. A jury's eyes would well.

"You sure?" Marco asked.

"Yes, yes I'm sure."

"I got hurt on the job. Cut by a band saw. Messed up everythin. Check it out." He held up his right hand, like a president swearing in. A finger was missing and there were other vertical scars across his palm. Anthony felt a quick stab of fear. He wanted to say, "My God. What's that like?" But he stuck to what was familiar. "Did you sue?"

"That's what I'm gettin to. Gonna love this. Ever heard of a third-party suit?"

"Only on a daily basis."

"Craziest thing if you ask me. If you get compensation and you got no reason to sue the company you work for, you look for someone else to sue. Am I right?"

"Yes."

"That's what I did. Got myself a lawyer. Thought I had a case against the company that made the saw. The Fliescher Company. See . . . I don't know if you're familiar with band saws, but they come with safety shields, so your fingers don't slip under the blade when you're trying to bang out table after table. Sometimes your boss needs you to move extra fast on a project, and the way you do that is by removing the safety shield. Everybody does it. Can't blame the boss. After all, he doesn't ask you to remove the shield. He just asks you to speed up. But a couple months after the accident, I looked into some things and found out those shields aren't supposed to be removable."

"If that's true, you should've had a case."

"Yeah? You think so? Cuz my lawyer said I had no case. I tell you what. Till this day, I think he had bigger things on his mind and didn't wanna bother with me. Know what I'm sayin? You know how guys like that can be." Marco smacked the steering wheel, "And that was the last nail. After my compensation payments ran out, I had nothin to fall back on. Not even the jockey thing. You need a good grip for that. I mean, take that guy Reeves. Guy was in perfect shape and look what happened to him. I tell you, we live our lives this close," he showed a small space between the thumb and pointer of his good hand, "every last one of us."

"And the wife?"

"Money. You know. Compensation only goes so far. She's an old-country type. Wife and mother. She moved in with her sister and brother-in-law. Didn't expect to have to go out and work."

Marco let that sit for a while. Ellis Island popped up on their right, formless and green behind the rolling fog. Marco jiggled the change in his hand as they approached the toll.

***

That evening, Anthony took a girl named Donna Dillard to a Japanese restaurant on the Upper East Side. He'd met her at a 10K run and picnic the firm had held in Purchase, New York, the week before.

Anthony had just poured her some sake, when Donna asked, "What makes up your ideal woman?"

Was this an icebreaker? So far they'd only talked about restaurants and whether or not Crunch was a better fitness complex than Equinox. "Well, I never thought of a type, but I know what I like when I see it." It was a good way to shoot her a compliment. "And you?"

"I've always pictured myself with someone tall and blond."

"Then you got the wrong guy," Anthony thought, feeling like a darker, shorter version of himself, but he didn't say anything.

"But you have to keep an open mind," she said.

"Charity?" Anthony quipped.

"Oh, nothing like that. Sometimes you've got to make sacrifices to find your soul mate. Look beyond appearances."

This wasn't getting any better. Anthony felt second-string. He knew her words would stick with him the way Marco's had. Anthony was aware that he could be too sensitive. A bad trait in a lawyer. "Speaking of charity . . . " If he couldn't be tall and blond, at least he could change the subject in a way she might recognize as WASP social grace. Then Anthony told her all about Marco and the third party suit, about wanting to help him out. "He's like a lot of guys from my old neighborhood. Smart, but with a weakness. Plays the horses. But he's got potential."

"I wouldn't waste my time."

Marco thought *snob* but he said, "Why not?"

She said, "If you think he's going to take his settlement and put it down on a house, you're crazy. If he's really a gambler, the more he gets, the more he'll blow."

***

Two days later, Marco kept Anthony waiting in front of the Federal Records Center, which sits on the Hudson River. The cold was no picnic. The wind off the water bit through his overcoat.

Where in the hell was he? Anthony checked his watch for the eighth time. He needed coffee. He'd spent the last two hours doing some extra work for one of the partners at the firm, sifting through case files for a few special memorandums. Although he hadn't exactly been briefed why these internal memorandums were so important to his partner, Anthony was willing to be a good company man and trust his partner's needs. On top of that, he'd given some good time to researching Marco's case although now Anthony regretted it. He'd gotten the name of Marco's former employer, a place called Woodshed. He checked on the accident. Marco's supervisor, Jack Cousins, told Anthony, "Marco Savella was drunk on the job the day he lost that finger. No lawyer in his right mind would take that case. Nothing but trouble, that guy. Too many gambling debts. Loansharks even after him . . . ate up our compensation to him in a minute. And we had to let him go."

Now, Marco was thinking of Donna Dillard's warning and felt a little foolish. He was almost grateful their first date was going to be their last, so he wouldn't have to explain any of this.

As he started back toward the building, ready to page Marco a second time, he heard a horn and turned to find Marco's cab tearing up the road, way over speed. Marco poked his head out the window as he pulled a U and stopped at Anthony's feet. "Sorry, sorry, sorry. Got tied up . . . I'll explain."

Anthony wasn't about to let Marco off that easy and stayed outside the cab long enough for Marco to read the displeasure in his face.

On the turnpike, Marco stuck his elbow out the window. "You don't have to get all quiet on me, guy."

"I'm tired and I want coffee."

"You want coffee? You got it. We're gonna stop for coffee. Right by the Journal Square there's Dunkin Donuts." Anthony was silent. "C'mon," Marco said. "Give a guy a break."

Anthony drew a deep breath. "Marco, my friend, everybody has a set amount of breaks in this life. Nobody's any luckier than anybody else." People didn't realize that the American Dream wasn't Lotto, or in Marco's case, hitting it big at the track. You work your tail off and maybe, if you really push yourself, you see pay-day. Anthony told Marco, "When your ship comes in, you've got to be on time for it. Now would you close that window? I've had my share of the cold."

Marco pulled his elbow in and did as Anthony said. "Look, I told you I can explain."

Anthony raised a hand, "No! No explanation. No excuses."

"That really ain't fair, guy."

"Fair? You want fair? Look at that!" They were passing Ellis Island. Today, the sky was clear and you could also see Liberty from torch to sandal. "You pass it just about every day. But do you ever think about it? Huh, Marco? Do you? What do you think liberty means? That the world's your oyster? No, that's not what it means at all. It means you're on your own, it's all up to you, you either show up for the prize or it goes to the runner-up."

"Listen—"

"No, you listen." Anthony felt his blood rise. All that work for this guy, and him just looking for a hand-out . . . "You know what an explanation means? It means you missed the boat. It's leaving, Marco. See it? It's in the middle of the ocean and there you are on the dock, going nowhere, shouting your excuses at the top of your lungs, but the boat, the boat just keeps going. Bad hand or no hand, you've got to pull your own load."

"Listen—"

"And what the hell have you been trying to put over on me, anyway?" Anthony's hands curled into fists. "Good Catholic, my ass. Drinking on the job . . . in debt up to your eyeballs. I figured you for a hard-working guy who'd just made a few mistakes. So I checked on your case. Do you know what my time costs people? But then you should know you don't get something for nothing. One hand washes the other. That's America. That's liberty."

"Listen, I never asked you for . . . " Marco started, but Anthony wouldn't stop.

"My old man never relied on anyone but himself—" The words slid back down Anthony's throat as Marco swung the cab off the road and threw it into park.

He flung his arm over the front seat and faced Anthony as fully as he could. "Who the fuck do you think you are? You don't know my problems. You're no better than me. So you had an old man who pushed your ass, but you're still a guinea, pal. You got that? You know who you're like? Those uppity types, get some fuckin' scholarship and forget all about where they come from. Forget all about real people with real problems and just blame us for everythin', so they don't have to feel guilty for their own cushy rides. I know what you white collar types get away with." A vein stood out on Marco's forehead. Traffic swished by.

Marco said, "You don't know me. Got that? You don't know my life and what I've had to deal with. You don't even know yourself. Face it. No matter where you live, you're a guinea like me. You're Vinny Barbarino, Sly Stallone, 'Lucky' Luciano. You sure-as-shit ain't no Robert Redford . . . and if you think so, you're living in Disneyland. So, before you go tellin me who I am, you better think about who you are . . . "

Ooooh, if Marco would only let him, Anthony'd give a list of answers to that one: A worker. A scholar. A man of stature. A man, period. A man who took what God and his old man gave him and ran with it. An independent man. A man who represented the growth of his people. And, most importantly, a responsible man. And there was more. Much, much more. If only Marco's eyes weren't so sharp, weren't such a sure sign that he was getting ready to say something else.

He Who Serves Two Masters
Disappoints One ... or Both
José Antonio Burciaga

This selection, from *Drink Cultura: Chicanismo,* explains the figurative and literal identity of Chicanos. Burciaga ends his essay with the ending logo C/ S, *con safos*—literally "with safety," which means, "anything you say against me will bounce back to you . . . whether you like it or not, this is my reality."

"This question may bother you," began the radio interviewer in Mexico City, "But do you write as a Mexicano or . . . ?"

The question trailed off but he didn't have to finish that one question forever asked of Chicanos by Mexicanos. "What exactly are you?"

The question was not only expected but welcomed, so the answer was quick and enthusiastic, "*Yo soy Mexicano!*" I answered, but added in Spanish, "And I am a *gabacho!* Culturally, I have as much of the Mexicano as I do of the gringo. I am as comfortable with the Mexican as I am with the Anglo-American culture."

Never before had I claimed to be a gabacho or even thought of myself as one, much less proclaimed it in a live radio interview. Yet at that instant I found it necessary to emphasize and reaffirm my cultural and patriotic allegiance to the United States of America. Not to U.S. policy in *Latinoamérica* but to the United States of the people. I am hamburgers and hot dogs.

The Chicano Movement was an act of identity and self-determination. It was meant to dispel the notion of inferiority of *Mexicano-Norteamericanos*. It was a reaffirmation of our indigenous ancestry as well as our Mexican ancestry. But we never claimed to be gringos. On the contrary, we fought the yoke of the gringo oppressor while aspiring for equal opportunities.

We are both. We are "the vanquished, the victor," wrote Corky Gonzalez in his epic poem, "I am Joaquín." Poet José Montoya said it another way, " . . . the theys are us," and

Pogo's famous line, "We have met the enemy and it is us," was all too applicable to the Mexican-American. Another friend said, "I'm Mexican by nature and American by nurture." We were caught on the razor sharp edge of two vastly different cultures, and in trying to identify with each side, while condemned by both sides, we denounced both and identified as a third alternative with a little and a lot from each side. We became Chicanos.

Born "razed" and "edgiekated" on the border, I crossed the Río Grande daily into *la madre patria*. It was the old world, returning to the past, nostalgic trips into day dreams of sights, sounds, street and kitchen odors. This is where grandmothers, aunts, uncles and cousins lived in Mexico. But through the brutal reality of childhood they opened our eyes to the fact that we were not Mexicanos. We were *pochos*, bastardized Mexicanos! A pocho, the Spanish dictionary states, is spoiled fruit. If anyone was vilified more than the Chicano, it was the gringo. Then I was a Mexicano to them because they would tell me the sins of Ango-American character I was picking up, losing my Mexicanness.

Years later, while I was stationed in Spain, a few Spaniards would tell me of their bitter dislike of the Anglo-American. "I tell you this because you are not an Americano!" You are a Mexicano! You are not like one of them. You know the difference!" My silence was one of humorous bewilderment to be considered *más* Español than Americano.

As occasional trips take me back to Mexico I continue to hear the bickering and complaints about the Americanos. Finally, I told one Mexican friend that I was tired of hearing my *paisanos gringos* insulted. She was speechless as I explained my earlier comment, that culturally, I had assimilated much of the Ango-American culture. Chicanos have the advantage of maintaining the best human values of both cultures.

Some people have always considered Chicanos gringos. Frank Del Olmo, the *Los Angeles Times* editorial writer, likes to tell about the time in Nicaragua when a *campesino* asked him if he was a gringo or not. Frank explained at length to the campesino that he was a Chicano. Then the campesino again asked him, "Well are you, or are you not a gringo?"

As relations between Mexicanos and Chicanos warm and grow each day, there is a tendency for Mexicanos to confuse what exactly a Chicano is. The word Chicano has caught on in Mexico.

According to Rodolfo de la Garza, University of Texas at Austin professor, Mexicans have begun to romanticize Chicano history as they understand it through the movies and literature. De la Garza compares this to the Chicanos' romanticization of Mexico during the Chicano movement.

More recently, the Mexican government and press have at times named all Mexicans residing in the United States Chicanos. The documented and the undocumented Mexican population in this country is enormous when it includes Chicanos. Thirty million by the 21st century? Our importance is critical to Mexico's future.

Mexico sees, or is blinded by, the potential lobby of both the Mexican residents in the United States and the actual Mexican-Americans, Chicanos. But the Chicano now seems to be saying, "*Un momento!* Not so *rápido!* Don't take me for granted. I am a United States–born citizen."

If Mexico thinks we have sold out, consider the other half of the story. In this country, Chicanos are Mexico's biggest defenders. After the recent formation of a Mexican Commission on Human Rights along the border, the Commission quickly realized that Chicanos in the United States have long struggled for the rights of Mexican citizens in this country. What Chicanos do not necessarily support is the Mexican government or the ruling PRI party.

While we may defend and protect the United States' national character in Mexico, we also defend and protect the Mexican national character in the United States. This may seem like a contradiction, but culturally we are tied to our mother country. "We are binational," say Luís Valdez. At the same time what flows in our veins is not necessarily what flows in our brains. We are a bridge with only one political allegiance—the United States. As the Spanish saying goes, "He who serves two masters, disappoints one of them, or both."

That narrow border where I grew up has expanded and has been sighted in Alaska. Mexicanos, Chicanos and their culture live in greater numbers in the interior of the United States. Our bilingual, bicultural, binational experience is a form of schizophrenia, rich and poor, sun and shadow, between realism and surrealism. To live on the border is to live in the center. The center unites and separates the four directions. To live on the border unites and separates two cultures, two worlds, to be at the entrance and the exit and to be able to accept both. These cultures cross each other not to assimilate one another, but to "transculturate."

C/S

The Shouting Within Us
Carolyn Flynn

Carolyn Flynn is a writer living in Santa Cruz, California. She is working on a book about her journey to discover her ancestors who were born during the Famine times in Ireland, and their descendants. Her work has apeared in *Earth's Daughters, Black Buzzard Review, Heron Lake Anthology* and Deena Metzger's *Writing for Your Life.*

The spring days are chilling, though outside the air is bright like crystal. It is green here in Washington, D.C., and after all the years I had forgotten. Upstairs in my bedroom I can see the tops of trees, like when I was a kid living in the attic, its third floor, and my kinship with all who lived in the uppermost regions of branches and leaves. No wonder I want to be with birds.

Going through the endless, disgusting piles of family history, I have found some jewels, though I don't have the historian's happiness or the researcher's calm. I go through the materials like a lion trying to rip something apart that insists instead upon getting bigger and more strong as I wrestle. I know the materials are pounding me down, that I am losing the battle though I continue, merciless upon my own faltering self, going through more, and more, as though, as though ... what? What is it I think will happen? As though some golden miracle will open up the sky and rain down the answers, if I just find that one key old photograph. Suddenly I will understand, having been alighted upon, and, floating home, I will sit down at my desk and write it all out, simple, like a tree growing, easy, like it is meant. As though the gods will say: You didn't know what you were doing but you came anyway and kept at it, so now we're rewarding you with it all. Here you go.

But of course such a thing does not happen and anyway how would I know if it did? I sit in that musty and dusty basement, oppressed and unhappy, aimlessly wandering through the scraps of this family, finding plenty of gold, probably, but there are so many unearthed piles, *so much still to look through*, it doesn't seem fitting to linger with what I've got in my hands. OK, I think to myself, there it is, that's good, OK, but *what's* over there in that pile? Finally I made a system of 20 or so labeled boxes so that I could go back and find again what I've unearthed, these boxes laid out on the double bed incongruously sitting smack in the middle of my parents' basement. The boxes used to house my mother's old checks. *They threw away everything that mattered, and kept the stuff that you could easily replace! Jeeesh!* my mother says of the fact that my father sent a handyman down to the basement and had him throw away anything dated prior to, oh say, 1980. Key financial records, gone, major papers documenting the history of the family business, what they did and when, and how . . . gone. This is the story of my parents' one big battle. She is an accumulator, he a . . . what? What is the word for him, or was he simply battling against her constant tendency to gather and keep *everything*, what he saw as a constant array of useless junk? Or did he have inside him an equal and opposite tendency to clean things out, keep life simple and organized, to disburse away from himself what was not essential? I think he did. And I feel these two tendencies working their way through my soul. For many years I was unequivocally on my mother's side—feeling my father's sometimes cruel tendency to throw away what mattered to my mother to be what it was, a real disrespect. Still, some new tendency has come upon me, I notice, particularly as I was cleaning out my house and my life to leave Santa Cruz for a year researching my family's history. *Here, take this*, I said endlessly to my friends. I sold all sorts of useless (now, to me) things at a huge yard sale. This was the act of someone about to die, and this was no little metaphor but the truth as I was going through a death of a certain self, a life, an attitude—in order to absorb an even older family truth.

So now I come to understand my father's instincts even as I hate his methods. Traveling with my mother to Ireland recently I watched in amazement as she collected little shampoo bottles from each hotel, to bring home and add to her collection of hundreds of equal little bottles and shitty little shampoos. Who knows, some day we could need these things, she tells herself of her hoarding, and everyone will thank god I saved them. On the Russian flight home the stewardess tried to hand me a little doll with a bottle of cheap perfume inside, and I said No, no give it to someone else, and my mother, to my astonishment, though she had one in her hands, said she'd like to have mine too. Why on earth? I asked and she said you never know, maybe she'd give it as a gift. And I shook my head and felt my father's disgusted grunt move through me. *OK, OK,* I said to his ghost traveling with us, *don't think I'll go all the way into your camp. But, it is amazing isn't it?* and he smiled and said *Yep you know now what I mean.*

And still I think, reading as I am Michael Ortiz Hill's *Dreaming the End of the World: Apocalypse as a Right of Passage,* that some end is coming—a change of an era and with it great upheaval—and there will be those of us who prepared by divesting ourselves, and those who prepared by hoarding. At my mother's it could be that those little bottles of shampoo save us from some dirt . . . assuming we have water . . . and who knows what else she has accumulated that will make a difference in that world where all structure has fallen apart and there is nothing left?

One dream Ortiz Hill quotes made me think of what it must have been like during the Great Famine in Ireland:

A terrible, apocalyptic time. Nature is being destroyed, everything is disintegrating, and we are all going to die. It could be the result of war or it could be something else. The most obvious aspect is the physical disintegration and chaos. In the house, everything is permeated with dirt and is disarranged. Our mood is that of people with a fatal disease who are waiting to die.

Last week I went to a lecture on the Great Famine by Joe Lee, a professor at Cork University and an Irish Senator. The figure: 1.1 million people dead. Ten times greater than any famine of this century. Over 2 million Irish emigrate to the United States and Britain. All of this in just four years, between 1846 and 1850. A population decimated and halved. Here is the trend it initiated and which continues today: 8.5 million people lived in Ireland in 1840;

4 million people lived there in 1910. Currently, 3.5 million Irish live in Ireland. And get this: *44 million* Irish-Americans live in the USA. 44 million. The Famine was the death knell of a country, Professor Lee said. The Irish-speaking Ireland, the poorer classes, the ancient and historic culture of the country, three-quarters buried.

Imagine the psychological torture, says Professor Lee. Does a starving family feed the breadwinner in the hope he could earn enough to buy food for the rest, or feed the weakest, the child in immediate danger of dying? These were heartbreaking day-to-day decisions, made within the family, by the mother usually. There were cases of cannibalism, Professor Lee said, but the bulk of the Irish died decently, *sometimes in one other's arms.* And this evoked for me Yeats in "Sailing to Byzantium":

That is no country for old men. The young
in one another's arms, birds in the trees,
—Those dying generations—

The famine decomposed a society, says Professor Lee, killed from the inside out. Although there were work-house deaths, deaths on the roads and in ditches, most deaths occurred at home within families. Death from starvation, he says, takes about two months. Death from famine fever, apparently the more common way famine struck, took 11 days. Think of the decisions regarding the allocation of food, think of it. The calculation necessary, a kind of constant form of life-boat economics—which loved one gets thrown overboard, and who first?

Professor Lee is interested in memory. By definition only survivors live to tell the tale. And who are they? How do they live? The poorest died, simply. Those with some little money sent one son or one young couple away. They held an American Wake, for those leaving were as good as dying, would not be seen again. There was tearful breaking away as the survivors were put upon a boat and all prayed it would arrive safely in harbor, for so many boats sunk in the rough Atlantic during the 1840s that they were called coffin ships. And what is the memory of a famine survivor? They have sailed away, and again the metaphors do not do justice, for they themselves *are* in a sinking ship, they may not survive the passage, and still, and still, it is the sinking ship of their mother country that they cannot bear to leave and must leave, to become the ancestors of those 44 million in America. To live when so many of the rest will die.

They were filled with a sense of guilt, not anger, but guilt—*why me? Why did I survive?* And here, Professor Lee says, Holocaust oral history helps, for though the Great Famine is by no means the Holocaust, still there is a common theme of response of survivors to great extremity. Irish-American history in the 1850s shows a "seething vortex of hideous memories . . . combustible victimhood, a sense of inarticulate rage." Letters that made their way from Ireland to America surely contained some hideous news, the death of a parent, often, and there was a sense of great failure, in a culture with family so central to identity, to miss a funeral. It was a rupture, the sense of breaking, with many a wound raked over anew. And the children in an immigrant family—Where's granny? Where are the memories? How are they transmitted? Where is the continuing relationship with Ireland, and what shall that be, if anything? How is collective memory transmitted? What is transmitted, Professor Lee asks, and what is lost?

We are the descendants of the dying culture of Ireland, of the survivors who ultimately sailed to these shores and stonily looked ahead. I am the granddaughter of a laughter-filled Irishwoman who arrived on this land in 1914, and whose throat was filled with silences. *They never talked about anything*, says my sister who spent her summers with Grandma Flynn and Aunty May. The silence was thick as the air, transmuted into family battles, alcoholism and despair. Silence consumed us, and flooded the family stories as they have been whispered over the years. It bled out of my Aunt Pauline's womb as she and her first child died in childbirth in 1945, rarely to be spoken of again. It exploded as my Aunt May as a young woman crashed head first into the windshield of a 1920s car. It rattled in the furious tremors as her sister Peggy died an alcohol-induced death four decades later. Silences explode us from within, like famine eats us, so that we die from inside out. The oppressor no longer need do a thing. What dies inside continues to kill, if it has not been able to die all the way, properly into the realm of the dark; to give over identity and a kind of hope. What has died but does not really die looks for any kind of refuge and crouches there. Whole selves remain crouched in those places for entire lifetimes, alone and unknown, even to themselves.

I find myself thinking of my Aunt May, who I loved, and the life she lost in the windshield and the life she could never recover because silence is a long-learned and harsh ruler. Her accident became confined to a black box, fairly bulging, of what was not to be spoken. What is not spoken cannot be grieved, healed, known or, ultimately, released. These were survivors, and descendants of survivors. As am I. Annie Breheny Flynn was determined to come to the U.S. and make a future out of air for her children. And I imagine May as a young girl living in a household with three families in two bedrooms—gazing in the mirror for afternoons at a time, seeing a beautiful, separate creature there, someone who had the possibility of escape. All cracked as the mirror shattered in front of her, as she was thrown through a windshield. Afterwards mirrors became death-wielding things which she covered in black, evoking a funeral, for a girl had died, and desperation had been born. It wore a face with scars that eventually healed but the eyes of a heartbroken soul.

Sometimes in those early days of our childhood Aunt May could glare at you across the room as though the devil owned you and only her eyes could begin to assess the damage. *It seems Aunty May was always yelling at us,* says my sister Pauline. *And there was some problem between her and Aunty Peggy, but they never talked about it so I never really knew . . .*

But of course you knew, dear sister, of course you knew, you ate it in your summer stew and shit it out each night in the little cramped bathroom. Of course you knew because silence looms so loud that children imbibe it via the pores of their skin, and through the openings of their souls that are so able to hear invisible songs. Children know everything and we forget this because we are the children who once knew everything and had to forget. There was steep punishment for coming near to truth. Ma Flynn could grab a grandchild by the ear and squeeze until she'd squeezed out the gallons of tears she wanted. She swam in those tears and us children did too, and we remembered, then—we remembered to forget; it wasn't to be spoken and it wasn't to be said and it wasn't to be known. We became adults who had known everything and who had swum in and drunk up our own forgetting.

And the children in our arms—we've forgotten too that they know everything, and when they show us their knowledge some forgotten fear rises up inside us to kill the thing, for that is what we learned all survival depended upon. *Kill the thing* the rage rose up inside us and however we managed it, we too tried to smother the knowledge in the young around us. We too, we could not escape, though the times were different and we'd drunk in the Beatles *All you need is love, everybody now* . . . And though the bitter juice my generation sipped was more likely from a synthetic bottle rather than our mothers' breasts, the formula as sure as ever contained the right combination of chemical-induced intoxication from truth. We were of a different era and we said we'd do it differently and we did, we did, we really did, but we were of a different kind not a different order. One cannot escape one's ancestors, the shouting within us, and voices strewn across the drowned landscapes of our souls. We all swim that landscape together, us and the dead around us, except now the dead are not so afraid of truth and are tired of the silences they taught us so well. *Tell the story!* they cry out but we all say *No Grandma! I don't remember! Don't you remember what you taught me?* And some remnant ghost of that accordion-playing Annie Flynn cries out *Tell the story! Tell my story! I don't want to die forever* . . .

And so this is it. This is what the ancestors want, and who can blame them? They don't want to die forever. They want to live in that elusive thing Professor Lee was talking about, they want to live in memory and who does that fall to but their descendants? It is our job to sing them into memory, and with them all who came before them, but we don't know their stories, we don't know their heartaches, their truths, and who cares about this, who cares, but the ghosts, the dead ones, the ones aching, aching. For what? They are now in a realm in which they see all. They are themselves and they are not themselves, they are like those children with open souls who could drink invisible songs, it's all around them now and it doesn't kill . . . *It doesn't kill,* they want to shout to us, *no matter what we thought when we were with you . . . The stories don't kill, but the loss of them does. You don't have to die that silenced, famine-struck death. You are not wrong to be the descendants of survivors, you are not wrong to be on this earth. Don't believe what I taught you! Don't believe what I inscribed on your soul! Listen past that to this song as the trees rustle next to you. That's me, I tell you, that's me! I'm trying to get to you! What are the tools I have but this earth, conspiring to help me tell my tale . . .*

And so, my father did his duty, threw out everything with stories, threw out anything that was dusty and ugly and shouted history. He was taught well and with strong, determined hands. He loved his mother Ma Flynn with the kind of love the Irish do so well—a kind of veneration bordering on sainthood and the equal sense that mothers are flitting creatures to be protected and chuckled at. Mother looms large and is ignored in equal parts by Irish men, and by mother of course I mean The Mother writ large, the She who inspired so much poetry and awe the first many millennia of human culture. Now dead in a bathtub, now imprisoned in someone's backyard. . . . *now I know that twenty centuries of stony sleep were vexed to nightmare by a rocking cradle,* writes Yeats in "The Second Coming." We are at the end of the twenty centuries and surely something is coming, some *rough beast, its hour come round at last. . . .* And we whose life purpose is to face this coming, this beast, this chaos born of change as some new cycle is painfully born and something old dies, what of us? I am the child of this apathy and this hostility, this twenty centuries of nightmare, and I sit in my parents' basement surrounded by the ancestors' lives and their stories and all I want is to flee in terror. The bile rises in my throat and wasn't I taught, too, wasn't I taught that it is sacrilege and the stories are dangerous? I sit in the burning basement and the hidden stories are full of heartbreak, though the people in the photographs are smiling, mostly, the stories are napalm to my skin and death to the song in my throat. Suddenly I can't breathe and I think it's the mustiness of the basement and I think *I've got to work somewhere else, I can't work here.* I open the little basement door and outside there is sunshine and dogwood blossoms and probably a mourning dove will sing to me if I wait long enough. In here are the stories and I say: *Forget it. What did you think, I could just simply fly out of your legacy and become someone else altogether? What did you think, that I was immune to the heartache, and the terror? Forget it. Isn't there sunshine outside that door? Why must I live here and drown here? Someone said a basement is like a fallout shelter, where one can go to escape, but in truth it is the place we face ourselves. Well, I don't like what I see. I've got to get a little sunshine or I will surely die, expire onto these piles of photographs screaming their unsaid stories, like so much flattened memory. Is that what you want, for me to join you prematurely? I'm getting out of here, and out of here and far away from here.*

And the ancestors say, Yes go. It is right. You are the instrument of our faith. So go, dear one, fly away. Surely it is us who taught you to fly all those years ago, and surely it is us who will bring you here again, down into this basement. But birds do need to fly and in that flight, look down and see what even we sometimes can't. So go, dear one. Go. You will be back.

Leaving California for Ireland
Carolyn Flynn

I pack my treasured items, preparing for the sojourn
across continent and ocean. I like to pretend
I'm traveling in a golden chariot, in some kind of glory.
I like to insist I know what I'm doing
because blind assurance is sometimes the only way
to climb to the top of one's own mountain.

I leave a life because another one calls.
I leave a life because something has to be sacrificed.
I leave a life because my face has begun to fall,
and there are lines about the eyes
and some sadness beckons me, says to come this way.
I want to hug and coddle him, this sadness,
I want to walk in the heart of the disappointed life.
I want to know grime and grit and the daily carrying
of water from a well to a house draped in poverty.

I come from the poor of Ireland. I do not go off
into some bright future, but into the arms of sadness,
the failure of a people and an island to flourish.
We're losing everything there: a language, a culture,
a myth, a story. Yet something tenacious holds on,
growing weed-like inside one of Ireland's granddaughters,
born on American soil, two generations from the land
and still heartbroken for it. They burn peat in Ireland
for fires, boggy land dried hard and ancient, they burn
the land and breathe the flames, drink in the land
and that night tell its tales to their young, who grow up,
leave the island, come to America, poverty-stricken
and alcoholic. They bear children who grow up
struggling and poor, who bear children who become
the new America, all white and shiny and *tabula rasa*.
Except some weed grows inside us, some great
yearning for something we can't name and don't know,

and all we know is the emptiness inside us,
that we are placeless and the landscape around us
does not know our name.

I like to believe I'm going in a golden chariot,
surrounded by glory and wild animals,
but in truth I'm straggling home,
looking, please god, looking, for the place I belong.
I have been expatriate, stranger, and orphan.
What I'd like to be next is someone at home.

ABCs
Deanna Tseying Fei

Deanna Tseying Fei is an aspiring Asian American writer.

Growing up
Getting to know the alphabet from the gang
at *Sesame Street*
Teaching my grandma how to read English
with my own narrow knowledge:
NO It's *h*our, not "our"!
You have to say the *h!*
Now read that over again fifty times.
(She humored me).
Then
reading stories to my little sister
in my own broken Chinese.
She has to learn Chinese first
(my mother says)
because later on she'll just forget anyway.
Better teach it now—maybe
she'll retain a little.
Well,
(my mother says)
I guess it's time.
So I teach her A, B, and C.
Apple Banana Coconut
Amy Brian Carl
American Born Chinese.
White people say,
with bad pronunciation,
—even worse than mine—
Ni hao ma? and Gung ho fat choy!
and think they are not only
multicultural, but witty
as well.
I go to camp
(black head among blonds)

Terri thinks we'll be best friends because
she can use chopsticks and knows
not all Orientals are Chinks
(there are gooks and japs too.)
Other Asian kids
(mostly my friends)
sing Korean or Chinese pop songs that are
all wannabe American
(all over the world that's the cool thing to be)
and think they're in touch with their roots.
I was born in Flushing Hospital
Queens
New York
the U S of A
and I think I am—American?
Christmas day, gazing
at the Rockefeller tree,
this redneck looks at us amazed.
You speak English real good!
(he says) Where y'all from?
Peking, I say as I turn away.
And it's *well*, not *good*.

Yard Sale
Faye Moskowitz

Faye Moskowitz is Chair and Professor of English at George Washington University. She is author of *A Leak in the Heart* (1985), *Whoever Finds This: I Love You* (1988), and *Her Face in the Mirror: Jewish Women on Mothers and Daughters* (1994). This selection is taken from *And the Bridge Is Love* (1991).

I never stop believing I'll find something worth keeping at a yard sale. Years of sorting through dusty depressing plastic flower arrangements and mismatched crazed crockery have failed to dampen my bargain hunter's spirit. among those impossible lamps a genuine Tiffany just might be hiding, somewhere in this world there exists a Rip Van Winkle type who doesn't yet know what an old patchwork quilt is worth.

That's why one lazy summer day out in the Virginia countryside where we have a weekend place for years I cruised the back road in search of the perfect yard sale. The professional looking signs that alerted me a half mile down the road, and eventually the house itself, a substantial brick rambler, gave promise of some better-than-average pickings, so I parked my car on the shoulder and made my way over the grass, past two rusty power lawnmowers and a red mower (for sale), and a white-painted tire planted with purple and white petunias (not for sale).

I felt wonderful, the scent of a potential bargain making blood sing in my ears. Leisurely, I circled the two aluminum folding tables that had been set up to display a toaster, a set of electric hair-curlers, a box of hair nets in their original individual packages, assorted greeting cards, children's clothing, plastic toys, *Readers Digest* condensed books, and Cozzens' ubiquitous *By Love Possessed*—in short, the usual yard sale fare. But that pitcher holding some kitchen gadgets might have been handmade. It was just ugly enough to be interesting, with its leaf-green base that burst into a crown of violet flowers at the lip and rim. Definitely a possibility. And what about that chenille bedspread, sporting a peacock with his trailing trail outlined in yellow and pink and lime green art deco colors. Wasn't it so hideous it might be fun?

Mentally, I put on my shrewd bargain hunter's cap, prepared to be ruthless in my dickering with whichever of the three gray-haired women sitting in plastic lawn chairs claimed ownership of either item. "Y'all live around here?" one of the women asked, approaching me. "Boston," I replied, naming the little village where we get our country mail. "Washington?" she said, not hearing me, but I insisted on establishing local credentials so I said "Boston" again, "Boston, Virginia." In moments she had me pegged, had located our farm, knew the people from whom we had bought it years before, told me her name—Dolly Corbin. We began jabbering away about nothing: the weather, how various garden crops were doing—the polite ceremonial talk before money is exchanged in the country.

And then my would-be saleslady was distracted by the small verbal exchange between one of the other women and a tall beefy man in Bermuda shorts and a loud Hawaiian shirt. I began looking in my purse. The asking price for the pitcher was four dollars; the spread was marked eight. Ten dollars seemed like a good price to offer for both items.

"Oh, no," the woman was telling Bermuda Shorts, and the third woman called out from her perch on the lawn chair, "What's he trying to do?" The tall man grinned sheepishly and said, "Wal, you're *supposed* to bargain at a sale." By this time they were all getting into the act. Dolly wiggled her tight gray curls, fresh from the beauty parlor. "You ain't a Jew, are you?" she asked playfully, looking the man up and down. "You're acting like a Jew, tryin' to jew her down!"

Now I ask myself why I didn't just turn around and walk back across the lawn and down the narrow highway shoulder to my car. I could have let them all put two and two together, as they say around there. I didn't need to become Mrs. Sixties Relevant again. But I was angry about my sweet day suddenly turned sour. Only the week before I had read a front-page article in the *Washington Post* that said Polish peasants remained stubbornly anti-Semitic, that the prejudice was in their folk culture, in their bones. "Who in hell have they got to be anti-Semitic about?" I had shouted at my poor husband, who was hidden behind his section of the morning paper. "The Polish Jews are all dead anyhow."

Shortly after my husband and I married, we moved to Oak Park, a new suburb of Detroit. There we helped form a local Democratic club and joined the county Democratic party in hopes of purging it of the Teamsters, who dominated the organization then. With others we formed a liberal/labor caucus and in a surprisingly short time I was chairman of our city club, while my husband was persuaded to run for state representative. We wore a track down Woodward Avenue, driving back and forth to Pontiac, the county seat, for meetings.

Our county chairman was an old party hack, amiable enough, a local businessman who had been around Democratic politics forever. Whatever he thought about the influx of young couples from Detroit, he must have realized that we were there to stay. So he patiently put up with our naïveté, our often sanctimonious insistence on being issue-oriented, our stuffy nit-picking to the tune of Robert's Rules. And we in our turn looked to the aging party bosses as relics from another time, with the same fascinating but distant relationship to us as the old iceboxes that still sat in our parents' garages in Detroit or the washboards in their basements.

Though we were drawn to the rich lode of political lore the old pols possessed, we often found the atmosphere in the smoke-filled rooms stifling. How could we fail to notice the patronizing way our chairman spoke to the few blacks who belonged to the party, or ignore his calling them "darkies" behind their backs, how many times could we listen to him brag about "buying low and selling high" in one breath and "jewing 'em down" in the next? My husband and I had long, very serious discussions about whether it would do any good to speak to Calvin. "He doesn't really mean anything by it," is what my husband said. "It's habit . . . automatic part of the local dialect. And anyway, he won't change."

Whether Calvin's attitudes were mere convention or not, they wormed at me, caused anger to burrow away somewhere deep inside. In the first place we weren't all that comfortable yet about being Jews in Oakland County. Perhaps we remembered how rigidly the lakes had been segregated out there: this one for Jews, that one for Christians only. For all I knew, protective covenants were still the order of the day, real estate agents were simply more discreet about it than before.

Nevertheless I couldn't let it go. One evening I managed to get my chairman alone for a moment before a county committee meeting. "Calvin," I said, taking a deep breath, "I know you don't mean anything by it," lying through my teeth, "but some of us are upset by certain ways you have of putting things. Now you and I both know it's just a way of speaking. Still I thought I'd sort of remind you that saying 'jew 'em down' and 'darkie' really offends people. You're the Democratic county chairman, you're supposed to set an example." Calvin looked at me with the same degree of concern as if I had just told him he'd picked up the wrong fork at the Dairy Workers' banquet, "Honey," he said, "nobody pays any attention to stuff like that. You're too sensitive."

By that time I was sorry I had bothered to bring the matter up at all. We walked into the meeting together, Calvin's arm around my shoulders. He did everything but give me a conciliatory pat on the rear. During the course of the meeting, Calvin made a progress report on his negotiations for the building where we were to have our county convention. "We're still some dollars apart on the price of the extra caucus rooms," Calvin said, "but I think we can jew 'em down a little more." Then he looked at me from over his half-glasses. "No offense, Faye," he said. That was consciousness-raising in the fifties.

Slowly Dolly Corbin came back into focus. "Look," I said to her. "Look . . . " finding it difficult to break into the conversation, as if it were enclosed in a membrane. "I was going to make an offer on that spread there. You're supposed to bargain at a yard sale, everyone knows that. It has nothing to do with being a Jew, though I happen to be one. People like a good buy. That's why they come to yard sales in the first place."

And all the while I was delivering my speech, Dolly Corbin was slowly backing away from me. Recoiling is what it was; I don't know any other way to describe it. "I was just kiddin' him," she said, pale suddenly except for the patchy rouge on her cheeks. "I didn't mean anything by it." Of course I felt instantly sorry for her, sorry I'd made a fuss, still something in me made me push on. "But we can't keep doing that to each other," I said. "Just because someone wants the best price doesn't make him a Jew. I'll bet you don't even know any Jews!"

"I didn't mean anything by it," Dolly said again with a strange small smile. "We was all kiddin' around." "But you hurt people," I insisted, surprised at the old pain welling up in me, the prickling in my nose, the sudden tears. "You hurt people, and you say you don't mean it, but you keep on doing it."

I turned and walked back to my car, conscious of Mrs. Corbin's "I'm sorry" trailing after me. "Yeah, you're sorry all right, sorry you lost a sale, you old bag," I muttered, just plain angry now, sick of the stereotypes, the assumption behind her remarks that everyone felt as she did, that she could say what she did as she probably had all her life without anyone calling her on it. On top of it all, I felt suddenly vulnerable. Dolly Corbin knew who I was, where I lived. Why had I made such a scene about being Jewish? Now she would send her redneck relatives to burn crosses in front of our house.

Driving back to our farm, I hardly noticed the Queen Anne's lace trimming the selvages of the fields, the patches of bright blue chicory and wild ox-eyed daisies everywhere. The day was ruined for me. I kept thinking that forty years had gone by since I argued with Calvin about the same kind of "harmless" labeling, and nothing had really changed except that Calvin was long dead and I was now as old as he was then.

This morning's *Post* carries an article with the dateline of Obergammergau, West Germany, where a passion play has been produced every ten years or so since the early seventeenth century. According to the story, Obergammergau residents are angry with Jews who boycotted the passion in 1970 and who continue to claim that parts of the six-hour play about the life of Christ are anti-Semitic. The article goes on to say that surveys show that there remains in Germany "a firmly anti-Semitic core of 15 percent." So what else is new?

Driving around a circle on Connecticut Avenue later in the morning, I pass two young women in picture hats waving picket signs from the sidewalk. Their placards read, "Free Tibet." The front pages are so crowded with bad news I have to maneuver the circle twice before the message registers. Free Tibet? Get serious, guys. What makes you think anyone will notice you in your silly hats, and more than that, what makes you think that anyone has time to worry about yet another injustice.

The funny thing is, I keep thinking about the women and their signs, and when I go around the circle one last time, they dip those placards at me once again. Free Tibet? Well, why not. Thumbs up, I say, sticking my hand out the window. It isn't much, but you can't believe how good that makes me feel.

Gorda, Mama and Victor
Angie Cruz

Angie Cruz, a Dominican-American writer born in New York City, has published two novels *Soledad* and *Let it Rain Coffee*. "Gorda," "Mama," and "Victor" are samples of her early work, *Voices on 164th Street*, about Dominican and Dominican-American women and men who have found ways to translate and transplant Dominican culture to Manhattan's Washington Heights.

Gorda

"Hola, Mujer." Gorda gestures for me to come into her apartment. She pulls off the new hair dryer that covers her head like a shower cap. "Look, I can walk around with it on." She turns around to show me the transparent tube that connects her to the wall.

I go into her kitchen and put the Tupperware container filled with rice and chicken my grandmother just made on the counter top. I peek inside Gorda's pots sitting on the stove. She's making beef stew.

"You hungry?" she asks me slipping her arm around my waist.

"No, just curious," I answer.

"It mustn't have looked too good. Eh?" I don't respond.

Everyone calls her Gorda, because her cheeks have lots of meat in them. Her real name is Luna. "My mother said I was born under a full moon, outside, on one of those long horse trips people used to take before cars. That's why she called me what she did." She doesn't mind being called Gorda. The name stuck, ever since she was a kid.

Some people say Gorda is full of nonsense. They say she doesn't know what she's talking about. She says they are afraid of what she has to tell them. She reads the patterns coffee grinds make in someone's cup after they drink from it; she holds palms and feels pulses. She can tell them what will happen in their immediate future. Sometimes it scares people away. "If they don't want to know the truth, why do they ask?"

Gorda looks at my face,

"Look at you, I sense you're in love."

"Actually I'm not."

"You just broke up with somebody?"

"No, Gorda, nothing's new. I would tell you if it was otherwise." Gorda has a way of pulling thoughts out of me, even before I know I have them. I am avoiding Gorda's ability to read my body language and sense of spirit. She says she stole a slice of my spirit when I wasn't looking. She keeps it in a bottle in her room, so she can pray for me.

"We're soul sisters, do you know that? You understand me and you are still so young." She said this many times, while we sat at her kitchen table and painted our nails in ruby red, sometimes champagne pink. She said it again when we spent hours looking outside her kitchen window, both our elbows rubbing on the concrete window sill, talking about how we both belong in the water. "We're both fishes you know. That is why no one understands us. We're out of our element."

Gorda treats me in ways that make my mother nervous, "Don't listen to her, she's crazy you know." My grandmother laughs about it, "She's not crazy, just misunderstood." My grandmother also belongs in the water.

Ever since I was a child Gorda talked to me like a friend. It's more than I can say for most adults who believed all I understood was, "Do this and do that, or don't, not yet, another time and I'm busy." Gorda always wanted to share stories with me about her daughter Flaca. Flaca is her name because her bones stick out around her neck and hips. She's three years older than me but Gorda always said she was born with a young soul. "Sole, you have an old soul. She's still a baby. She's got to make lots of mistakes before she can learn."

Gorda tells me everybody's secrets after I promise not to tell anyone else. She told me Johnny was with another woman and Marzo was going to talk or to get some advice. After they leave, we sit and discuss their lives; "What do you think, should Margaret leave her husband?" I remember when she told me that I had brains, unlike her daughter,

Flaca, who couldn't ever keep up in school. "Too busy messing with those boys," she'd say. Gorda told me she had a feeling that I was going to be smart enough to ignore all those horny boys. She said I was smart enough to guard that special gift all women have. That is why she talked to me like she did and still does. "That's your property." she'd say, pointing to the spot in between my legs, after women came to her crying over the men that left them.

Gorda pulls out a chair for me.

I sit at her dining room table, right next to the kitchen. I watch her get some cups from the pantry so we could drink some juice. "I paid $19.99 for a juicer. I used it yesterday for the first time. It took me ten minutes to make the juice and an hour to clean the machine. I'm returning the thing. The commercial said, satisfaction guaranteed." She pours pulpy carrot juice into the cups. Flaca's daughter, born two years ago, hides behind her grandmother's skirt, peek-a-booing smiles at me.

"I'm glad you here. Maybe you can help me figure something out."

"I need money, what else is new? I'm trying to scrape a few dollars to put Flaca's daughter into Catholic school. I need to make sure she's locked up in a good school. Not one that lets their students run out and cut class. Look at you, you went to Catholic school and now you're in the university. I'm so proud of you. Look at my Flaca, she's working as a cashier trying to go to school at night. Pasando trabajo, because she didn't listen to me about those boys. You see how right I was. You listened to me and you turned out good." She holds my hand in a familiar way, caressing the wrinkles on my knuckles. I watch Gorda. She looks old trying to make things different for Flaca's kid, who is now her problem. Flaca has to work and go to school almost every day of the week.

"Do you know, yesterday, I went to get some lunch around where I work. I saw this sandwich in the hands of una blanquita. It looked so good. So I tell the guy behind the counter to make a sandwich just like the one the lady have. The guy look at me all funny and tells me it's nine dollars. So I tell him, 'I didn't ask how much it is, I said I wanted one just like it.' Maybe he didn't understand me. My English don't sound so good. So I tell him again. He look at me, in the funny way he look at me before and he tell me to pay first. He don't tell anyone else to pay first, but I go and take out my money. I have pride, you know. I didn't want him to think I couldn't pay for the stupid sandwich," Gorda says.

We hear a whistle coming from the hall outside. "I know that whistle," she whispers to me. The doorbell rings. Gorda doesn't respond. She covers her lips with her finger, signalling for me to be quiet. The doorbell rings again. She crawls over to the door and makes sure the crack under the door is clear before she say anything to me. "That was Jesus."

Everyone knows that Jesus has been in love with Gorda for years. Every once in a while he comes by with a handful of the prettiest flowers. I've seen him knocking at Gorda's door from my kitchen window. She hardly ever opens the door for him. After a few attempts, Jesus gives up and walks away until he gets the courage to come over again.

"Can't Jesus lend you money?"

"Jesus," she says, "wants to take over my life and my house. I want to teach you something and this is a lesson my mother taught to me. You let men in and they will never leave. They take over your heart and soul and if they leave they leave you with nothing. It's like borrowing money from the devil. Once someone gives you something they own you and you should never forget that."

"So what are you going to do?" I ask her. She says she will pray to her saints that sit behind her bedroom door on a table with pictures of her mother who just recently passed away.

"The saints will help me find a way. They always do." She picks up Flaca's daughter and sits her on her lap. "Isn't that true," Gorda coos, rubbing her nose against her granddaughter's cheek. She hands me my grandmother's empty Tupperware container and walks me to the door. "No te pierdas," she says, in a way than means more than not to forget to visit her.

"Don't worry about me," I tell her, knowing she will.

Mama

"Men say they like pretty women but I tell you that pretty keeps no man. It's the woman that feeds him that keeps him coming back. Listen to me child, I am old and know these things." My grandmother told me this when I was ten. She and I would spend afternoons in the kitchen talking, chopping, cooking, washing.

"Now to make mangú take the plantain like so. The key is not to cut corners. You make sure you boil the plantain in salt water. If you forget the salt, all is lost because it's no good salting the plantain once it's cooked. It's not the same. You take the boiled pieces and mash them. Add some of the salt water and butter if you have it. Mash again until the texture is nice and smooth. You can chop up some left over pork rinds or fried chicken and mash it inside the mangú. This is good because men like meat in everything, but do it only sometimes, not always, because then they get used to it. Remember don't tell him when you're going to make it or when you're going to put the meat in it, give him something to wonder about. Men like mysteries. Don't let him peek in your pots. You are feeding him and you control your kitchen."

Victor

My grandmother watched Victor walk into the apartment with his left eye black-blue, and his hands holding his stomach. He sat himself on the leather covered rocking chair in the living room and rocked himself soft like a baby.

"You see him? He come dressed like that, with his shirt hanging out of his pants, alcohol on his breath. What kind of son I raise? Tell me what kind?" My grandmother stayed in the kitchen pretending to be busy. I heard her move pots around and run some water. She had seen Victor get himself into trouble too many times. After what seemed like a long time, she came out and looked at him with his head in his hands.

"Get yourself into trouble again, eh? Get yourself in

trouble?" She gave him a terry cloth rag filled with crushed ice. She pushed his head back and held the ice on his eye. Victor didn't respond.

"Can't talk? Eh?" She took his hand and made him hold the rag. She untied the laces of his shoes and slid them off his feet.

"Mama, they took my car. They bumped it from behind and I got out to yell at the guy and . . . " Victor said the words slow. He was crying. Nothing more vulnerable-looking than a thirty-year-old man that thinks he's so macho, cry.

"You fight them?" she asked. "Why they hit you for?" She paced in front of the rocking chair with a worried look in her eyes. She looked at me sitting on the sofa facing the television that I wasn't watching. She seemed relieved that Victor did not get himself into another fight like the one he had last week at work.

It all started when Victor's new manager told him to work in silence. He told Victor that if he must say anything at all he should say it in English, not Spanish. The manager knew very well that even though Victor had been living in the States for seventeen years, Victor didn't speak much English. Victor told us that the manager was nothing more than a college-grad punk, who's never worked a day of his life and unlike Victor who has worked seven years at the chocolate factory and knows more than the manager himself, the manager was insecure and just wanted for Victor to quit.

So when the manager told Victor to talk only in English, Victor began to talk more than ever, and when he had no one to talk to, he would sing Latin love songs getting other workers to join him. After a week of Victor singing, the manager came over to Victor, grabbed him by the arm and told him that unless he stopped, he would have to fire him. Victor grabbed the manager and said, "I'll give you something to fire me about," and punched the guy right on the jaw bone.

Victor did not regret standing up for himself and that worried my grandmother even more. "He's not going to make it in this country with that attitude." He lost his job last week and the chances of getting a job that paid him as well as the one he had is low. In his seven years there, he was promoted three times. He was a mechanic with a pension plan and benefits.

"They tried to take my wallet. I couldn't just let them take it like that." Victor told us a little more about what happened. He said he didn't recognize the guys. He said they weren't armed, but he was too drunk, tonight, to fight them. My grandmother came back with black coffee and an aspirin. He put his fingers over his eyes that were now spidery red and wet from all the tears. She combed his tight curly hair with her old fingers.

"Life is hard on my boy. I can't be mad at him. Life too hard."

The Handkerchief
Elise Marie Ficarra

Elise Marie Ficarra, the daughter of a Swiss mother and Sicilian American father, has thought a good deal about what it means to be an "American." Her first book of poetry *Swelter* (2005) won the Michael Rubin Award in Poetry. Her work has appeared in *Bird Dog, Commonweal, 14 Hills, Small Town;* and *Hinge,* a BOAS anthology of eight Bay Area experimental women writers. She lives in San Francisco and is the business manager for the Poetry Center at San Francisco State University.

Shoved in the closet is a small chest of drawers, an unremarkable piece of furniture, no more than two and a half feet tall. When it was new, and I was a child, it smelled like Christmas, filling the house with a sweet tangy pine odor. This humble chest has traveled for nearly twenty years, following me like a loyal dog, though its contents have long exceeded its capacity to contain them. Now the top drawer holds a gaggle of underwear, an assortment of faded bras, mismatched socks, a couple of old tee shirts. Digging further down I find little sachets of herbs and lavender, brightly colored bandannas, holey longjohns. Buried somewhere near the bottom is a small cotton handkerchief, white with pale purple flowers. Although crumpled, it still bears the creases where a hot iron once pressed it into a neat flat square.

I imagine her hands moving the steaming iron over its flat surface, folding once, the corners all lined up, pressing, folding again, pressing, all neat and even.

This drawer where the handkerchief lives defies order. To open it, I have to tug and jostle with one hand, the other pushing the garments down, so the drawer can slide clear. Once I tried to organize it, but the chaos reemerged, erupting like the contents of a jar someone had shaken. This compression of intimate life inside the drawer could not be more unlike the interior of the drawer from which the handkerchief originally came, everything neat and tidy, folded soldiers in orderly rows.

Grandmaman ironed sheets. She ironed dish towels. She ironed underwear. She ironed handkerchiefs.

I've barely used the handkerchief since it arrived in

the mail. For one thing, it required laundering which didn't suit my lifestyle. And I never felt right, blowing my nose onto those delicate flowers. Still I wanted it, with a power I didn't understand, like a magic talisman that could connect me to her life. After her death, I wrote Aunt Madeleine in Switzerland, staking my claim as an absent granddaughter.

"I want something of Grandmaman's. Could you send me one of her handkerchiefs?"

"Those are old. I will send you a new one."

"No. Send me an old one, one of hers."

I was nine the first time we went to Switzerland, in January, 1968, my mother returning to her parents' apartment after fourteen years of absence, bringing with her an American husband and three children. When we were growing up, in California's Central Valley, Mother never spoke to us in French. But she taught us a few things she felt we ought to know, like how to count, tell time, say *please, thank you,* and *my name is . . .* When it came time for the trip, she stepped up our "lessons." At the kitchen table, after dinner, and before we washed the dishes, she drilled us on pronunciation. "Not 'too,'" she implored. "'*Tu*' like this . . . Say the letter 'U,'" she commanded. "No! Push your lips out like this," puckering her lips for a kiss. "Now keep your mouth like that but say 'EE' instead of 'U.'"

"EU," we repeated after her "EU." "EU," cooing like a flock of migrating birds.

My sisters and I practiced our "r's" each night by gargling, after we brushed our teeth. "Grrr" we'd say, taking water in our mouths from plastic green cups, "Grrr," spitting into the sink. None of us wanted to sound American. On the weekends, Mother organized the scrubbing of walls until they were free of dirt, finger prints and smudges. We dusted, vacuumed, polished, shined. Then one winter day in the middle of fourth grade, she directed our whole family in the packing of suitcases. I was finally going to see where my mother came from.

Uncle Louis met us at the train station. He led us down

Rue Des Portes Rouges (Street of the Red Doors) on foot, to our grandparent's apartment. We climbed a mountain of stairs, stone stairs cut straight into the side of the hill, tier after tier, then three more flights of cement stairs inside the building. They stood in the doorway, waiting, Grandmaman, expectant, in her apron, Grandpapa, his big square hands firmly grasping us by shoulders one by one, as he planted kisses on our cheeks. Immediately we were enveloped in a kaleidoscope of sounds and smells, slurred S's swishing like the drawing of large drapes, accordioning in and out as you pull the cord, the guttural "rrr's" rolling and crashing back and forth, none of it making sense. *"Qu'elles sont grandes!"* Grandpapa exclaimed. *"As tu faim?"* Grandmaman queried, her eyes moist. *"Est-ce que tu veux quelque chose à boire?"* The kitchen was right by the front door and the smells of *pommes de terre au gratin* and *saucisson* wafted through the apartment, having an hypnotic effect. They led us past their bedroom down a short hall to the only communal room. The adults took our coats and shoes, and we girls sank down onto the narrow couch.

A fully set table with a white linen table cloth and smoothly ironed cloth napkins filled the room. Behind it was a small balcony that overlooked the street. I wanted to go and look out over the rooftops, but was afraid to move, to touch or break anything. Soon Mother started carrying in platters of food from the kitchen. "Sit at the table," she told us. I took the heavy white cotton cloth napkin and placed it over my legs; it had a comforting weight. Grandmaman began offering the food, Grandpapa the *vin rouge*, until soon all the plates and glasses were full—mountains of fluffy potatoes, tender cooked carrots, slices of roast, bathed in dark red juices, salad with mustard dressing like how my mother made it, only stronger. I was dizzy and the food swam on my plate. Grandpapa kept filling the glasses and toasting, the clinking chime of glass on glass reverberating. Then he started telling stories, his face animated, his eyes big and round and full of mischief, while Grandmaman sat quietly in her chair, her arms folded across her chest, clucking her tongue at him disapprovingly, and my mother laughed until she cried.

Grandmaman's eyes were blue and sharp, and vigilant. She monitored each plate, how fast each person was eating, and quickly offered more as soon as any portion diminished. "She says you say 'no,' but your eyes say 'yes,' " my mother translated for my father as Grandmaman refilled his plate despite his protestations. I stared at my father in disbelief, as he accepted Grandmaman's verdict. She had seen right through him, beneath his words to the truth: he wanted more. Could she see right into my mind, too, even though she didn't speak English? I willed my mind to be blank, just in case she had supernatural powers, and could discover some secret defect in my thoughts. When the plates were cleared, there appeared bread, sharp cheeses, chocolate, and finally the rich old-man smell of Grandpapa's pipe.

After the meal, Grandmaman put her hand on my forehead. I was running a fever. She led me into a small room with a cuckoo clock adjacent to the dining area. She moved her pile of sewing, and the teddy bear, pulling back the blankets on the narrow twin bed, and tucked me in. She sat there for a while stroking my forehead, and talking to Mother in their strange language. "She's going to take care of you," Mother said, "it's OK." I nodded. Grandmaman came back with cotton balls soaked in warm oil, and gently put one in each of my ears. Then she produced a bag of *sugus* chewy fruit-flavored candies, individually wrapped in waxy paper, and offered them to me with words which, despite my mother's lessons, I did not understand. *Merci,* I said. *Ça va bien.* Grandmaman picked me. She kept me with her and Grandpapa in the apartment, when the others went back to the hotel. I wanted to stay there forever, watching the cuckoo bird come out of his hole in the clock and do a little song and dance, every fifteen minutes.

I recovered quickly under Grandmaman's care, and soon I was up, wearing a pair of borrowed slippers, and watching Grandmaman knit, her hands deftly pulling the yarn back and forth with the needles. She made socks, slippers, blankets, scarves, sweaters. I wanted them all! I stayed with them three days. The rest of the family came over at noon every day for mid-day meal, and left again in the evening. Whenever Grandmaman asked me a question, I would nod my head "yes." She put a towel around my shoulders and washed my hair, both of us kneeling over the edge of the tub. Her shampoo smelled like the rosemary from our yard at home. *Est-ce que tu veux que je te coupe les cheveux?* She asked. I nodded. Out came her scissors, and clip clip, my tangled curls covered the bathroom floor. I was new.

Our last day in Switzerland was solemn. Grandmaman pulled Mother aside, gave her cheese wrapped in white butcher paper, and seven blocks of chocolate. Then Grandmaman looked at the clock, and pointed to the balcony, giving her instructions. My mother's head nodded up and down, her cheeks reddened, as she held back tears. I bit my lip. Why did we have to go back? Grandmaman dabbed her eyes with her handkerchief. Then the kissing of cheeks, like bobbing for apples, in and out, one, two, three times. We walked back to the train station in silence. "Grandmaman will be on the balcony, watching," Mother told us. "In seven minutes after we leave the station, you have to remember to look up. The train will pass by their apartment, but fast. I don't know if you'll be able to see her." I pressed my face to the window, watching building after building pass by. "There!" Mother pointed. Grandmaman stood next to Grandpapa on the balcony, waving, smaller, smaller, as the train shuttled us away. I remember her handkerchief, clutched in her knobby hand, flapping in the wind, a white, one-winged bird, above the window boxes of red geraniums.

I returned to Europe thirteen years later, at twenty-two, so much more an "American" than when I left. I had tried many things by then: dropping out of college, marijuana, and hitchhiking across the United States, a diet of Kerouac's *On the Road, Zen and the Art of Motorcycle Maintenance* and all of Carlos Castenada. In the late 1970s I discovered Mary Daly and Adrienne Rich, feminism, and love between women. Now I wanted to go "home" but where was it? My mother had left my father, and fled to England. Both my father's parents, Sicilian immigrants, were dead. So I turned to Switzerland, determined to learn my mother's language, hoping Grandmaman would have the key.

I spent three months in France, studying French before venturing to Switzerland. *The Swiss are so cold, not warm like the French,* I was told on the eve of my departure. That night, I stayed up late, drinking with my fellow American students, and took the night train to Geneva. Sitting in the train compartment, I pressed my forehead to the glass and watched the countryside roll by, bathed in darkness. Shapes and shadows spun and whirred, sad and old with the rhythm of the train rocking me. I arrived in the morning with a hang-over and no passport. Aunt Madeleine was anxiously waiting at the gate, and had to persuade the customs officer to let me in. "Her grandfather was a customs officer in *L'Auberson*" she told them shaking her head, disapprovingly. *La grande-fille d'un douanier!* After a calculated hesitation and stern words, the man finally relented.

We took the next train to Neuchâtel, and walked the same path from *La gare* down *Rue Des Portes Rouges* to my grandparents' apartment. The buildings looked drab, smaller, and a new *Migro* supermarket had sprung up on their block. "Since Grandmaman broke her hip last year, she doesn't leave the apartment anymore," my aunt told me. "There is no elevator." We climbed the three flights of stairs, to the open door, and there they were again, the two of them side by side, Grandmaman much thinner now, in a navy blue flower print dress, and apron, the lines on her face deeper, a quiet blue flame in her eyes. We sat down to a simple meal of soup, and bread and cheese. "We don't cook so much, anymore," Grandmaman told me. I could see the great effort it took for her to move around the apartment. She refused to use her walker, and instead braced herself on the furniture, placing her hands one at a time on the backs of chairs, swinging the fractured hip around, her mouth set in determination. "Her right leg is four inches shorter than the left now," my aunt whispered when Grandmaman was out of the room.

I stayed with them a week, going to bed early, as they

did, with the sun, and rising at six a.m. for *le petit déjeuner*. I adjusted with difficulty to the slow rhythm of daily life inside their apartment, organized by routines of cooking, eating, washing up, and television, each moment measured by the ticking of the clock, and Grandpapa's low, loud breathing. I knew if this life were my own, it would be intolerable, to live so quietly, so close to the body, yet in that week each day was precious. Unable to knit anymore, Grandmaman folded her arthritic hands in her lap, her thumbs chasing each other in wild circles. Grandpapa sat at the table, playing solitaire, or reading the newspaper, slowly moving his large magnifying glass over the words. "He thinks he's the king." She said to me, one afternoon loud enough for him to hear, "but he's not." I looked over at him. "Eh, you, you think you're the king?" she asked him. But he didn't look up.

Then she turned the full force of her gaze onto me and looked deeply into my eyes. *C'est dur, en, Elise? Tu as beaucoup souffrir.* I nodded, pierced, as pools formed in my eyes. I didn't know what she had seen in me, only that it was true. I wanted stories, and sat with her at the foot of her rocker while she paged through her photo albums, showing me mountains at *Château d'Oex* where she and Grandpapa grew up, later a handsome Grandpapa in his uniform at the border, picnics in the woods, and then her children. We paused for a long time on a snapshot of my mother, from the early fifties. She was perched on the balcony of their apartment, smoking a cigarette, a half-smile on her lips, a look of hunger in her eyes. "Your mother," she tells me, "right before she left."

"It's good you speak French," she said, later.

At 11:00 each day I followed her into the kitchen, to prepare the mid-day meal. I helped, washing and scrubbing carrots, slicing them into thin rounds, laying them out, one at a time in the bottom of the casserole dish.

"I'm not afraid of death," she told me, vigorously stirring the mustard into the salad dressing. "One day it will come. Why be afraid? I'm ready."

---

*It's been hard for you, Elise. You've suffered a lot.

I nodded, thinking the way young people think that there is always more time, that I would come back, that she would still be there.

She died of a heart attack, a couple of years later, just before Christmas, no time for good-byes. It was like her, my mother said, to go out fast. A few days later, Grandpapa was hospitalized. I borrowed money for plane fare.

He was seated outside his room on a chair, paper thin, in a hospital gown. I walked down the hall towards him as if through a dream. There was one moment when he turned his head, and saw me, his eyes lighting up with tears.

"You came!" he pronounced with such joy, pushing himself to his feet. I offered my cheek for his scratchy kiss. Then the clouds moved over his face again. I sat by his bed for half an hour. We didn't speak.

"She loved you very much," he said, softly, as if finally, this was the most important thing.

I wanted to stay there, quit my job, move to Switzerland and take care of him until he died. But I heard her voice in my head.

No. Go back. You have your own life.

How could I tell her that my life eluded me, that I was drowning in my own freedom—this American illusion that I could do anything—My own weightlessness as heavy as the ordered life my mother fled from.

An ordered life.

He died without leaving the hospital.

Their grave is on a hill, with a view of the lake, a detail I find comfort in, as if the dead are limited to where we put them. Among the rows and rows of small stone markers is their tiny plot, identical to all the others—*For our beloved parents,* the marker reads. Ashes under stone, neatly clipped grass, and plastic flowers. The grave is rented. My grandparents are allowed to stay there for thirty years. Then, as is the procedure, the authorities will unearth them and deposit their ashes in a communal plot to make room for the next occupants, unless the family pays again. Efficient. In a small country, space is a commodity, why be sentimental? I feel cheated that a culture so steeped in convention would honor the dead so little. But then maybe it's not so strange, for the dead are a messy business, tugging and pulling on the heart, leading the mind into dark corners and back alleys where *les déchets* pile up, old shoes, vegetable rinds gathering flies as they rot and decompose unseen. We are meant to see only the neat store fronts, newly swept walks, manicured rose bushes, all at high noon, without shadow.

Indeed there is something comforting about an ordered life, kept agreements, and the simple act of cleaning up after one's self. The smooth surface of a clean sheet, pulled taut over the mattress is refreshing. It feels better than laying in a bed of wrinkles. That the mind could be as clear as a freshly ironed sheet! Of course, I wouldn't find Grandmaman in a cemetery. She's a part of me now, my blood, my memory, keeping her alive. The teacher and poet Thich Nhat Hanh advises Westerners practicing Buddhism to return to our own traditions, to find our spiritual roots. Now that they are gone, I go back to that room in my mind where she sits in her chair, rocking and twirling her thumbs, surrounded by things of the past; and I re-enter the slowness of time, of life lived in the body, where the constant intake and release of the breath is a ground note, supporting life. Here each small ritual is an anchor, the preparation of food, eating, cleaning up, digestion, elimination, sleep, and waking. In meditation, my mind slowed to the sound and rhythm of my own breath, I re-discover what Grandmaman taught me at the end of her life, and didn't consider extraordinary: the knowledge of death and the passage of time, the certain peace that one day, one breath will be her last.

The lessons of time and the body are cyclical. When I visit my mother now, and open the door to her linen closet, I see her dish towels are ironed. Coming to America, my mother left whole lives and histories behind her. As a young woman, I retraced her steps to discover what she had left. There is a freedom in America, and a terrible loneliness, to be separated from the chain of generations. Any day could be a new beginning, in a new place, another break.

Since Grandmaman died, my journeys have taken me many places, up mountains, across deserts, into the halls of universities, and through the jungle of urban living. What do I carry of hers? A small cotton handkerchief, white, with pale purple flowers, thin with age but durable; there when I need it. It travels well in my pocket. I plan to take it with me, next time I climb a mountain. I will dip it in cool water, press it to my forehead, wrap it around my neck to soak up the heat. And when I get home, I'm going to wash it, iron it, fold it, and gently tuck it into my top drawer.

Remembering My Spanish
Elena Perez

Elena Perez is second generation Mexican American. She wrote this essay when she was a student at San Jose City College in California.

I remember running home after my first day of school when I was six years old. I said to my father quickly in Spanish, "La profesora dijo . . . ," but my father scolded me and said, "It's the teacher, say it in English . . . " I didn't quite understand, except that to please him from that moment on, I had to stop saying things in Spanish.

Another incident happened around the same time. I was at my aunt's house and I was reading, or should I say trying to read a magazine in Spanish, and I mispronounced several words. My cousin, who was a year older than I, laughed and repeated to my aunt what I had said until they both laughed at me. I felt rather stupid, especially in front of the whole family. They called me "Pocha," which is a Mexican who doesn't speak Spanish and an insult in Mexican culture. I was confused to say the least.

My father was born in El Paso, Texas. He left home when he was seventeen to join the Navy. The only Spanish he knew was slang. Being away from home, he forgot most of the Spanish he had learned growing up. So when he met my mother, they didn't communicate very well. She was born and raised in Mexico in a small town just outside the capitol of Sonora. Unlike my father, who had little, if any schooling at all, mother was educated in her native tongue. That didn't matter much. My father told me the story of the day he first saw my mother: "Your mother was so beautiful I couldn't help falling in love with her. She thought I was a perfect gentleman because I would let her go first; what she didn't know is that I wanted to watch her walk." Needless to say, my father quickly learned to speak more Spanish and my mother learned English, which became "her kind of English." After their first few years of marriage, my father was stationed in San Diego, California, where I was born and raised.

My father became very Americanized. For example, he pronounced our last name of Perez, "Paris." He also became very critical of my mother's culture. If we had a small hole in our clothing, my father might have said, "You're from Sonora, take that off and put something decent on." To make sure we didn't wear it again, he sometimes made the tear larger. He would also do this to himself, and say, "Oh no. I'm from Sonora," and he would tear his own shirt. Although he did this in a joking fashion, I grew up with the impression that being Mexican meant you lived in poverty and wore raggety clothing. I was almost ashamed to acknowledge that I was Mexican.

Then there was the time when my mother went to school for her citizenship. I remember it well because she had to recite the order of all the Presidents over and over again. To hear her saying them in "broken English" was sometimes so funny, and we tried not to laugh. Yet, my siblings and I would crack up about the way she pronounced "sandwiches" to sound like "sonwitshes." Even now we all say, "Let's have some sonwitshes" when we joke around. If you were an outsider to our family, you probably wouldn't get this humor.

Looking back now, I realized that I avoided the Spanish language as a teenager. Especially around my mother's side of the family, I just knew that if I said anything in Spanish, they would only laugh at me. Yet, they criticized me because I only spoke to them in English. They said something like, "What, you're ashamed of your true language? It's not good enough for you?"

In my twenties I met and married "a pocho." He was of Mexican decent, looked Mexican, but did not speak a word of Spanish. And that was fine with me. I didn't have to speak anything but English. Our children, however, did not benefit from this. I'm sorry to say that they were also exposed to the criticism of the family. Then my husband took a job in Orange County and we moved two hours away from San Diego. Being away from home, I somehow felt free. I took a job working in an office for a toy manufacturing company. There were only two Mexicans working there at the time, a man named Jorge, who worked in the warehouse, and Luz, our cleaning woman. Their English was very "limited," and I was asked quite often to interpret, which made me all nervous and tongue-tied. I really didn't want to do it because I didn't think my Spanish was any good. To my surprise, they didn't laugh or make fun of me; on the contrary, they were very supportive. It didn't matter that I wasn't pronouncing each word just "perfectly." For the first time I was accepted and that felt good. So I started asking Jorge and Luz how to pronounce and how to spell certain words that I had problems with and, in turn, I helped them with their English.

One day, the manager of the company decided to do business with Mexico. He gave me a list of "sewing factories" with the names of the owners. He asked me to send them a typed letter, asking them if they would be willing to sew doll clothes for these dolls we were getting ready to market (later known the "Cabbage Patch Dolls"). Although my Spanish was getting much better, I still could barely carry on a conversation without going into English. I didn't know how to tell him that translating "mop" or "chair," was one thing, but translating business language in Spanish was another. My confidence wasn't very high. I don't know how long I just sat there staring at "the end of my world," but it seemed like it to me. Then I thought, "Wait a minute, what about Jorge?" Jorge was born and raised in Sonora, not very far from where my mother lived. He was a very intelligent man, and from our conversations I could tell he was well educated. I always thought that if he would learn to speak and write in English, he could successfully own and operate any business he put his mind to. Well, Jorge did come to my rescue. Between the two of us, we came up with a very professional letter. I was so proud of it, I even kept a copy and had it framed!

If I learned anything from all of my experiences, it was to not be so quick to criticize someone just because his or her "English" or, as it was in my case, "Spanish" isn't perfect. It does not mean a person is slow, uneducated or stupid. Powerful historical forces have moved my people. I will always remember those who touched my life without judging me. With their acceptance of me, I am learning to be more accepting of myself, as well as accepting of others . . . their Culture . . . their Language. Mine.

Poppa's Girls
Lesléa Newman

Lesléa Newman is a second generation Ashkenazi Jewish American. She has written over 20 books and edited five anthologies. Her titles that explore the themes of immigration and identity include the children's book *Remember That*, the short story collection *A Letter to Harvey Milk*, and the novel *In Every Laugh a Tear*. "Poppa's Girls" dramatizes several common sources of conflict between first and second generation Americans.

"Don't speak to me in that tone of voice, young lady."

"What tone of voice?"

"Amy, I'm warning you. You know exactly what tone of voice I'm referring to."

"To which I am referring."

"What?" Mrs. Goldstein whirled around, the wooden spoon she was stirring the sweet and sour meatballs with raised in mid-air. Amy fixed her eyes on a drop of grape jelly (the sweet of the sweet and sour) that was sliding down the edge of the spoon toward her mother's hand. "What did you say, young lady?"

Amy sighed and looked up from the cucumber she was slicing. "I said, 'to which I am referring.' Mrs. McKay says ending a sentence with a preposition is incorrect English."

"Oh she does, does she?" Mrs. Goldstein slammed the cover onto the meatballs, threw the wooden spoon into the sink and yanked open the silverware drawer, causing the knives, forks and spoons to rattle against each other. "So that's what this is about, I don't talk good enough for you? Is that it? You're ashamed from the way your mother talks?"

Don't talk *well* enough, Amy thought silently as she cut the cucumber into thin, even slices. Ashamed *of,* not ashamed *from.* Why can't she talk normal English like everyone else's mother?

"Well let me tell you something, Miss High and Mighty." Mrs. Goldstein slapped three knives and three forks into her hand as she spoke. "You think you're too good for the rest of this family? You're so anxious to forget where you came from? As anxious as you are to forget, believe me, someone will be just as anxious to remind you. You think when the Nazis came they gave a damn about where you put your prepositions? You think they cared if you ate with your fingers or cocked your pinky around a teacup?" Mrs. Goldstein shoved the drawer shut and turned to set the table. Now she slammed each piece of silverware down as she spoke. She wasn't addressing her daughter so much now as she was the world in general. "A poor Jew, a rich Jew, a Jew with manners, a Jew without manners, what did they care? Into the oven you'd go, right along with the rest of us."

"Ma." Amy was now cutting a tomato, first slicing it in half, then halving the halves, then halving them once again. "Ma, all I did was ask you where my red sweater is." Amy spoke more gently now, for she knew when her mother started in on the Nazis, she'd better watch her step.

"How should I know where your red sweater is? What do I look like, the maid?" Mrs. Goldstein had finished setting the table and now returned to the stove where a large pot of water was boiling. She snapped a stack of spaghetti in two and threw it into the pot. "Did you look in your dresser?" she asked, turning to face her daughter. "What about in the hamper?"

"Yes, I looked in the hamper and in my dresser," Amy said, not hiding the annoyance that had crept into her voice.

"Amy." Her mother shot her a warning glance.

"What?"

"Don't get smart with me." Mrs. Goldstein took the lid off the meatballs, added some barbeque sauce (the sour of sweet and sour) and stirred them again. "To everyone else she's polite; the mailman, the garbageman, a stranger on the street. Only to her own mother does she talk to like dirt. To her I'm a *nebbish*, a nothing, a piece of *shmutz, feh*." Mrs. Goldstein brushed an imaginary speck of dirt off her sleeve.

"Oh, Ma." Amy shook her head and scraped the tomato slices off the cutting board into the big green salad bowl with the edge of her knife.

"Don't 'oh Ma' me. I want a little respect from you, young lady. I work plenty hard around here to keep you and your father happy." Uh-oh, here she goes, Amy thought, ducking her head as if she were about to receive a blow. "You think the house cleans itself? You think the food jumps into the pot, the books you leave all over the house hop onto the shelves? What, a magic show I'm running here, a circus?" Mrs. Goldstein's voice rose to a shrill pitch. "You think the floor sweeps itself? In addition to everything else," Mrs. Goldstein placed one hand on her hip and shook the other hand at her daughter's back. "I should know where your red sweater is. Her red sweater, her blue sweater," Mrs. Goldstein, having gotten no response from her daughter, now addressed the simmering meatballs. "Her trouble is she's got too many sweaters. Spoiled rotten she is. When I was growing up, I was lucky if I even had a sweater. I should know where her red sweater is." Mrs. Goldstein turned off the flame under the meatballs and covered them again. Amy, now finished making the salad, put a partial head of lettuce and the unused half of a cucumber into a plastic baggy and returned the vegetables to the bottom shelf of the refrigerator.

I hate her, she thought, as she leaned against the counter and started leafing through the TV Guide. It's not my fault she's wasted her life being a housewife. She could get a job or go back to school or something. But no, she'd rather sit in the house all day and *kvetch*, I mean complain, I mean bitch all day long, bossing everyone around. She knows what's best for everyone. Amy scowled and flung the TV Guide back onto the counter. "I'm going upstairs to do my homework," she announced, started for the doorway.

"Your father will be home any minute," Mrs. Goldstein reminded her daughter.

"I don't want dinner. I'm not hungry."

"Amy Rebecca, you will sit down at that table and eat supper with your family like a normal human being." Mrs. Goldstein's words were stretched to the breaking point.

"I'm not hungry!" Amy whirled around and flung up her hands. "Why do I have to eat just because it's six o'clock?"

"Because," her mother's voice was almost a hiss. "Because I said so, and because I want us to be a normal family that sits down and has supper together at the end of the day. Your father works very hard to keep you happy. Who do you think pays for all your sweaters? It's time you started thinking about someone else for a change. It wouldn't kill you to sit down at the table with a smile on your face and be pleasant for once in your life. Your father deserves a little *naches* when he come home from the office. He's got plenty aggravation at work, he don't need more when he steps into this house from you or anyone else."

Amy pressed her lips together. Only three more years until I'm off to college, she thought, folding her arms across her chest. I can't wait. She walked back to the counter, leaned her behind against it and picked up the TV Guide again, not to read it so much, but to have something in her hands to protect her from her mother's anger and her own hurt. Nothing I do is good enough, Amy thought bitterly. I have to be happy all the time. Pleasant. Be a clown. Amy snuck a glance at her mother who was now making herself a cup of instant coffee. She tore open a pink packet of Sweet'n Low and poured it into a yellow mug. Sweet'n Low, Amy thought, inspecting the tips of her long red hair for split ends. Sweet 'n Phony is more like it. That's what she wants me to be. Well, I won't do it. She looked at her mother again, who was staring out the kitchen window, waiting for the water to boil.

All of a sudden both mother and daughter heard the sound of Mr. Goldstein's big brown Buick pulling into the driveway. Instantly Mrs. Goldstein's posture changed. Her shoulders dropped and her neck relaxed. When she turned from the window toward her daughter, there was a pleading look on her face. Amy refused to meet her eye, but stared down at the toes of her purple high top sneakers instead. Mrs. Goldstein followed her daughter's gaze and almost said something about her horrendous footwear but then changed her mind. The two of them stood still, as if frozen in time, listening to Mr. Goldstein's footsteps approaching the house. They heard him turn the key in the lock, open the front door and shut it behind him. They heard him call "Yoo-hoo, anybody home?" in a sing-song voice and rattle the hangers in the hall closet, trying to untangle one for his coat. They heard him walk through the foyer and they saw him enter the kitchen with a hesitant smile on his face and his hands extended, palms up, in a grand gesture of welcome, as he asked the same question he asked every evening at six o'clock and seldom got an answer to. "How's Poppa's girls?" Mr. Goldstein said, and then shook his head in bewilderment as one of them burst into tears and the other one shrieked, "She's impossible!" as she ran out of the kitchen, through the hallway, and up the carpeted stairs.

A Pipe
Kirby Congdon

Of Irish descent, Kirby Congdon has compiled bibliographies on small-press poetry and a reference file of poetry-in-the-news. Over 350 of Congdon's publications have been collected by the Spencer Research Library of the University of Kansas.

He found the small ceramic pipe in the cluttered room that was plastered and partitioned off at the end of his grandmother's long, dark attic, and he took it for himself. Affecting a French poet's mien, although he had not been to France nor heard much of French poets, let alone seen one, he took up smoking. It gave him an air. He wanted to have an air.

"Where do you think this came from, Daddy?" he asked, trying, with the studied casualness of his words, once more to fill in the gap that seemed, always, to be between them.

"It was mine," he answered, leaning back on his spine to ease his backache from bending in his grandfather's fields.

The son then tried talking as men do, from one side of their mouths with the pipe in the other, but the pipe was either too light or it was too heavy and it fell from his lips and broke apart on the huge stone ledge that rose up in an exhausted wave of history. His grandfather's acre of potato plants had fallen like an old hope whose light liquid foam had turned to a million hard, mean grains of gravel.

"I had it when I was eighteen," the older man said as if in some final accusation. The silence had in it that kind of reply that is complete, whole and impenetrable. It says everything there is to say for those who hear it, even more, which is the unsayable. But the pipe was in pieces.

"Can it be repaired?"

"No, it can't," his father replied.

The Cockfight
Rosemary Ybarra-Garcia

Rosemary Ybarra-Garcia, an educator for over twenty-nine years, is Dean of Student Advancement at College of San Mateo in California. Her writing has appeared in *Lighthouse Point: An Anthology of Santa Cruz Writers.* "The Cockfight" suggests more than a straight-forward description of cockfighting, a gambling sport and long-time tradition in the Latino, Filipino, and rural southern U.S. white cultures. Although the cruelty of this sport appears indisputable—attaching metal blades to the roosters' legs to make the fight shorter, bloodier and more exciting—it is not considered cruel by people for whom cockfighting is a tradition, a part of their culture not easily left behind.

I could see the shadow
of their hats and cigars
against slivers of moonlight
Carmen was inside crying

her father was inhaling
the smoke from anxious bets
and the cool September night air
from my window, I could hear
the mumbling, rapid syllables
bounce off the night fence,
the fire torched
the smoke-filled sky,
and I could see felt hats
wearing faces,
blending into noses and red eyes,
fuming away a dream
Carmen was inside crying

like weather vane statues,
the cocks perched to strike
with knightly claws
one was struggling
toward its prey,
bold and burning
like a macho, two-fisted man

Carmen's father
took his cheap cigar
and needled it into the cock's ass
like a whip
the cock lashed into the oncoming bullet
two knives flashing, slashing
bird feathers fraying
blood oozing
hats in a frenzy
fists in the air, goading
the cock with the bold eyes
and the crooked mane
dead warriors stiff
in the dark dust
Carmen was inside crying.

Exotic or
"What Beach Do You Hang Out On?"
Tara L. Masih

Tara L. Masih lives in Andover, Massachusetts. She was the assistant editor for the national literary magazine *Stories* for three years, and has an M.A. in Professional Writing and Publishing from Emerson College. A regular contributor to *The Indian-American*, she now writes for *Masala*. Her piece "Turtle Huntin" from *Hayden's Ferry Review* was nominated for a Pushcart Prize in 1992. Her other awards include the Lou P. Bunce Creative Writing Award (1985) and First Place in *The Ledge's* 1995 fiction contest. This essay originally appeared in *Two Worlds Walking: Short Stories, Essays, and Poetry by Writers with Mixed Heritages.*

When you are of mixed parentage—one parent dark-skinned, one light—you come out looking like café au lait. You become one of those gray areas people struggle with; they struggle with their compulsion to categorize you, label you, and place you neatly on the shelf in a safe spot, safe because the species is one that has already been identified. Yet while humans have always feared the unfamiliar and foreign, times are forcing us to change.

"Your look is in," I'm told by friends. "I like exotic-looking women," I'm told by men. I still have not learned how to react to these well-meaning comments. I bite my lip, smile, and nod vaguely, hoping they'll take my expression as a thank you.

What that expression really reflects is a reaction to my own struggle, a reluctance to be placed in any category to satisfy the comfort of others. Now I am labeled, and they can rest easy. Everything's safe.

Fear of the stranger goes back centuries. In her essay, Susan Sontag uses this metaphor to explain the fear of AIDS victims: "The fact that illness is associated with the poor—who are, from the perspective of the privileged, aliens in one's midst—reinforces the association of illness with the foreign: with an *exotic* place" [my italics].

There is no doubt that words have power, or rather, we imbue them with power. As the Bible proclaims, the word is flesh and dwells among us. Like humans, words are either accepted or rejected, synthesized into culture or banished. For instance, during the McCarthy era, the term *communist*, like the person it labeled, was claimed to be evil, and therefore every effort was made to eradicate it from the American vocabulary.

The word exotic is derived from the Greek word, exō, meaning "outside." "Exotic" itself carries several meanings in modern times, and, as cultural and collective views change, terms and phrases, chameleon-like, are made to reflect and adapt. (*Communism* is no longer an evil word, communists no longer exist in an "evil empire.") According to *Webster's Ninth Collegiate*, there are four modern definitions of *exotic*:

1. *Introduced from another country: not native to the place where found*

It is amazing what a short-term memory we Americans have. Our history begins with the discovery, by Italian explorer Cristoforo Colombo, of this land and its exotic American Indians (and we all know he was looking for a quicker trade route to my ancestors, those other exotics in India proper). But by definition it was Colombo and his followers, religious refugees and convicts, who were the exotics. In essence, all Americans are exotic. Our history, riddled with convenient lapses in memory, takes a great leap to the American Revolution, discounting that the non-native Europeans, with "savage-like" enthusiasm, slaughtered the natives (now rightly referred to as Native Americans). Our fear of foreigners is no doubt a projection of our fear of ourselves.

2. *Archaic: outlandish, alien*

By this definition, exotic is hardly a compliment. The word again addresses the fear of the unfamiliar. (The *Oxford English Dictionary* uses the words barbarous, strange, uncouth as synonymous with foreigners). It's why we seek to erase differences in this culture. By covering our bodily smells with the same scents, by following the current trends in hair styles (witness all the media coverage recently devoted to *Friends* star Jennifer Aniston's retro haircut), by spending all our energy/time/money to wear the same clothes during the same season, and by keeping up with the latest profanity, we are saying to our compatriots: "Hey, I'm just like you, therefore I'm *safe* and *familiar*." (Note how these two adjectives are often paired.) It is no accident that most of the women and men accused of witchcraft during the hysteria of the seventeenth and eighteenth centuries were citizens who lived by themselves, outside of the community—social lepers. In our own century, Michael Jackson is the epitome of one who has tried, literally, to erase his exotic features, even going so far as to erase his gender—he is generic in every sense, and therefore can be marketed to a broader audience. His attempts, nevertheless, backfired. In erasing all differences he has become that which he tried to avoid. A true alien, living a solitary life away from society, he is like the witches of old—a target for outlandish rumors and supernatural speculation.

3. *Strikingly or excitingly different or unusual*

The word's own definitions contradict each other. While the unfamiliar can be frightening, it can also be exciting. As psychologists have discovered, love and lust are heightened in the presence of fear. Now we know how to make someone fall in love with us—take them on a walk over a shaky bridge. And as fear and excitement appear to be in opposition, so do different cultures' concepts of beauty. In the States it is considered an asset to be tan, though the tan shouldn't be natural. It should be achieved through leisurely hours of sunning on tropical beaches or through the assistance of artificial means. Americans brave melanoma, carcinoma, early aging for this brief stain of color. I enjoy being the barometer every summer for my friends to measure their tan by. With what glee some of my white friends greet their achieved goal—to be darker than I am. But only in the summer, when it's acceptable. Or if they've been to Florida. I went to the beach once with another friend. "Look how everyone's staring at me," she said. "Black people aren't supposed to go to the beach, it's only for whites trying to look black."

I find it ironic that meanwhile, on the other side of the earth, people are doing their best to appear light-skinned. Hindu gods are rendered by artists with a blue tint to their skin, and Indian movie stars are lighter than many Europeans. I was appalled to find my own cousin, in preparation for her wedding, spreading hair bleach all over her amber-tinted face and neck. "I'm too dark," she said. "It's not pretty."

If we go beyond the outward schizophrenia of these opposing ideals, we find a sad explanation—it is class related. In the States, a tan is a sign of wealth. It takes money and leisure time to be able to noticeably tan—not burn, but tan, like the model in the Bain de Soleil advertisements.

But in equatorial countries such as India, a tan is a sign of the lower caste. The wealthy stay indoors, cooling themselves under rotating ceiling fans, while the rest of society works beneath a branding sun.

4. *Of or relating to striptease*

This meaning is so repugnant it's comical. Is an exotic woman expected to dance her version of the seven veils for the edification (or destruction) of men? Visions of Salome arise, and again that fear of what is different, or man's fear of woman. As Jung noted, we give women all the characteristic that "swarm in the male Eros." Because of the sexual connotation, it has become de rigeur for a man to be seen with a foreign-looking woman. The advertising community, taking note of this, has littered their ads with exotic women, the cosmetics industry is cashing in on their growing number, and the film industry is giving more roles to women who don't look like Cindy Crawford, beautiful as she is.

Which brings me to the real definition of *exotic*.

A growing segment of the U.S. population being targeted for consumerism

As the discussions of the previous definitions reveal, in our society industry and consumerism build the foundation from which change evolves. The foundation for consumerism began with the colonists' revolt against taxation. A

growing consumerism held our country together, forcing a
civil war: according to some social historians, the North
didn't want to lose the South's textile or agricultural contri-
butions, which fed the Northern industries. It met the de-
mands of the civil rights and the women's movement dur-
ing the sixties, when the work force was in dire need of re-
plenishment. Today, consumerism is behind the efforts to
manufacture environmentally safe products, fake fur, and
to provide dolphin-safe nets.

And it now causes publishers to compete against each
other so that they may proudly announce that thirty-five
percent of their authors are minorities; it causes politicians
to include minority policies in their political platforms, it's
behind the slight darkening of the skin and rearranging of
models' features; and it drives fashion designers to steal
other cultures' traditional attire, reproduce it, and sell it for
a criminal price. Are women aware that they're wearing a
mini sarong from Africa? Or *shalwars* from India? These
pants cost as much as $200 in the States, but in India, de-
pending on how well you can bargain, you can get them for
$5. Westerners don't see the women sitting crosslegged in
dark rooms and on thin mats, a useless protection from damp
floors, embroidering or weaving their own fallen hair into
the materials. And they never haggle with a street vendor
for 5 rupees (the equivalent of about 25 cents), until the boy
says earnestly, with that tilt of the head peculiar to Indi-
ans, "Look, miss, to you 5 rupees is nothing—to me it is
everything." True.

The *melting pot* is recognized as an anachronistic term.
The new buzz-word for the nineties is *multicultural* or *mul-
tinational*, because we know that soon minorities will be
the majority. They are gaining economic independence and
buying their way into acceptance. So out of fear, our culture
is adopting their clothing and jewelry, eating their foods in
restaurants with purple decors, and taking up their causes
to the point where we will forget who it all really belongs to.
But I hope that we will fight the desire to have these groups
assimilate, and that the prefix *multi* will begin to take power,
allowing this country to exist as many rather than as one

generic, incestuous mass. May the words of *M*A*S*H*'s Frank Burns be banished to an unenlightened past: "Individuality is fine. As long as we do it together." No one should be labeled and shelved. I hope that we open our minds to learn from other cultures, accept what each has to offer, not because we can make a profit from them but because it will enrich our own culture. As Richard Rodriguez writes, "Diversity which is not shared is no virtue. Diversity which is not shared is a parody nation."

Perhaps the real definition of *exotic* should be "a recognition of that which is especially unique to each culture." For if someone calling me exotic meant a recognition of a proud people who persevere in the face of terrible poverty and disease, if they saw in me even a spark of Paul, a disfigured leper who, every evening, sits on the leprosarium stairs to take in the beauty of the Himalayan foothills during sunset, with no bitterness at his lot, then I would smile widely and say, "Thank you."

From City to Suburb America
Abby Bogomolny

it's so pretty near the bridges
just like the pictures
but those rat-dirty streets,
the broken glass of going nowhere,
fast runaway madness
of worlds upon worlds upon one street,
first stop for immigrants
just happy to be somewhere
they don't shoot on sight

they don't yet know
the American train
runs underground,
moldy tile echoing
the deafening of others,
they don't yet taste
the blood in our coca cola
or stretch in a bed built
from the brittle bones
of other people's destitution.

perhaps the next generation will discover
that stores, filled with the gasoline
chemistry of free trade labels,
and the sprawl across suburbia,
will not save anyone's children.

Chapter 6
Looking to the Future

National attitudes toward immigration changed abruptly on September 11, 2001, when four airliners were hijacked. Two of them destroyed the World Trade Center in New York; the third slammed into part of the Pentagon outside Washington DC, and the fourth crashed in a rural field in Somerset County, Pennsylvania.

Prior to September 11, immigration had been debated mostly in terms of its economic and cultural effects. On the economic side, Americans disagreed about such questions: Were immigrants lowering the wages of Americans, or were they merely taking jobs that Americans did not want? Were they stimulating economic growth, or were immigrants draining the tax revenues of local and state governments? On the cultural side, Americans also disagreed. Some wanted to tighten immigration because they saw their communities changing in ways they did not like. On the other hand, many Americans welcomed the changes in customs, culture and language, and some Americans were happy to see more people of their own ethnicity arrive and prosper.

After September 11, the old debates remained, but they were joined by a new one, relating to national security. The hijackers, we soon learned, were all foreigners in the U.S. on student and tourist visas—most of them from Saudi Arabia—and members of a terrorist network called Al Qaeda. On the surface, foreigners seemed to be attacking the United States. A new question emerged: Did the survival of the country require much tighter controls on immigration?

The federal government took the position that it did, although many questions about ignored intelligence and the executive branch's response to September 11 still remain.

Regardless, the federal government began to impose a wide variety of new restrictions on immigration. Within a few weeks, for example, it became much more difficult to obtain a visa to enter the United States as a permanent immigrant or in a temporary category such as tourist or student. In major east coast cities close to New York, Boston, and Washington, DC, Middle Eastern and South Asian immigrants were detained in police dragnets and held for questioning. For hundreds, it would be many months before the status of their cases, or even their names, would be released.[1] In addition, entry at the border became a more onerous process. A vast databank of foreign students was established, requiring the expenditure of many millions of dollars by universities, although it was not clear that the databank served any purpose related to national security. Universities soon noticed that the number of foreign students enrolled in their institutions fell, and they faced increased difficulties in hiring foreign scholars and professors.

In short, the government reduced the rights of both legal and illegal immigrants. On October 25, 2001, Congress passed the USA Patriot Act of 2001. Only one vote in the Senate and 66 votes in the House of Representatives dissented. Hastily passed, the Act was difficult to understand at first, but Law Professor Richard Boswell explains its impact well: "The Patriot Act supplemented 1996 laws that limited immigrants' access to the courts, countered foreign terrorists, and provided for the removal of immigrants for relatively small offenses."[2] As a result the number of deportations increased, some for the most minor of infractions and some without judicial review. The government also asserted the right to keep foreigners in prison without access to the courts, as well as the right to intercept telephone conversations—of Americans as well as immigrants—without a judicial warrant.

Then on March 1, 2003, President Bush dissolved the Immigration and Naturalization Service (INS) and integrated it into three areas under the Department of Homeland Security (DHS), the largest U.S. government restructuring since 1947 when President Harry S. Truman combined areas of the armed forces into the Department of Defense. The Bureau of Customs and Border Protection (BCBP) would handle border enforcement; the Bureau of Immigration and Customs Enforcement (BICE) would manage interior enforcement, and the Bureau of Citizenship and Immigration Services (BCIS) would oversee immigration benefits and services.

The new emphasis on immigration as an issue of security immediately frayed relationships between the United States and its two neighbors, Canada and Mexico. Since the Canadians refused to copy the newly restrictive immigration controls instituted by the United States, American policy makers worried increasingly that terrorists could enter Canada easily and then come to the United States through its relatively open northern border. In response, they instituted new restrictions on entry through Canada: restrictions that threatened the considerable flow of commerce and tourism between the two neighbors.

With Mexico, the problems were much more serious. Mexico is the source of more than half the illegal immigration into the United States, and the American government now had a new reason to restrict that immigration. In the period between President Bush's inauguration in January 2001 and September 11, the president appeared to be coming to an agreement with Mexican President Vicente Fox on a plan to regularize the flow of Mexican workers into the United States, and to provide some form of access to legal status for those who had previously entered illegally. For several years after the terrorist attacks, those plans were abandoned, to the increasing dismay of Mexican leaders. Instead, border enforcement budgets swelled.

Eventually, in 2005, President Bush tentatively reopened the issue of providing a legal way for Mexicans to work in the United States. This time, however, these initiatives were to be coupled with measures to increase surveillance at the border and reduce entry of the undocumented.

Vigilante groups such as the Minutemen Project called for "volunteers" to come to Arizona "to help secure" the southern border. With more than 80 percent of the volunteers carrying weapons, sometimes joined by members of white supremacist organizations, the Minutemen Project delivered a chilling message. In short, relations with Mexico were greatly set back in the aftermath of September 11.

Many compare the political climate after September 11 to previous periods of wartime concern over national security. For example, considerable anti-Japanese sentiment broke out after the attack on Pearl Harbor in 1941, and the United States cited national security as a rationale to intern Americans of Japanese ancestry in "hospitality centers."[3] After September 11, increased profiling of South Asians, Arabs, and Muslims in all walks of life became a sore point of debate, later aggravated by the U.S. attack on Afghanistan in 2001, the treatment of prisoners at the Guantanamo Bay Naval Base Prison Camp, and the subsequent 2003 invasion of Iraq. In 2006, a $385 million contract made to Halliburton subsidiary KBR (Kellogg, Brown and Root) expanded the possibility of detention facilities for "an emergency influx of immigrants." At approximately the same time the Sensenbrenner Bill (HR 4437) was introduced in Congress that proposed criminalizing undocumented immigrants and charging anyone aiding them with a felony. In response to HR 4437, student walkouts, followed by protests in New York City, Los Angeles, Chicago, San Francisco were held on May 1, 2006 in most major U.S. cities. Tens of thousands of immigrant families and their supporters marched to urge lawmakers to enact less punitive measures and institute easier routes to legal residency. With many competing plans and no agreement, congressional work on a comprehensive immigration reform bill will take place in a future legislative session.

Whether or not Americans view immigration as an issue of national security, it is clear that immigration will continue. Immigrants will continue to change the face of the country in many ways. They will make the population bigger, and they will change its racial composition. In the early years of the 21ˢᵗ century, non-Hispanic whites (or "Anglos") make up just over 70 percent of the American population; the Census Bureau estimates that by 2050 they will account for about 50 percent, and some time in the second half of the century they will become a minority. The population descended from Latin Americans will become the next largest group after the white population, and the proportions of those of African and Asian descent may be roughly equal.

Immigrants, their children, and grandchildren will be transformed by the experience of coming to a new country— and so too will the country be transformed. While questions still remain about September 11 and its impact on immigrants and American-born residents alike, immigration is central to the American experience: its culture. its politics, its demography, its ideals and much more. Immigrants deserve and morality requires that we find ways to enact reasonably fair policies that also protect us.

[1] See the Department of Justice's Office of Inspector General Report (OIG), June 2, 2003, detailing the abuse of 762 South Asian, Arab, and Muslim immigrants.

[2] Richard Boswell is Professor of Law and Director of the Center for International Justice and Human Rights at the University of California, Hastings College of Law in San Francisco. His explanation of the Patriot Act appeared in *The Network News*, Spring 2002, published by the National Network for Immigrant and Refugee Rights.

[3] See Executive Order 8802, issued by Franklin D. Roosevelt, June 25, 1941.

A Tapestry of Hope
Jeanne Wakatsuki Houston

Jeanne Wakatsuki Houston co-authored *Farewell to Manzanar* with her husband James D. Houston, and is the author of the novel *The Legend of Fire Horse Woman*. "A Tapestry of Hope" is an adaptation of the inspirational commencement address she gave to DeAnza College graduates in June, 1996.

Many years ago—43 to be exact—when I stood on the ground where DeAnza College now stands, I looked out onto lush orchards, fragrant with blossoms in springtime and ladened with plump fruit in summer. I viewed acres of foliage carpeting the earth with green—patches of beans, tomatoes and squash, and long furrows of strawberries, glistening red under their leafy canopies.

In those days I knew this area well, for I had spent several summers picking those berries at a large strawberry ranch called "Esperanza," located not far from here. Esperanza, the Spanish word for "hope," was farmed by Japanese families in partnership with the Driscoll brothers. They were sharecroppers. My father sharecropped with the Driscolls at another ranch in South County from 1951 to 1955.

In 1945 when our family re-entered society after three and a half years of incarceration at Manzanar, a concentration camp for Japanese-Americans during World War II, my father's fishing license was revoked. It forced him to seek a livelihood outside a successful pre-war fishing occupation.

Starting at economic zero, at age 59 he seized the opportunity to begin again and brought his family to San Jose from Southern California to farm strawberries. Although my father had been in this country for more than 35 years, and his family, including my mother, had been born here, we arrived at this luscious valley like new immigrants, refugees from another world.

Why do I tell you this? I tell you this because when I picked those berries I never dreamed I would be speaking at a college that someday would rise up within view of where

I knelt in the dirt. It was beyond my imagination. But here I am sharing with you some thoughts and insights I have accrued since those days in the strawberry fields more than 40 years ago.

As Santa Clara Valley's landscape has changed, so has its consciousness. I'm not going to lecture about how tough it was then to be Asian, to be poor, and to be a woman. But I would like to say a few words to remind us how we have changed, how things are different—especially in attitudes toward ethnic diversity.

When I was growing up in the '50s, being "American" and acceptable to mainstream society meant one had to assimilate, melt into one great pot where the broth was predominantly Anglo-European flavored.

No one talked about the concept of cultural diversity as a mosaic or as a tapestry of multi-colored threads that when woven together created a brilliantly rich and textured fabric. "Real Americans" were white. People of color had to think and act "white" to prove their "Americanness." And while I was growing up after the war, muted by the internment experience, it never occurred to me to question this attitude.

Not even when I was told I should not continue with a journalism major at San Jose State because I was "Oriental" and a female. There were no jobs in the field. So I changed my major to social welfare. And when I was told again by the head of Juvenile Probation Services that they would not hire me as a probation officer because the community was not "ready" for "Orientals," I did not protest—although I had been educated enough by then to know it was wrong. But that was the '50s.

Equal opportunity laws were non-existent. I remained silent, returning to the safety zone of invisibility and "don't make waves" mentality.

Then in the '60s, the Black Power movement changed forever the way racial and ethnic minorities thought of themselves. Black leaders led us to rediscover our cultural backgrounds and our histories. We rediscovered our participation in, and our contributions to, the development of this country, and with this recognition came a sense of pride and identity.

For the first time in U.S. history, an awareness of values inherent in America's sub-cultures rose into public consciousness. We began to see that when individuals have a strong sense of identity, of pride in one's heritage, this sense of self-worth strengthens the larger society. Not only were attitudes changing in the dominant culture, but also subgroups themselves began to recognize that America is a land of immigrants, and that all immigrants had a hand in developing it.

Thirty years ago the word "immigrant" seemed reserved for people of color, individuals from the Third World. Today, this still seems to be the prevailing myth. I hear so often the comment, "America is becoming—so multi-cultural with all the immigration from Asia and south of the border." Some people are surprised or mystified or threatened by the idea that the country is becoming so diverse, when in fact, it always has been.

From the moment Portuguese and Italian sailors landed in the New World to mingle with indigenous people in what we now call the West Indies, American began its cross-cultural heritage. And up North, more than 500 indigenous tribes, speaking as many different languages, for centuries had lived on the vast and fertile continent.

Ethnicity is not the exclusive property of people of color. We all have ethnicity. We are descendants of individuals from China, Ireland, Ethiopia, Vietnam, El Salvador, Canada—to name a few. Ideally, Americans should not have problems with identity; we must realize there is no need to "wanna-be-ethnic"—because, in fact, we all are.

I would like to share an experience I had two years ago when I was in Japan. I met a Japanese man, a visionary who founded a grass-roots movement called "the Sweet Potato Movement." It was a calling back to the land from the cities, the dense urban area he referred to as the "fourth world."

He surprised me with this comment, "The world is

watching America deal with its diversity. For the Japanese, America is the role model for democracy. We may be strong economically, but we need your country to lead us to human rights and values. You must succeed if democracy is to succeed around the world."

I like to view our diversity as a metaphor, a microcosm of the macrocosm of a world of nations. I like to see America as a great experiment, a laboratory for testing ideals—the big test today being tolerance and cooperation. If we can't get along in our own communities because of our cultural differences, how can we expect nations around the world to co-exist peacefully?

One of our greatest challenges is to embrace our differences while seeking out the common bonds that hold us together. What are those bonds? What are those threads, the warp in the loom that sets the pattern for who we are as Americans? For me, those threads are the ideals of freedom, equality, opportunity, justice. I also include the human qualities of gratitude, generosity, curiosity and love. Those threads together provide the strength and foundation around which our individual cultural differences weave, making each and every one of us unique and interesting Americans.

As I noted earlier, there was a major shift in perception to reach the point of agreement that we are, indeed, a multi-cultural society, that we began with diversity. But there is a difference between cultural diversity and cross-cultural understanding. They are not synonymous. The great opportunity now is to seek out ways to enhance cross-cultural understanding and not fall back on separatism and attitudes of "our tribe against theirs."

Today, in a time of economic crisis, there are those in our political leadership who are all too ready to find scapegoats.

More and more, it seems, these scapegoats are immigrants. The voices of fear echo daily on the front pages of newspapers, in our television broadcasts. "They are different from us. They have no idea of democracy and freedom. They won't speak our language and they keep to themselves."

Those are the words used today to describe the newest Americans. How many of us who lived through the racism and internment of Japanese-Americans during World War II remember what it was like to have those words directed against one innocent group?

In 1942, we had no one to speak up for us. But after the war, empowered by the Civil Rights movement of the 60s, Japanese-Americans began a 10-year drive for redress from our government. It culminated with the passage of the Civil Liberties Act of 1988, which officially apologized for the internment.

Japanese-Americans were vindicated in the eyes of history. But this victory was not for Japanese-Americans alone. It was a real victory for all Americans, for it proved our Constitution is not just a piece of parchment under glass in the National Archives. It is a living, vital contract that binds us all together as Americans.

And if that contract is broken—as it was in 1942—it is not just the rights of individuals that are threatened, but the very fabric of this nation. And we know that the fabric is woven from threads representing many different groups. If one of these threads is cut, stretched out of proportion or bleached of color, the design becomes listless and in danger of unraveling.

I began this talk with a memory, a powerful memory, which should underline one of the ironic possibilities of living in America. Who knows what the future holds for any of us? But whatever measure of success we have achieved is because we own a certain capacity. That capacity is hope.

When I was a teen-ager picking strawberries on that ranch, so appropriately named "Esperanza," I did not have vision. I could not envision the future I have today. Yet, I did have an unexplainable pull to fulfill some possibility, some unknown challenge. I now know that urge to fulfill was hope, a submerged belief in my own power, in the possibility I could accomplish "something."

Today I salute the accomplishments of all people and their faith—their faith in themselves and thus, in a future for this country.

They Shut
My Grandmother's Room Door
Andrew Lam

When someone dies in the convalescent home where my grandmother lives, the nurses rush to close all the patients' doors. Though as a policy death is not to be seen at the home, she can always tell when it visits. The series of doors being slammed shut remind her of the firecrackers during Tet.

The nurses' efforts to shield death are more comical to my grandmother than reassuring. "Those old ladies die so often," she quips in Vietnamese, "every day's like new year."

Still it is lonely to die in such a place. I imagine some wasted old body under a white sheet being carted silently through the empty corridor on its way to the morgue. While in America a person may be born surrounded by loved ones, in old age one is often left to take the last leg of life's journey alone.

Perhaps that is why my grandmother talks mainly now of her hometown, Bac-Lieu; its river and green rich rice fields. Having lost everything during the war, she can now offer me only her distant memories: Life was not disjointed back home; one lived in a gentle rhythm with the land; people died in their homes surrounded by neighbors and relatives. And no one shut your door.

So it goes. The once gentle, connected world of the past is but the language of dreams. In this fast-paced society of disjointed lives, we are swept along and have little time left for spiritual comfort. Instead of relying on neighbors and relatives, on the river and land, we deal with the language of materialism; overtime, escrow, stress, down payment, credit cards, tax shelter. Instead of going to the temple to pray for good health we pay life and health insurance religiously.

My grandmother's children and grandchildren share a certain pang of guilt. After a stroke which paralyzed her, we could no longer keep her at home. And although we visit her regularly, we are not living up to the filial piety standard expected of us in the old country. My father silently grieves and my mother suffers from headaches. (Does she see herself in such a home in a decade or two?)

Once, a long time ago living in Vietnam, we used to stare at death in the face. The war in many ways had heightened our sensibilities toward living and dying. I can still hear the wails of widows and grieving mothers. Though the fear of death and dying is a universal one, the Vietnamese did not hide from it. Instead, we dwelt in its tragedy. Death pervaded our poems, novels, fairy tales and songs.

But if agony and pain are part of Vietnamese culture, pleasure is at the center of America's culture. While Vietnamese holidays are based on death anniversaries, birthdays are celebrated here. American popular culture translates death with something like nauseating humor. People laugh and scream at blood and guts movies. The wealthy freeze their dead relatives in liquid nitrogen. Cemeteries are places of business, complete with colorful brochures. I hear there are even drive-by funerals where you don't have to get out of your own car to pay your respects to the deceased.

That America relies upon the pleasure principle and happy endings in its entertainment does not, however, assist us in evading suffering. The reality of the suffering of old age is apparent in the convalescent home. There is an old man, once an accomplished concert pianist, now rendered helpless by arthritis. Every morning he sits staring at the piano. One feeble woman who outlived her children keeps repeating: "My son will take me home." Then there are those mindless bedridden bodies kept alive through a series of tubes and pulsating machines.

But despair is not newsworthy. Death itself must be embellished or satirized or deep-frozen in order to catch the public's attention.

Last week on her 82nd birthday I went to see my grandmother. She smiled her sweet sad smile.

"Where will you end up in your old age?" she asked me, her mind as sharp as ever.

The memories of monsoon rain and tropical sun and relatives and friends came to mind. Not here, not here, I wanted to tell her. But the soft moaning of a patient next door and the smell of alcohol wafting from the sterile corridor brought me back to reality.

"Anywhere is fine," I told her instead, trying to keep up with her courageous spirit. "All I'm asking for is that they don't shut my door."

Growing Old in an Alien Landscape
Ann Cooper

Anne Cooper, past "Brit" and present resident of Colorado, is a teacher-on-the-trail. She has written eight natural history books for children. Her poetry and essays have appeared in the *Christian Science Monitor, Poet Magazine, Sistersong, Frogpond,* and *Piedmont Review.*

I am alien, but this is not science fiction. I do not have five eyes or antennae, neither are my limbs ameoboid nor my skin reptilian. For twenty years I paid my Green Card dues, swearing not to live on immoral earnings, swearing to uphold the constitution, renouncing all other allegiances–(reporting to the authorities each January). I've just passed the thirtieth anniversary of what turned out to be the defining moment in my history. I've spent more than half my life in this adopted landscape as a hybrid—a hyphenated American.

I never expected to stay this long. Anywhere. Come to think of it, in some of my pessimistic moods I didn't expect to live this long. In the beginning—as portentous and biblical as that sounds—in the beginning I didn't know I was an immigrant or that I would be an alien—forever. I was coming for two years with a husband who had been offered a temporary, high-tech job. He was part of the mid-sixties brain drain. I was the traditional female follower. In tow was a small daughter who, as the grandparents were at pains to point out loudly and often, we were *ripping from the bosom of the family.*

"What's the big deal?" acquaintances here have often said. "It's not as if you were from Vietnam, or China, or Mexico." The implications in this statement fascinate me, for the implications are so many.

I don't come from an ethnicity that looks different from them, they mean. True. I am white, as are 90 percent of the people in the town I adopted through happenstance. Actually, I am brownish-pink with freckles and red hair. I am neither taller, nor shorter than average. Not fat, not thin, not old, not young, not fashionable, not frumpy, just ordinary. Nondescript. Unmemorable. Walking along any street in the west wearing my mall-bought jeans and T-shirt, no one could tell my national origin by looking at me. But no one can glance at a person on the street who looks Asian or Mexican and know whether they have just arrived—to visit or to stay—or have been American for generations. It's only the hasty who make judgments. It is only the hasty who ask of an obviously Asian colleague—one hopes in the spirit of inclusion and welcome—*where are you from?* only to discover the colleague was born and raised in Omaha. It has been said often, in many ways, and many believe it: we are all Americans, with our black, brown, pink or freckled faces, with our slanted eyes, with our Slavic cheekbones, with our multitude of backgrounds, voices, hopes, ambitions, fears and failings.

What's the big deal? I don't speak a different language, my friends point out. I don't speak a language incomprehensible to them, they mean. I and my family don't rattle away in what might seem a private code, excluding friends from our intimate conversations. My language, British English, sounds nothing as exotic as Vietnamese, Laotian, or Japanese. The impression that my friends and I speak the same language is deceptive. Mine *is* another language. Even after thirty years, I am still caught out by subtle and delicious differences. Some are harmless and funny, others potentially embarrassing—differences that lead to serious social gaffes. All of them enrich my life. As a writer my English labels me, something as different-good, other times as incompetent, illiterate, or just plain ignorant. Spelling I can deal with. My spell checker, constantly alert, prevents me from getting off "centre" and weeds out the "colours" and "flavours" in my writing that tell of my early rote-learning at the Leasgill Church-of-England Parochial School.

I look "right" and sound "right" (whatever that might mean)—except for the weird accent that I will never lose. But I don't fit completely and know I never will. Does any first generation immigrant ever belong anywhere ever again? What makes me a misfit? What makes me the puzzle-piece from the wrong jigsaw? I see life from both sides of a great divide.

On this side of the Atlantic, I've studied enough history to understand the War of Independence. (I used to know it as the American Revolution on the other side of the divide). There is nothing new about dissenting Brits, whether from the wrong class, the wrong religion, or merely the wrong mind-set, to succeed back home, deciding to make this epic journey. It started in 1607 and continues still. It is commonplace and has no novelty or paranoia factor. "Oh, British, so let's move on with the conversation. . . ." Or people notice the accent, wonder if it is British (or maybe Australian, or New Zealand, or South African)? They ask me "where are you 'from?'" "Colorado," I say. "No, really from," they insist. So I relent and confirm with a quick phrase—*Britain a long time ago*—and tell them I grew up in the English Lake District. As I say it, I see the lush, Wordsworthian landscapes of soft greens and grays, see stone cottages nestled into folds of sheep-cropped fellsides, feel the silvery mist drizzling into my parched skin. The whole area is a mere 40 miles across. It would piece into the Southern Rockies ten or twenty times over. Yet it is the small jewel of my childhood.

Other people related their European travels to me, or share their *I've been there* and *do you know so-and-so in such a town?* stories. Elderly men reminisce of being stationed in Britain during World War Two, their war. "Do you know the air base at Brise Norton, or Lakenheath, or Hethel?" they'll ask. "Yes," I'll say, "that's in my husband's part of the country." I'll tell them my husband remembers Christmas parties on the base put on for children in the village—that he still recalls his first Crackerjack with toys in it; that he'll never forget the strange, blackened fruit you had to peel that the American GIs told him was banana; and that for years, his prize possession was a pocket knife given to him by an airman from Iowa. What I do not say is that, as a five-year-old, he remembers hiding in the nearest ditch when the American Super Fortress bombers returned from raids over Germany. Many planes, damaged by anti-aircraft fire, would limp home with half wings or half tails, scattering fragments as they skimmed the tree tops and wobbled in to land. Friendly fire of a kind, I suppose. Conversations like this are amicable, but illustrate the chasm between our experiences of the same events. Our cultural base has very little overlap.

Once these kinds of pleasantries are out of the way, in the minds of casual acquaintances I am thoroughly established as "not quite one of us." My accent marks me alien, and perhaps suspect? People call it charming or cute—using it, I know, as nothing more significant than a way to start a conversation—but their comments make me feel less American. My accent also denies me permission, except among my very best friends, to openly criticize American institutions or customs. What if I speak my mind about the stupidity of a particular piece of legislation? What if I suggest that the local high school really should push for academic stringency? At the moment I let my passions flow in offering opinions—even if they are opinions my company-of-the-moment share—a wall of hostility rises to separate me from previously-amiable people. I am one. They draw together, closing ranks, and are a solid block. Different. I feel strong wafts of the unstated. *Who does she think she is to say that? What right has she to suggest?* And the ultimate, *if she doesn't like it, why doesn't she go back where she belongs?* The conversation develops a bristly antagonism until we move on to safer topics.

I *do* belong (don't I?) I *am* American after thirty years. I've raised three American kids who have grown up to be good American adults, full of enterprise and ambition, doing their darndest to live the dream. They grow strong and confident on hot dogs, peanut butter and jelly sandwiches, space and freedom. They expanded their horizons with Big Bird and Bert and Ernie. They played little league baseball, not cricket. These kids were enriched by having a foot in two worlds, by having the chance to know where their parents and grandparents fitted in the grand scheme, to taste another way of doing things. On our visits to Britain, they experienced castles and stone circles, unheated houses and temperamental plumbing, hedgerows of wildflowers, fish and chips in newspaper, (and, later, the dubious delights of warm, thick beer and a game of Aunt Sally).

All this time, enthusiastically, I did American Mom stuff. I baked cookies for the homeroom, became den mother to a rowdy bunch of cub scouts, sewed the prom dresses, cheered the marching bands—and raised funds for new band uniforms by selling turkeys for Thanksgiving—that most American of celebrations.

I cared about being American, wholeheartedly and with passion. I fought for causes and volunteered for more tasks than I had time for. I marched in candlelight parades against the war in Vietnam; I encircled Rocky Flats to protest the making of plutonium triggers for nukes; I wrote letters to save spotted owls, whales, wilderness.

Despite this ongoing dedication to being a full participant in the here and now, I find myself living in a small, cottage-y home surrounded by a struggling half acre of heartbreak. I try ineffectually to recreate an English cottage garden, although I know it is hopelessly nostalgic to plant foxgloves, hollyhocks, Christmas roses, and love-in-the-mist in barren, bedrock soils on the edge of the Great American Desert. I long for the scent of damp, emerald mornings. I lust to hear a true dawn chorus of thrushes, yellowhammers, and English robins and blackbirds in a tangly wood full of bluebells and blackthorn. Day after day I wake to that damn-blue continental sky, that tawny, parched hillside with coyotes and cougars, that—desert. Or I hear a wintry forecast and know we'll get heavy snows in May. I am almost resigned to flattened daffodils.

Shall I go back when I am old? Shall I return, full circle, to the climate in which I sprouted, the landscape that nurtured my growing years? I doubt it could work. The England revisited is not the England for which I sometimes long. That England existed thirty years ago. That England held a village centered on a church, reached through a lychgate old before Shakespeare, a churchyard with towering yew trees and lichened tombs. That village contained a house built in 1638—a gracious house of apricot stone festooned with clematis—where I was born and grew in spirit and imagination. That England was gentle and full of freedoms, or so it seems in memory, for memory is nothing if not selective. Visiting now, I am aware that England has grown out of me, grown up and moved on. I am left behind with outdated images. The culture has changed. Hustle has invaded. I am an outsider. I no longer laugh at the jokes and cartoons. The politics bewilder me. The changes in education baffle me. I am barraged by unfamiliar slang. In conversation, I listen and learn, for there are changes in attitude that come as a shock to me. Social encounters have the wrong feel. I risk misinterpretation. This is not home.

Contact with friends and family distances me too. I am, they think, still English. They take up where we last left off and assume I know the score. They expect me to fit in their gatherings, after all, it's not as if I'm "foreign." They are absorbed in their lives and want me to slip quietly back without waves. They ignore my other life, because they neither share nor understand it. Sometimes I resent their lack of curiosity about my life in Colorado. If they meet "real" Americans (real in their assessment) they ask politely and with genuine interest about the culture, the scenery, the politics, the way of life, the movies. If these topics arise in conversations with me, English friends are harsh and critical of America and Americans. They joke about Americans as tourists, rushing around Europe with frantic and farcical desperation. How absurd, the English think smugly, to imagine you could "do" Edinborough or London in such a short time. I want to shake them from their arrogant complacency. We Americans, I say, we save for these trips for a lifetime and want to see everything in case we never come back. If we think we can do England, Scotland, Wales, and Ireland in quick succession we are remembering the drives from Pennsylvania to the Rockies, from California to Texas. Different geographical and cultural parameters define us. I am met by blank looks and lack of understanding.

When they are with me (and not with real Americans, they imply) my family and friends openly deride American politics, scoff at the gun culture, and scorn the brash, frontier mentality. At these times I am ferociously American, and most insulted and offended by their lack of sensitivity. Are they being nasty or insular? Yes. But they wouldn't dream of being openly rude to other-culture people, they say. They just assume I am English still, and see things from their point of view. Too often I keep my peace, but it is at these moments I am most deeply diminished as an American. I am closed out of small courtesies of interest shown to born Americans and asked to conspire in whisperings about my adopted country. In the family's grip, I have little left to talk about safely but our shared memories of growing up in an England that has ceased to exist.

Where does this leave me after thirty years of journeying? I think about possibilities and wonder when it becomes too late to start again. If I were to go back, I would distance myself from my kids, my grown-up life and accomplishments, (my shriveling garden, my flattened daffodils, and the damn, blue sky) and would still never reclaim my Englishness. If I stay, I'll never again live with the mists and greens, the villages settled before William the Conqueror, the sense of walking on history. I'll never return to the ease of sharing cultural icons and trivialities with people who grew up with the same heros, the same fashions, even the same silly quotations culled from theater and radio. I will never return to my roots.

I think I understand a little of what other, more easily-identifiable hyphenated Americans mean by cultural integrity and the importance of language, ceremonies, and traditions. I know this, although my reality contains none of the deep, true separation and alienation described by many newcomers from other cultures. If I stay in this adopted landscape, and year by year it becomes more likely, I'll keep on fighting to belong, to be heard, to be known for myself and not for a clutter of national stereotypes and misconceptions. I'll enjoy driving distances inconceivable in Europe to see my kids and grandkids—all unthinkingly assimilated and un-hyphenated—all unidentifiable as part-alien. Still, I have no illusions. I know, without doubt or hesitation, that whether I choose to spend the rest of my life on this side or the other side of the Atlantic—my Great Divide—I will be growing old in an alien landscape.

All Educated With No Place To Go
Tony Diaz

Tony Diaz's work has appeared in the *Los Angeles Times* and *Houston Chronicle*. His novel *The Aztec Love God* won the Nilon Award for Excellence in Minority Fiction, and was published by the University of Colorado at Boulder and Fiction Collective Two. He is also the founder of *Nuestra Palabra*, Houston's forum for the Latino writing community.

I thought I was a hyphenated American because I chose to call myself a Mexican-American. But looking over my résumé, I realize I earned this designation because I've worked as a free-lance journalist, teaching-assistant, and assistant-editor.

That's why I'm on un-employment.

Always a bridesmaid, never an executive. That's my story. Employers don't want to pay me to be an editor, a professor, or president because they think I'm too easy to hire. I've been around. But really, I'm trying to settle down.

Back during that naïve spring quarter before I finished graduate school, my fiancé was anxious to set a wedding date.

"How about a year after I've been working full-time," I said. I thought I could use the 52 weeks to get adjusted to my new job, make sure our grad school chums and my work chums got along, get my finances straight, play the lottery.

Well, the fall quarter has just ended. I've got three un-employment checks left and I'm hassling her to come with me to the justice of the peace so I can be covered by her university plan. (She's a teaching-assistant and has a year and a half left with that hyphen.) Slowly but surely, she's warming to the idea.

Since I earned the degree in May, all I've been able to do with my master of fine arts is visit museums and say, "Yes, that art's fine. That's fine too." And I still have to show people my degree for them to believe me. Earning just a bachelor's degree might've meant I'd be single forever.

We wanted to have the wedding out here in California, but some of my relatives in Texas were wary of visiting since

Proposition 187 passed. I told them not to worry. As long as they mispronounced the Spanish names of towns they'd be just fine. "San-Joe-Say." I told them to practice "Sand-Lewis-Abyss-Po."

My parents are very supportive (grocery money when we really need it), but I can see the desperation in their eyes even though they try to hide it behind their tears. "All those diplomas," my poor *mamacita* cries in Spanish, "Kindergarten, eighth grade, high school, regular college, graduate school and still, still you're not married."

I've had three graduations more than anyone else in my family, but I'm also the only one to have three part-time jobs that don't add up to 40 hours a week. I'm an intellectual migrant worker.

When I was still in grad school (remember that näive spring quarter?), folks told me I wouldn't have a problem finding a job; I'd not only have a master's degree, but I spoke Spanish too.

So far, being bilingual has meant only that I can read the back of the unemployment insurance claim form as well as the front. And to the folks at all those cocktail parties who told me it was a "hot time to be Latino," I must admit that it seems as if our Nielsen ratings are suffering.

But I'm keeping the faith. Instead of scrambling for 25 jobs leads next week, I'm going to hustle 50. Instead of six hours' sleep, I'll settle for five. (That's still a luxury. My dad says he never slept until he turned 30.)

I know that soon I'll come across my dream employer's want ad for the position I perfectly satisfy. She'll write: "Looking for a writer who can handle day after day of exciting challenges and irregular hours, high pay and a thrilling environment. Unpublished preferred. Who wants this post?"

If only she'd give me a ring, I'd shout, "I do! I do!"

What it trickles down to is that some guys are married to their jobs.

I'm just trying to get a commitment.

Histories
David Kherdian

What do we gain from our parents
that was never ours
but in being theirs was ours,
I wonder about the food and music
and especially the tongue
that never ceased to make me laugh or weep—
because I realize now that our tongue
has always been a member of the heart,
not the head;
a language for histories and passions
spent, perhaps, but alive
alive always in the body of each man.

I put all that aside because so many
others could say it as well—
and take one thing, one thing alone
that is mine, that no one else can touch
or want to understand:
my father at an Armenian picnic, dancing,
round and round and round,
his whirling arms in a speech I could not
understand
with a knife tightly clenched in his teeth
held fast forever
in his bald and spinning head.

It Begins Right Here
Morton Marcus

Morton Marcus is the author of nine books of poetry and one novel. He has published more than 400 poems in such periodicals as *Poetry, Triquarterly,* and *the Nation,* and in over eighty poetry anthologies. Born in New York City in 1936, Marcus taught English and Film at Cabrillo College for thirty years in Aptos, California. His two latest books of prose poems are *Moments Without Names: New and Selected Prose Poems* (2002) and *Shouting Down the Silence: Verse Poems 1988-2001* (2001). This selection was taken from *Pages from a Scrapbook of Immigrants: A Journey in Poems* (1988).

1
My grandfather drops
the lighted cigarette
in the muddy wheel rut
outside his house the day
he decides to leave Russia.
I had forgotten this,
although it has been told me
countless times by my mother,
the six-year-old watching
from the kitchen window.
"He is looking to the west,"
she says, "toward Vilna.
I see it clear as yesterday."
It begins here, and I
will not forget it again.
What the old man chooses—
dropping the cigarette,
kicking at clods with muddy boots—
is what I will become.

He harnessed the horse cart,
tumbled in baggage, crockery,
sons, daughters, wife,
sweat and garlic sliding
beneath his undershirt
and holy prayer shawl,
his rancid sheepskin coat

billowing like wings;
and clopped past hamlets,
villages, towns, and cities;
past continents and oceans;
past storage tanks, tool works,
corner diners after dark;
past cancers, wars,
no bread in the cupboard,
roaches, tetanus,
children leaving home—
clopped past everything
to where I sit now
in this house above the bay
where the green Pacific
emerges from the fog.

My grandfather has been dead
for more than fifty years.
He died without knowing
where California was.
But sometimes I think he comes
to the door and with cap in hand
stands outside with sightless eyes.
At such times, I'm convinced
that his eyes are in my head,
and that for both of us,
and for my mother, whose vision
is diminishing to memories
in a city on another shore—
it begins again right here.

2
In the mountains above the bay,
both my daughters murmur in sleep.
Moonlight is sailing through the window.
Their mouths are open as they dream.
I don't know if they dream of Russia
or of the tenements of New York
or of the continent that ends here,

the water's beaten silver
slipping outward from the shore.
The mountains breathe around them:
honeysuckle, mustard, clover,
lilac, rhododendron, mint,
and the musty leaf pack
on the shadowy forest floors—
redwood, pine, and bay.
All these scents stream skyward,
and with them, like voices in a choir,
rise my daughters' dreaming breath.
For both my children adrift in sleep,
for whatever lives in them of me,
the dream begins right here.

3
With a friend, I wandered out
to watch the evening sun.
He had a special place in mind
and led me to a cliff above the bay
where cypress held a rusty light
and gray pines swayed.
"There," he said and pointed
to a black cloud
wheeling low above the sea.
The water was flat and polished pink,
dark hollows shifting here and there
like changing currents in a dream.
"See?" The cloud was spinning
like a wheel of ash,
and I saw it was composed
of sharp-winged birds,
thousands of sooty shearwaters
skimming the surface of the bay,
feet and wing-flick ruffling up a froth
or detonating the surface when they dived,
until hundreds wrestled with the water,
snapping beaks and fanning wings
beating up a storm of waves and surf

as others fell like a blizzard,
crashing through to "Fish! Fish!
There must be millions of them!
What a feed!" he said and looked away.
There was a stain beneath the water,
a school of anchovies
three hundred yards long,
sprawling this way and that
beneath the clamoring birds,
whose shadow hugged the stain so closely
that an image fluttered through my head
of the bay lying open
for thousands of years beneath the sun
like an old chipped serving bowl
where the feeders were no different
than the food on which they fed.

Next year on the wharf,
I was leaning against a rail
just as the fog burned off,
and it began:
                    a rustle,
static across a widening gulf,
a cloud low and far away
but as it approached
whipping up small peaks
and racing above what seemed
its shadow on the bay,
until I was engulfed:
starchy wings and battered surf,
beaks chopping water
and shredding it to froth
as they snatch at fish.
I was spattered and stained.
I couldn't breathe. Below me
were eyes, acres of eyes,
eyes smeared with an oily light,
edged in sediment, in winy mud;
everywhere eyes streaming by,

thousands of silvery disks
with black holes in their centers
like mine shafts hurtling
to the end of the universe;
eyes that neither beseeched
nor accused, but watched
from the outskirts of the present
as they sank into the past.
And the bay, suddenly,
in a tinfoil shift of wind,
was a sky full of drowned stars.

For me, each day begins
right here.

4

   Teeth have been found,
human teeth, in the tidal mud,
and flints, hand axes, arrowheads,
burial grounds in the hills.
The words *aptos* and *soquel.*
Not much else. The Indians
followed their eyes beyond the sun.
Their irises flashed for a moment
and then they were done.
The grandees and conquistadors,
the padres in rough robes,
have shriveled with their land grants
beneath adobe walls.
They spice the earth around us.
They are smoke or wind or waves.
They are leaves that tongue the breeze
like tiny bells, chimes
that are felt as well as heard,
like bee stings beneath the skin,
endings in which, each moment,
all things once more begin.

5

A student, grinning,
shows me an old photograph
of his Italian grandfather.
and I think, *My grandfather
must have looked like that.*
Surrounded by family, braced
against the back rest of the chair,
big-knuckled hands gripping the arms
as if he were about to spring,
the old man glares at me.
There's arrogance in those eyes,
defiance in that out-thrust chin,
and the usual costume
to accompany the pose:
handlebar mustache,
high stiff collar,
silver watch chain
across a black wool vest.
The print is muddy brown.
It could be Sicily
or Spain or even Russia,
but it's not. Outside
the photograph, it's Monterey.
A muddy daylight shifts
across a muddy bay:
                    Sardines,
silver-sided shoals of them,
pack the waters.
Canning factories
clatter and shake and steam.
Discarded fish heads and fins.
Scalding fish oil
that leaves a greasy film
on every townsman's skin.
Twenty-five tons
were canned every day.
The old man knew Ferrante;
used the zigzag lightning
of his lampara net;

was one of the colony
of Sicilian fishermen
that Ferrante, like Moses,
led to this fog-swabbed bay
and to whom Ferrante said, "Here.
You have been promised this."
For thirty years, the old man
fished and overfished the bay.
Then it was done. Arrogance
and promises were not enough.
For sardines and fishermen,
it ended where it had begun.

6
The fog removes a hill
beyond my neighbor's fence.
Out of sight behind the house,
the road and redwood grove
have been missing for a week.
And there, across the bay,
the entire mountain range
has vanished overnight
to be replaced by nothing
but a gap of ragged gray.
It is the fog, then—the fog
that makes the countryside
a landscape we invent,
a jigsaw-puzzle scene
where pieces are always missing
or constantly rearranged,
exposing absences
that take us unaware,
gaps our minds must fill
with landmarks we remember
or places we invent.
Now and then, the land
shifts beneath my feet,
the house around me trembles.
There can be fog outside or sun,
but a such moments I think

the landscape and the elements
contrive to make us dream.

Downtown, last month, near
a women's clothing shop,
a girl in beaded buckskins,
hair braided like a squaw's,
padded up beside me, and stared
through the plate-glass window
at the gold glitter pumps
and genie pants on display.
She was eighteen or so
and white as a picket fence
and could have been the sister
of the boy across the street
who sat cross-legged on a bench
in beard and hemp-tied robe,
as if he were Jesus begging
in front of the five-and-ten.
I see them everywhere:
carrying blankets and guitars
to somewhere else, dressed
like apparitions in a dream,
or like foreigners, or like the dead.
When he was young, my grandfather
must have looked like them.
What he was looking for,
they look for now. No,
it isn't quite the same.
But who am I to talk,
who have lugged an old man's dreams,
and the dreams of the old woman
who was once his daughter,
across a continent
to resurrect them here
above a foggy shore?

Who are these children,
these actors without a play,

these masquerading bands
who traipse past cairns and graves
and all the unmarked places
in a shifting countryside
where dead men's dreams
are flowering around us
in trees and rocks and weeds,
where the stares of birds and fish
remind us of the eyes
of that vague, fog-laden form
who shambles from our sleep
and whom we almost recognize?

More and more I think
that if I looked closely
at the tapering face bones
of that buckskinned white girl,
I would find a daughter.
Weren't those our skeletons,
costumed in their separate skins,
who wandered here, hauling
our parents' crockery and clothes
to this fogbound place?
And aren't these children
the ones we dreamt about
who have tumbled onto a landscape
more authentic than the one
on which our imaginations
could put down houses?
Our dreams like fog
swirled around them
and clung, clung to these children,
these muscles of our eyes,
these skins of our breath,
whose only hope now—
and our own—is to feel
the trembling beneath their feet
and recognize
that the land is as unsure
as they are, and as young.

No Memories At All
Eva Metzger Brown

Eva Metzger Brown, Ph.D, is a psychologist, mediator and Child Survivor of the European Holocaust. She was born four months before Kristallnacht (1938) in Nurnberg, Germany, and arrived in the U.S. three years later. As an adult she founded the Intergenerational Healing in Holocaust Families at the University of Massachusetts. This poem illustrates some of the reasons for her work with members of European Holocaust families, and families of other Holocausts.

I listened to others talk about their childhood,
sharing what they had lost in the War

about cousins no longer there
and families that never laughed . . . again

about his father who walked into the forest,
only to fall in a knot of black bullets
about his mother who did not come back from
Theresienstadt,
without a record of her death, he searched for her still

about hiding in convents, closets, cubby holes
not like games of "hide and seek" but for hours, days,
years . . .
one woman, who was placed in a convent at six and left at
ten,
simply said "And then I was adopted,"
not . . . "I lost my parents."

the first time I heard their stories
I did not ask them what had happened to their grief,
kept silently to themselves, no,
they had leapt over their pain
to get on with their lives

the first time I heard their stories,
I did not ask
because I could not find my words

I had no stories to tell about what I had lost in the war
somewhere between earth and sky, in my mother's arms,
then someone else's and someone else's again, an infant, I
lived through Kristallnacht, but I had no words,
lived through the race across Europe, but do not remem-
ber
orphanages and explosions in France
only this . . .
one day my mother came
one day my father came
one day we got on a boat to Casablanca to Martinique and
then America

we were children
we were children
ALL OF US

how could this happen to children?
how could this happen to parents?
how could this happen to the world?
why did no one stop what was happening in the world?

how come it is happening, again?
happening to other children—now?
look at today's explosions . . .

I may not have had words, then
but there is an echo to the past,
hear it and listen to the words of my echo, the words of
their stories
so that another generation of children will never
have to tell stories filled with suffering,
losses, murders, and starvation again.

Enforcement: A Tool to Control the Flow of Labor at the U.S.-Mexico Border

María Jiménez

María Jiménez is the Director of the American Friends Service Committee Immigrations Law Enforcement Monitoring Project (ILEMP) in Houston, Texas.

Immigrants and immigration are buzz words in the U.S. public debate that stir emotions, polarize relations between ethnic and racial groups, and evoke hostility toward anyone foreign-born. Ironically, the process of globalization, economic integration and economic restructuring gives rise to an increasing movement of persons across international boundaries. "International labor migrant" is a more precise term to describe those who move in the complex web of a global economic system. Since the 1960s, economic migrants from developing countries to industrialized nations have quadrupled, reaching about 940,000 per year.

Worldwide immigration policies have made it possible for a small group of people to become more and more mobile by providing the legal flexibility for the exit and entrance of business owners, executives, administrators and technical labor. However physical and other barriers to the movement of poor people have proliferated. The *inequality of mobility* is a part of the maintenance of the larger socio-economic and political inequalities on a national and international scale.

The movement to industrialized countries is not a movement seeking a "transition to prosperity" but rather a response to the politics of economic integration created and imposed by global economic elites. Migration cannot be separated from the policies of debt collection by multi-lateral agencies like the World Bank and International Monetary Fund in acquiescence with domestic elites and national governments. Such policies have caused untold human suffering and widespread environmental destruction, rendering these countries with few resources to invest in economic recovery.

Border control is sought as a policy decision not so much to stop unauthorized migration, but to frame the condition in which international labor participates in economic, social and political spheres. No other border control policies better illustrate this complex facet of global integration and the inequality of movement of persons than those of the United States with respect to its border with Mexico.

These nations share the most integrated relationship between a rich and poor nation, in terms of debt, trade and migration. Mexico's debt to U.S. banks totals about 150 billion dollars. From 1965 to 1990, some 1.9 million Mexicans were admitted as legal permanent residents. During the same time period, there were more than 36 million undocumented entries from Mexico and more than 31 million departures. The process of social capital formation, human capital accumulation and market integration between the two countries has so far advanced in over 100 years of continuous migratory flows, that stopping the flow of migration is impossible.

Increasing the INS[1] budget by 75% to enhance border enforcement reflects more of a rejection of the presence of working poor, Spanish-speaking immigrants than policy decision based on fact. Traditionally, concern for "borders out of control" has always been about the 2,000 miles of the U.S.-Mexico border and never the 4,000 miles of the U.S.-Canadian border. According to the Urban Institute, only four out of ten individuals who are illegally in the country entered by crossing the southern border; the other six entered with legal visas that later expired. Yet 85% of all the resources of the Immigration and Naturalization Service, including the Border Patrol, are located in southern border communities.

Walls, more agents and military support as tougher border enforcement measures only redirect the flows of undocumented immigrants to other parts of the border, delaying entry and increasing the risks to migrants as they move toward more dangerous and remote areas of the border. A recent University of Houston study estimated that 190 to

300 persons died annually attempting to cross the Texas border; countless more die crossing the deserts of Arizona and mountains and highways of California.

At the same time, enforcement of immigration laws is selectively applied to persons of Mexican origin and/or descent. Mexican nationals represent 39% of the undocumented immigrants in the U.S., but they are 90% of those arrested for illegal entry by the Immigration and Naturalization Service. The Mexican-origin population bears the burden of civil and human rights violations. Deaths, beating, sexual assaults, illegal arrests and other cases of abuse of authority are often reported by those confronting immigration authorities. In a recent study by the University of Arizona, 18% of 200 randomly surveyed persons in South Tucson indicated that they had been mistreated by immigration officials. Of these 60% were citizens born in the United States.

Violence on the U.S.-Mexico border reinforces temporality and control of Mexican labor on both sides of the border to ensure high profitability in industries on both sides. U.S. immigration policy is an artificial and misdirected effort to intervene in economic transactions between willing sellers of labor and willing buyers by interposing armed force both at the border and at worksites. It is the only aspect of employee and employer relations that is enforced through the use of guns. Ultimately, dependence of many U.S. industries on undocumented labor encourages contempt for the law, fosters contraband in human beings and the widespread falsification of identity documents. The international labor workforce is placed in a position of illegality, vulnerability, exploitation and socio-political marginalization.

In a historical continuum, this is nothing new for the Mexican-origin population in the United States. Racism, exclusion and segregation are all too familiar. The only change currently is that this fervor takes place in the context of the inequalities produced by a global economic system. In the short run, a realistic approach to border control on the U.S.-Mexico border is to recognize the movement of labor as an inevitable consequence of the ongoing processes of the market integration presently occurring and formally recognized by NAFTA.[2] Binational agreements on migratory flows within both countries must move toward developing a flexible legal framework for the movement of labor in both directions, guaranteeing equity and respect for the human rights and dignity of all human beings. In the long run, the construction of immigration control policies must evolve as a product of mutual agreement and acknowledgment between the people of both countries that together work to construct a world of economic equity, social acceptance and peace.

[1] Immigration and Naturalization Service.

[2] North Atlantic Free Trade Agreement.

Ethics and Interests
in the Immigration Debate
John Isbister

John Isbister is Dean of Humanities and Social Sciences at Laurentian University in Sudbury, Ontario, Canada. He received his Ph.D. from Princeton University, and then taught in the Economics Department at the University of California, Santa Cruz, where he was the Provost of Merrill College for 15 years. He is the author of *Promises Not Kept: The Betrayal of Social Change in the Third World, Thin Cats: The Community Development Credit Union Movement in the United States* and *The Immigration Debate: Remaking America.*

Immigration is a controversial subject in the United States. Although we are a nation of immigrants, many of those who are already established in the country want to close the door against new entrants. Today, as many times in the past, voices are rising in protest against immigration. Some of the voices make a distinction between legal and undocumented immigration, and speak only against the latter—but many others claim that all categories of immigrants should be cut back.

I favor immigration, and I want to argue for it here principally on the grounds of ethics. This is not how the case is usually made, whether for or against immigration. Usually we argue from the point of view of interest: our personal interest perhaps, or the interest of our ethnic group or class, or perhaps even the national interest. Seldom do we look beyond the interests of Americans to the question of what is right.

Even when one restricts oneself to the national interest as the criterion for judging immigration, the debate is complex and confusing. Both proponents and opponents of immigration can be found on all sides of the political spectrum. Liberal opponents of immigration are most worried about the effect of immigration on the wages and employment opportunities of low-skilled and poor Americans, including most centrally African Americans. They also worry about the effects of increased population growth upon the natural environment of the United States. Conservative opponents are mostly worried about the cultural impact of the immigrants. They would not mind more immigrants from Europe, but they worry that the newcomers from the third world are changing the languages, ideas and customs that Americans are used to and have a right to retain.

The defenders of the new immigration have equally varied ideologies. Liberal defenders tend to favor the United States' becoming an increasingly multicultural society. They welcome the variety and the new stimuli that immigration brings with it. Organized ethnic groups in the United States are not of one mind about immigration, but most are concerned to preserve the right of families to be reunited with their kin from abroad. The conservative case for immigration is based mostly on the interests of employers who face potential labor shortages. Immigration allows them to hire unskilled labor at low wages, and also in some cases skilled workers.

One of the reasons it is hard to resolve this debate, even when it is restricted to the level of interests, is that the relevant facts are not clear. Do immigrants take jobs that Americans don't want and won't fill, or do they displace Americans from employment? Do they stimulate the economy and help all to prosper, or do they widen the gap between the American rich and poor? Do they exploit American taxpayers by claiming government services in the areas of health care, education and welfare, or do they pay their way (or perhaps even more than pay their way) in terms of tax payments? Participants in the debate generally have strong views about these factual questions.

The empirical research on the factual questions has not led to definitive answers, however. It is interesting that most econometricians in the field can find virtually no quantitative impact of immigration upon the wages and employment opportunities of Americans. These findings do not absolutely prove the case, since the econometric studies probably suffer from unavoidable methodological problems, but they should at least give pause to those who think that immigration necessarily impoverishes Americans.

When we formulate the debate in these ways, however, we are for the most part avoiding the most important question: what is right? National interest is, after all, just a fancy name for national selfishness, and selfishness is hardly the same as morality. How does the immigration debate look if we consider it from the point of view not of national selfishness but of morality, or ethics?

We are on slippery territory here, since we do not agree about the foundations of morality. Surely we can agree, however, that the interests of people in the rest of the world, including the immigrants themselves, should have some standing in our assessment of the value of immigration. How much standing? As it turns out, the founding document of the United States is clear on this question. "We hold these truths to be self evident," wrote Thomas Jefferson in the Declaration of Independence, "that all Men are created equal." He did not argue the point; it was "self-evident." The importance of equality was that equal rights accrue to all people. "They are endowed by their Creator with certain unalienable Rights, that among these are Life, Liberty and the Pursuit of Happiness." If we transform Jefferson's "men" to "people," we are confronted with a document proclaiming that every single person in the world is of equal value. Of course Jefferson did not completely believe this; he was a slaveholder. Rare is the American today who completely believes it either. But somewhere deep in our hearts we know that it must be true, that it is self-evident, that it is the basis of morality. In another section of his subconscious, Jefferson may have thought something like, "all Englishmen are created equal," but that is not what he said, and had he said it his words would not resonate so strongly to us through the centuries. The United States was founded on the axiom of the absolute equality of all people. Almost a century later, the idea found a reprise in the most famous speech in American history, Lincoln's Gettysburg Address: "Fourscore and seven years ago, our fathers brought forth upon this continent a new nation, conceived in liberty and dedicated to the proposition that all men are equal."

If it is an American precept that people are of equal

value, and being of equal value consequently have equal rights, what gives Americans the moral authority to restrict the movement of non-Americans? Some of the world's equally worthy people would like to move to the United States. Surely the freedom to move is one of the "unalienable rights" that accrue to equal people. We would all agree that the people of California lack the right to exclude New Yorkers from their territory. Why, therefore, should the people of the United States have the right to exclude Mexicans? I am talking here of the moral right, not the legal right. Americans do have the legal right to exclude people from entry, whether temporary or permanent, onto the national territory. More than anything else, that is the definition of sovereignty, and when countries try but fail to enforce such restrictions, their sovereignty is called into question. But that is a matter of international law, and the law does not necessarily embody the highest standards of ethics. Ethically, it is hard to argue that one group of people has the right to restrict the movement of others. When white South Africans controlled the movement of blacks through a system of pass laws, they were almost universally condemned by the outside world.

Let me make the case stronger, and argue that it is actually less defensible for Americans to exclude Mexicans than it would be for Californians to exclude New Yorkers. Californians could argue that New Yorkers who are excluded from their state have many other options that are comparable; the New Yorkers could move to Oregon, for example, or to Washington or Arizona. They could stay in New York which is, after all, a state with much the same amenities as California. The United States, however, is in a remarkably favored position, compared to Mexico and to most of the countries from which today's immigrants come. Americans are privileged, vis-a-vis Mexicans, in a way that Californians are not in comparison to residents of other U.S. states. The United States is one of the world's richest and most advantaged countries; many foreigners want to come to the United States for exactly that reason. Americans, for their part, maintain restrictive immigration laws because they fear that unrestricted entry would lead to a major influx of people, that the newcomers would compete for scarce resources and jobs in the United States and that they would drive down the standard of living of residents. No doubt it is in the interest of the privileged to protect their privileges, but it cannot be ethical, if that protection has the effect of further disadvantaging the unprivileged.

"Not so," an American might reply. "We built this country with its enviable standard of living, and we have the right to defend it against people who might diminish it by sharing in it." That reply has some merit but it does not settle the case, at least on ethical grounds. Note first that there is no convincing evidence that immigration of the magnitude we are currently experiencing diminishes Americans' standard of living. Still, it is likely that completely open borders would lead to such a large inflow of newcomers that many American residents would pay a price in terms of wages, employment and the cost of public services.

What gives us the moral right to avoid that price? Perhaps we could argue that we are morally justified in artificially retaining the structure of advantage and disadvantage in the world from which we benefit as if we ourselves were responsible for building up our national wealth. But few of us can claim that responsibility. Most Americans today did not create the country's great riches—they inherited them, and inherited privilege has only the most dubious moral justification. Think of different privileged groups who claimed they were justified in restricting other people's rights, lest the recognition of those rights would diminish their own privileges: southern white slave-owners before the Civil War, white Afrikaners in South Africa before the transition there to democracy, the aristocratic class of France before the Revolution. All those groups argued in favor of the restrictive laws and social practices that surrounded their positions of privilege; they believed that they should not have to bear any sacrifice. When their societies were fundamentally changed, each of those groups did bear a significant sacrifice. Most of us would agree, however, that the cost of that sacrifice was not of sufficient moral weight to justify avoiding the social change. The fact is that any adjustment of a privilege-disadvantage relationship necessarily results in a sacrifice on the part of the privileged, and the prospect of that sacrifice is not a strong moral argument against the change.

It is one of the overwhelming features of today's world that there are enormous differences of privilege and income. Most (not all) Americans are on one side of that great divide, and most of today's immigrants come from countries that are on the other side. The principal purpose of our immigration laws is to maintain the gap. It is here that we see most obviously the conflict between interests and ethics in immigration policy. It is in the interest of most Americans to restrict the flow of immigrants into the country, at least to some extent. These days, almost every potential immigrant who is excluded by the restrictions is a person who is less privileged than the typical American. Our self-interested immigration policy therefore has the unethical effect of reinforcing the structure of privilege and disadvantage among the world's people, people who are of absolutely equal moral worth.

Does this reasoning lead us inevitably to the moral requirement that we eliminate our immigration laws and open our borders? Several moral philosophers who have considered the question have concluded that it does, that open borders are an ethical imperative. I am not so sure. I think there may be a morally defensible case for at least some restrictions on immigration. I am worried that open borders would impose disproportionate costs on the most disadvantaged native-born Americans: the poor and some ethnic minority groups. Unskilled and semi-skilled immigrants might compete with them, to an even greater extent than they do today, driving their wages down and their unemployment rates up. How can it be ethical, one might ask, to embark on a policy that has a good chance of lowering wages, raising profits of American companies, increasing the already unconscionable gap between the rich and the poor in this country and disproportionately harming minority groups, particularly African Americans? Do we not have an obligation to attend to social justice at home, before we look to the world as a whole—and does this not justify at least some restrictions on immigration?

I think there is considerable validity to this point of view. To date, empirical research has not been able to identify a negative effect of immigration upon wages, income distribution and the prospects of the least fortunate Americans. My guess, however, is that with completely open borders we would begin to see some negative impacts.

I think, therefore, that we find ourselves in a situation in which moral rights conflict. Foreigners who come from disadvantaged backgrounds have a moral right to try to improve their situations and to provide for their families by coming to the United States. At the same time, disadvantaged Americans have the right not to see their prospects diminished by the country's immigration policy.

Before suggesting a strategy that responds to this ethical dilemma, let me turn to two related ethical problems. First, suppose we conclude that there is a defensible case for at least some restrictions on immigration. It follows that our immigration policy will be discriminatory. That is, we will discriminate in favor of some people who would like to immigrate and against others. Discrimination—the unequal treatment of morally equal people—is always an ethical concern. How can we set up a discriminatory immigration system that does the least moral harm?

Immigrants are currently admitted in several different categories, some of which correspond closely to the interests of at least some groups of American residents. The majority of authorized immigrants come as a result of family sponsorship; they are the children, spouses, parents or other kin of U.S. citizens or legal residents. Certainly many people with relatives abroad have a strong interest in the reunification of their families, and other Americans are right to respect those interests, at least to a certain extent. Another large group of immigrants come because they are sponsored by employers; they fill gaps in the American labor force and allow American industries to expand. These are perhaps worthwhile goals, although the existence of employment-based immigration has some ethical ambiguities, since it may in some cases result in the displacement of American workers. To the authorized entries in these two categories we should add the undocumented immigrants, the great majority of whom come either for family reunification or to get a job, or both.

Another category of immigrants exists, people who have a stronger claim on our moral sympathies. The people for whom entry is most urgent—even sometimes a matter of life and death—are the refugees. They are people who face persecution in their home countries, for no fault of their own, usually because of civil strife or dictatorship. Few Americans have a self interest in admitting refugees. While the United States has accepted some refugees, it has not done a good job with its refugee policy. Too often people have been classified as refugees by the U.S. authorities for ideological, anti-communist reasons, rather than because they were in danger of persecution. For many years, for example, every entrant from Cuba (a country with no internal warfare) was classified as a refugee, while almost no one from Guatemala and El Salvador (where vicious civil wars raged) was accorded that status. With the end of the cold war, the opportunity exists for the United States to reform its refugee policy along humanitarian lines, and thereby use its immigration policy to do the most possible good that it can in the world.

The last ethical issue has to do with the treatment of the immigrants in our midst. However the debate unfolds in the future, immigration is here to stay. While the anti-immigration forces are strong, so too are the pro-immigration forces, and they are unlikely to permit a severe reduction in authorized immigration. Even if the authorized levels were to be reduced, the reduction would likely be attenuated by increased levels of undocumented immigration. As long as foreigners want to work in the United States, and as long as jobs are available, they will find a way of coming.

So while the immigration debate will rage, we will not be able to avoid the question of how we treat the people who will continue to come. In the recent past our record has been poor. We have adopted laws and passed propositions intended to exclude immigrants—both legal and undocumented—from access to schools and social services, and to limit their rights to appeal their situations through the courts. It is almost as if we are saying to potential immigrants, "Please come and work for us, and expect to be exploited." That is a shortsighted, indefensible position for a nation built upon the foundation of immigration.

What would an ethically defensible U.S. immigration policy look like? We would accept more immigrants than we do now, on the grounds that they deserve a chance at the American dream. We would monitor closely the effects of immigration upon the status of the least well-off Americans, and be prepared to limit immigration to the extent that the effects became negative. If we had to limit immigration, we would increase significantly the number of refugees, even if that meant reducing the number of people admitted for reasons of family reunification and employment. We would allow no legal distinctions—except the right to vote—between citizens and legal immigrants, and we would provide generous transition assistance to help the newcomers get on their feet in their new country.

I am under no illusion that ethics, as opposed to interests, will guide the development of American immigration policy. To the extent that the two principles lead in different directions, however, and to the extent that we follow our interests, we should understand clearly the fact that our country, in our name, is acting unethically.

Migrant hybridity
Rubén Ríos Ávila

Rubén Ríos Ávila is Professor of Comparative Literature at the University of Puerto Rico, Rio Piedras, where he writes about contemporary Spanish-American writers and publishes *Postdata,* a journal of Cultural Studies and Theory.

It was 17 years ago, on a hot Summer afternoon in Central Park. The Gay Parade had reached its final destination; we were tired and exhilarated. The march was over, the political speeches were over, our job was done and we were ready for some action. So Grace Jones came out of a stretch limo and was hauled on top of the roof wearing black leather pants and spiked boots. Of course, she was singing "I Need a Man," the gay anthem that year, and suddenly I felt that I needed one too. I drifted away from the place of the concert and started crossing, not to mention cruising, that most erotic area of the park known as The Ramble in order to get (I told myself) a breath of fresh air and also (the truth be said) a glimpse of fresh bodies, intermittently available, humid and glistening in the shade.

As I walked through this Victorian maze, pushing the bushes with a certain trepidation and a feeling of confident anticipation, a "polemically persistent smell" distracted me. It smelled of lard and fried flour, of salted codfish. It was unmistakable: somebody was frying *bacalaitos* in Central Park. I could not help it: my nose took over against the wishes of my lower body. If it is true that the brain started out over a million years ago as an extension of the olfactory tissue which warned us of strangers and indicated where food was on our first nomadic forays, then I was experiencing a true primitive epiphany and as a result of it I no longer needed a man. I smelled, therefore I was, and I needed a *bacalaito.* Or perhaps I wanted both.

On the other side of The Ramble, equidistant to my first gay parade, Puerto Ricans in New York were celebrating the eve of San Juan Bautista. The sudden recognition of an intonation, the glimpse of a pose, the gradual saturation of familiar noise began to ground me. The sounds of the gay parade became dim and distant. I must have reached the middle of the Ramble when the story became impossibly allegorical. On one side of the park the celebration of a certain sexual heroism: the public vindication of the right to enjoy a particular brand of intimacy. On the other side of the park the celebration of a certain kind of ethnic heroism: the massive Puerto Ricanization of Central Park, not Jackie O's park, nor Woody Allen's, but the colonized territory of Loisaida, El Barrio, El Bronx y La taza de oro. It felt like the strength of both sides pulling away at the center made the park infamously and perversely central.

I also felt magnetically hemispherical. The wavy beat of salsa started to compete with the bacalaitos, and Grace Jones became a distant echo, curiously syncopated against the ever louder refrain of "Maestra Vida," all of it amusing and sweetly confusing. There I was, mid-way along The Ramble, adrift amidst two powerful organizers of my then recent adulthood, Puerto Rico and homosexual desire: two roads converged and I took the one most rambled by.

And it could only happen in New York. I was one of so many Puerto Ricans in their twenties who partially used the opportunity to pursue graduate studies in the States as a way out of the closet. It was the mid-seventies, and I had recently begun to present myself as gay and as Puerto Rican. Both identities were, I guess one could say, inaugurated, at roughly the same time. In the island I was not marked as either one or the other. There was no apparent need for it. I was not ready or willing to pay the price of coming out of the closet and Puerto Rico was not an ethnic option there, but a powerful, albeit troublesome national given. I became a Puerto Rican subject for the Office of the Registrar of my new American University, and a homosexual subject for its newly founded gay allegiance.

Expatriation can be a powerful form of estrangement. One is either invited or forced to divest oneself of the comforts of automatic self-effacement and the body becomes foregrounded, systematically de-familiarized. These days it is not so much a matter of radical exclusion, and even more so in the case of those of us who have migrated within areas of the U.S. territory, it is also not a matter of losing contact with a cultural or national origin. In modern times, as Edward Said has aptly pointed out, exile is not character- ized by radical distance, but by a sort of fluid in between- ness. One is neither out-nor-in, but constantly traveling up- and-down the seemingly opposite roads of departure and return. The migrant becomes the site of tense and some- times contradictory mediations. Luís Rafael Sánchez has developed the metaphor "guagua aérea," the flying bus, for the new site of Puerto Rican migratory exchange. He still regards this situation as a crisis, as an unresolved duplic- ity. But perhaps it is no longer so. My contention is that today's migrant is a hybrid, not a divided self. A divided self is a torn, tragic disruption of an identity that envisages it- self as a whole, but is either doomed or forced to lose its true image. A hybrid is made up of different, sometimes clashing identities that become available, necessary or pos- sible at different or alternative times and places, according to need and desire. Manuel Ramos Otero, a gay Puerto Rican writer, has a story titled "The Other island of Puerto Rico." At some level the story refers to the island of Manhattan as a potential geographic metaphor for the new migrant Puerto Rican subject, as an alternative operative ethnic synecdoque. But I think the story moves even further than that. All Puerto Ricans are today, in one way or another, inhabitants of some other island of Puerto Rico. Hybrid identities no longer float in a flying bus, waiting for their eventual land- ing: their only true self is the rough and dirty territory of their radical alternancy. Hybridity has become the marker for a new type of visibility, the evidence for a new kind of valid experience. Hybridity is migrant, but not because an original self is exiled from home and has to survive in the transitory shelter of nostalgia. It is migrant because it is made up of constantly movable and expandable borders.

Take, for example, the gay Puerto Rican migrant hy- brid. Can one trace the lines of intersection of these two different kinds of eccentric subjectivities, the ethnic and the sexual, can one identify the shape or the depth of these marks, the trace of their particular indentations and the ways through which they each limit, project, intersect and cross the borders of a very specific gay Puerto Rican migrant body? What is the status of this particular breed of migrant hybridity?

Historically speaking, Puerto Ricanness and homosexuality have been thought of as mutually exclusive. Bernardo Vega's memoirs, as Carlos Gil has brilliantly demonstrated, builds the first Puerto Rican identity outside of the island during the first half of this century precisely by marking the notion of a Puerto Rican ethos against the shady, decomposed, suspect abjection of effeminates and homosexuals, men of dubious masculinities hovering around the exemplary subjectivity of this international socialist, politically progressive new Puerto Rican that he represents through the abnegated, almost abstract utopian center of the memoir who is no other than the narrator himself. The very trip from the island to New York on the *Vapor Coamo* is symbolized around the emblem of masculine empowerment: Bernardo, following somebody's advice, throws a beautiful wristwatch into the ocean, because only effeminate men wore those in the city, he was told. Later he was surprised to find out that it was the kind of wristwatch everybody was wearing in New York. Gil reads in this a gesture of detemporalization of the migrant body. In order to found the new, utopian international Puerto Ricaness, Bernardo has to abandon the intransferable body of marked sexual desire and authorize himself as the representative of a homogeneized, meta-corporeal Puerto Rican consciousness.

Homophobia becomes a grounding limit for Bernardo Vega. The body of the effeminate marks the ultimate border against which to mobilize and crystallize a Puerto Rican presence in New York. Gil does not give Vega enough credit, I think. The memoir assigned itself the task of recognizing, of witnessing a new subjectivity: the Puerto Rican in New York, a new Puerto Rican that would not only become a contributing element within the rich ethnic hybridization of New York, but would also promote and configure the cultural and national hybridization of the island. A task of such magnitude needed a worthy antagonist. And the homosexual subject will play that role. The effeminate becomes a perfect other for this subject proposal. Subject formation is not only the birthing of a new, improbable creature; it is also a war. Homi Bhabha draws his program for a transnational location of culture through a close reading of Heidegger's dictum: "A boundary is not that at which something stops, but, as the Greeks recognized, the boundary is that from which something begins its presencing." It is a positive reappropiation of postmodernism, no longer perceived as the demolition site of meganarratives, but as the foreshadowing of new, promising borders, borders which begin to blur the hardened edges of the traditional national perimeter, displaced now by a veritable host of peripheral subjectivities, inaugural and full of promise, because their borders are no longer limits, but expanding signifiers.

But what happens when hybridity becomes the ground for an eccentric but nonetheless violent antagonism of marginalities? What happens when someone like Bernardo Vega re-territorializes the Puerto Rican subject by de-territorializing the homosexual subject? Borders are, yes, inaugural spaces, zones of presencing, but they are also the rough, volatile surface of an imagined bastion, the edge of the abyss of fear. The border is also the narrow interstice of agreed neutralization, out of which the other's differential status is entitled. A border is always negotiable.

Tension, violence, fear of dislocation become central in the pursuit of a safe haven for the marginal subject, and sometimes the border of a parallel marginality functions as the clearer frame of reference. The border is no longer a fixed demarcation, but an imaginary line always expandable and movable, drawn according to the intensity of a given, but also movable fear. It is also drawn according to the intensity of a given but movable allure.

The migrant hybrid rambles along a complex scenery, where various identities become available. Esmeralda Santiago's powerful memoir is at the opposite end, at the latter edge of the 20th century, of Bernardo Vega's memoirs. *When I was Puerto Rican* is the first work that presents being Puerto Rican as an option, no longer an ontological given but a phenomenological construct. And

Esmeralda has a choice. She even has the choice of becoming a different sort of Puerto Rican: one that sells books in Spanish, while at the same time being a successful ethnic American writer writing in English.

I recently saw a play titled "Motherlands" in Boston; it was written, directed and performed by Brenda Cotto, a lesbian Puerto Rican teaching in New England. It tells the story of being the daughter of a fervent Catholic Puerto Rican lady who claims to see the Virgin Mary every now and then. The mother claims to see the Virgin in her daughter, and her daughter begins to claim that she is a lesbian. When the tension becomes unbearable, the daughter moves to the States, in order to study and to be what she wants to be. She comes out as a lesbian, finds a lover, and talks to her mother on the phone. The play moves with the help of one simple, basic device: a long rope that in Puerto Rico functions as a clothes line where mother and daughter hang their dresses, and where the wind blows a blue sheet on the daughter every time she becomes the Virgin to her mother. And the rope also becomes the telephone line when she moves to the States, and the umbilical cord, and the tangled web that ties mother and daughter together across distance, as part of one same tight knot of fear, dependency and love. But one day mother decides pay her daughter a visit. The play then becomes a study of the different selves that compose this migrant hybrid. After a tense and sometimes even excruciating process of mutual accusations, mother, daughter and lover finally learn to negotiate their borders. And at some point, side by side, the mother and the lover feel the urge to kneel down in front of the virgin daughter they each adore so differently.

Sometimes Mother has to land in a foreign territory in order to discover that desire builds more than one motherland in a daughter's heart. The motherlands of desire drawing borders across the heart: national and ethnic and sexual borders crisscrossing and indenting and highlighting each other, like the multiple paths of a Victorian maze. If the converging borders become too hard to read, one has to relax and learn to enjoy the Ramble.

We Are the Miracle
Abby Bogomolny

One day the god of north america said,
"You will do the work of the empire six days a week,
burning fossil fuels in my name, but on the seventh day,
you will park your car in the driveway. If on the seventh
day, you long to run errands, try a movie, prozac,
cell phone, implant, a virtual miracle."

The next day we could no longer pray.

But the god of north america spoke again,
"You will hear messages of the empire as they wind
their way, moving like quicksilver, colorless
and electric. You will drive by, and buy,
believing your hands to be clean, another miracle."

How could we buy, and not buy in?
We have seen the god of north america maul farmland
and destroy what it cannot objectify or buy,
seen the lower ninth ward, guantanamo,
seen the worship of DOW over Tao.

Right there, behind the commercial curtain
we became the miracle— minds that can not be bought;
blood and bone that can not be sold for the empire.

No longer do we drive by, and buy
from the rack of overseas pain.
We are the miracle behind the commercial curtain.
Together we pull it aside and renew the dream.
God help us. *We* are the miracle.

Your Chosen Land
Stanley Nelson

Stanley Nelson has written thirteen books of poetry, among them *Immigrant: Book III* and *Book IV*. He is the recipient of New York University's Thomas Wolfe Poetry Award.

Immigrants!
>   how quickly your chosen land
grew to an empire
>   whose native sons and daughters, indistinguishable,
acquiesce in a society
fixed
>   as in the days of the manor lord. Your island
has become the pale
>   of a federal commission. Congress has
claimed
it as a national shrine
>   Already
uniformed guards
>   patrol its boundaries; radar
scans the harbor; military jets
hover over

>   Liberty   Isis

>   to the eternal immigrant.

First Writing Since
Suheir Hammad

Several weeks after the September 11th attacks on the World Trade Center in New York City, Suheir Hammad emailed this poem to her network of friends, artists, and writers across the country.

1. there have been no words.
i have not written one word.
no poetry in the ashes south of canal street.
no prose in the refrigerated trucks driving debris and dna.
not one word.

today is a week, and seven is of heavens, gods, science.
evident out my kitchen window is an abstract reality.
sky where once was steel.
smoke where once was flesh.

fire in the city air and i feared for my sister's life in a way
never before. and then, and now, i fear for the rest of us.

first, please god, let it be a mistake, the pilot's heart
failed, the plane's engine died.
then please god, let it be a nightmare, wake me now.
please god, after the second plane, please,
don't let it be anyone
who looks like my brothers.

i do not know how bad a life has to break in order to kill.
i have never been so hungry that i willed hunger.
i have never been so angry as to want to control a gun
over a pen.
not really. even as a woman,
as a palestinian, as a broken human being.
never this broken.

more than ever, i believe there is no difference.
the most privileged nation, most americans
do not know the difference

between indians, afghanis, syrians, muslims,
sikhs, hindus.
more than ever, there is no difference.

2. thank you korea for kimchi and bibim bob, and corn tea
and the genteel smiles of the wait staff at wonjo — smiles
never revealing the heat of the food or how tired
they must be working long midtown shifts. thank you
korea, for the belly craving that brought me into the city
late the night before and diverted my daily train ride
into the world trade center.

there are plenty of thank yous in ny right now.
thank you for my lazy procrastinating late ass. thank you
to the germs that had me call in sick. thank you,
my attitude, you had me fired the week before. thank you
for the train that never came, the rude nyer who stole
my cab going downtown. thank you for the sense
my mama gave me to run. thank you
for my legs, my eyes, my life.

3. the dead are called lost and their families hold up
shaky printouts in front of us through screens smoked up.

we are looking for iris, mother of three. please call
with any information. we are searching for priti, last seen
on the 103rd floor. she was talking to her husband
on the phone and the line went. please help us find george,
also known as adel. his family is waiting for him with his
favorite meal. i am looking for my son, who was delivering
coffee. i am looking for my sister girl, she started her job
on monday.

i am looking for peace. i am looking for mercy. i am
looking for evidence of compassion. any evidence of life.
i am looking for life.

4. ricardo on the radio said in his accent thick as yucca,
"i will feel so much better when the first bombs drop over
there. and my friends feel the same way."

on my block, a woman was crying in a car parked
and stranded in hurt. i offered comfort, extended a hand
she did not see before she said, "we're gonna burn
them so bad, i swear, so bad." my hand went to my head
and my head went to the numbers within it of the dead
iraqi children, the dead in nicaragua. the dead in rwanda
who had to vie with fake sport wrestling
for america's attention.

yet when people sent emails saying, this was bound
to happen, let's not forget u.s. transgressions, for half
a second i felt resentful. hold up with that, cause i live
here, these are my friends and fam, and it could have
been me in those buildings, and we're not bad people,
do not support america's bullying. can i just have a half
second to feel bad?

if i can find through this exhaust, people who were left
behind to mourn and to resist mass murder,
i might be alright.

thank you to the woman who saw me brinking my cool
and blinking back tears. she opened her arms before she
asked "do you want a hug?" a big white woman, and her
embrace was the kind only people with the warmth
of flesh can offer. i wasn't about to say no to any comfort.
"my brother's in the navy," i said. "and we're arabs."
"wow, you got double trouble." word.

5. one more person ask me if i knew the hijackers.
one more motherfucker ask me what navy
my brother is in.
one more person assume no arabs or muslims were killed.
one more person assume they know me, or that
i represent a people.
or that a people represent an evil.
or that evil is as simple as a
flag and words on a page.

we did not vilify all white men when mcveigh bombed
oklahoma. america did not give out his family's addresses
or where he went to church. or blame the bible
or pat robertson.

and when the networks air footage of palestinians
dancing in the street, there is no apology that hungry
children are bribed with sweets that turn their teeth
brown. that correspondents edit images. that archives
are there to facilitate lazy and inaccurate journalism.

and when we talk about holy books and hooded men
and death, why do we never mention the kkk?

if there are any people on earth who understand how
new york is feeling right now, they are in the west bank
and the gaza strip.

6. today it is ten days. last night bush waged war
on a man once openly funded by the cia.
i do not know who is responsible. read too many books,
know too many people to believe what i am told. i don't
give a fuck about bin laden. his vision of the world does
not include me or those i love. and petitions have been
going around for years trying to get the u.s. sponsored
taliban out of power. shit is complicated, and i don't know
what to think.

but i know for sure who will pay.

in the world, it will be women, mostly colored and poor.
women will have to bury children, and support
themselves through grief. "either you are with us,
or with the terrorists" — meaning keep your people under
control and your resistance censored.
meaning we got the loot and the nukes.

in america, it will be those amongst us who refuse blanket
attacks on the shivering. those of us who work toward

social justice, in support of civil liberties, in opposition
to hateful foreign policies.

i have never felt less american and more new yorker —
particularly brooklyn — than these past days. the stars
and stripes on all these cars and apartment windows
represent the dead as citizens first — not family members,
not lovers.

i feel like my skin is real thin, and that my eyes are only
going to get darker. the future holds little light.

my baby brother is a man now, and on alert, and praying
five times a day that the orders he will take in a few days'
time are righteous and will not weigh his soul down
from the afterlife he deserves.

both my brothers — my heart stops when i try to pray —
not a beat to disturb my fear. one a rock god, the other a
sergeant, and both palestinian, practicing muslim, gentle
men. both born in brooklyn and their faces are of the
archetypal arab man, all eyelashes and nose
and beautiful color and stubborn hair.

what will their lives be like now?

over there is over here.

7. all day, across the river, the smell of burning rubber
and limbs floats through. the sirens have stopped now.
the advertisers are back on the air. the rescue workers
are traumatized. the skyline is brought back to human
size. no longer taunting the gods with its height.

i have not cried at all while writing this. i cried when
i saw those buildings collapse on themselves like a broken
heart. i have never owned pain that needs to spread like
that. and i cry daily that my brothers return
to our mother safe and whole.

there is no poetry in this. there are causes and effects.
there are symbols and ideologies. mad conspiracy here,
and information we will never know. there is death here,
and there are promises of more.

there is life here. anyone reading this is breathing, maybe
hurting, but breathing for sure. and if there is any light
to come, it will shine from the eyes of those who look for
peace and justice after the rubble and rhetoric are cleared
and the phoenix has risen.

affirm life.
affirm life.
we got to carry each other now.
you are either with life, or against it.
affirm life.

We Have It
Opal Palmer Adisa

The dream
began before
Africans were tracked
on the coast of Ghana
the Middle Passage
flesh for sharks

The dream started
before 1619
when the first slaves docked
before
we knew Mississippi
fed her blood
for passage
before Rosa Parks
the Montgomery Bus Boycott

The dream isn't
a singular vision
it lives in the Dozens
Second Line
Praline and Fat Tuesday
It's the beat of our walk
the slang of our tongues

This dream is us
we got it from old people's eyes
the way their fingers knuckle
the glee and laughter
of black children
starched and oiled for church

The dream lives
in sisters
their heads held sure
in brothers
their confident bop

We all have the dream
Martin Luther King, Jr.
gave it voice

Index of Authors

Printed in the United States
134040LV00002B/184-213/A